Copyright © 2022 Rod DesJardins

Design by Chris Wetton

Printed in Marquette,
Michigan U.S.A.
By Lake Superior Press

All rights reserved.
No part of this publication may be reproduced or used in any form or by any means—graphic, electronic, or mechanical, including photocopying, recording, taping, or information storage and retrieval systems without written permission of the author.

ISBN 979-8-88627-169-0

First printing 2022

For Deanna,

RDJ

Deanna Nelson — 1721 Windstone

What's this Book About

Well, this book is about a lot of things but mostly it's about living up here in the U.P.

It's about living and working and playing in the woods around Alger County and out on the Big Lake. It's about the changing seasons, especially Winter and how we survive and amuse ourselves up here in God's country. It's about pick-up trucks and camps and pontoon boats and islands. It's about fishing and hiking and just wandering around in the woods. It's about old friends, new friends and absent friends. It's about old dogs and young pups.

It's about growing up and growing old and it springs from roots sunk deep in the bedrock of this peninsula. It's about uncles and nephews and great uncles and great nephews. It's about growing up in a tar paper shack and coming of age in the 70s. It's about fire and rain and a lumberjack's troubles. It's about being called "your honor" and marryin' people.

It's about music from space and landing on aircraft carriers. It's about underwear, or the lack thereof, and it's about Sauna. It's about history and the marks we have made on the land in this place we call home. It's about critters and COVID and change. It's about living up here above the land that's down below the Bridge.

It's about the sun and the moon and the stars and planets too. It's about old submarines and old submarine sailors. It's about having your heart broken when you're young and re-plumbed when you're old. It's about buckets and guardrails and the difference between a shitload and a gazillion.

Some things might make you laugh, but that depends on how warped and twisted your sense of humor is. Mostly I've tried to just make people smile or sigh, or hark back and remember, or maybe just say "yeah." If my words are rough around the edges it's because I was trained as a reporter and I'm too old to care very much about polishing them any further. You can ruin a thing by fixing it too many times.

These "stories," if you can call them that, got started in my convalescence after heart surgery in 2018 and I've compiled them over the last couple years on my web page. I hope you like them enough to read them and recommend them to your friends. Make them buy their own copy though. If I can sell enough books it may keep me out of the poor house in my retirement. I'd like that. So would my wife. My alternate retirement plan is to be a colorful character at my nephew's pub.

I'd like to thank my wife Shawna for putting up with my wandering on a daily basis, and special thanks to the world's best High School English teacher, Helen Peters, for teaching me that we learn the rules of grammar so that when we break them we do so deliberately, intelligently and effectively.

And remember, life's short. Drink the good Scotch first.

CONTENTS

What's this Book About	iii
Lake Effect	1
I Walk These Hills	5
The Big Lake	9
A Good Man in the Woods	15
My Father's Enemies	21
The Continuing Adventures of Charlie Bear (Prologue)	27
Sentenced to Matrimony	31
Etched in Stone	37
The Long White	41
Ice Monkeys	45
Fresh from Hard Water	51
The Chapters in my Closet	59
The Scar	63
Pussy Willows, Crows and the Ten Dollar Hill	65
Wandering in the Winter Woods	69
The Warm Smile of Early Spring	73
Spring in the Valley of the Left-Handed Echo	77
Trilliums and Trout	83
Hanley Field	89
Sentinels	95
That'll be Two Dollars	101
These Scars on the Land	105
Speed of Arrival	111
I'll Take the Dirt Road	119
The Bear Dog and the Wolf Hounds	125
Down Below	129
Fire and Water, Earth and Sky	133
Dear John	139
Stop Helping. Please!	145
Pigs in Space	151
Underwear and Satellite Radio	155
U.P. Road Warriors	159
The Old Soul	165
A Random Chorus of Trumpets	169
. . . and I Learned it All in the Navy	175
Buckets of This and That	183
Makin' Wood	187
Guardrails	195
No Snot, No Lace Panties	209
I Knew Your Dad	213
The Last Ride	217

Life's Short! Drink the Good Scotch First!

Lake Effect

My dad worked outside for most of his life, either on the lake, on the farm or out in the woods, so knowing tomorrow's weather was important to him. Every night after supper he would slump heavily into his chair and sit quietly while he got his news without comment from Walter Cronkite. Then he would wait patiently through the local news and sports report, though neither interested him very much, so that he didn't miss the next day's forecast.

Many times each winter, when describing a snow event from the north off Lake Superior, the young weatherman on TV-6 would confidently predict "with heavier accumulations near the lake," and my old man, who had little tolerance for masters of the obvious, would get up from his chair and say "well, no shit Commander!" a phrase he no doubt picked up when he was in the navy during the war. Then he'd walk out in the kitchen mumbling something to himself about the relative merits of educating a young man who still didn't know shit from apple butter.

"Of course, there's going to be more snow near the lake," he would mutter to no one in particular. "It's a northwest wind fergawdsake!"

My dad lived in the U.P. for most of his life and like everyone else up here he understood lake effect snow. We all do. If you live near Lake Superior you can't help but understand and appreciate the lake effect; colder air from Canada blowing over the relatively warm waters of the lake creating bands of heavy snowsqualls along the south shore.

Lake effect snow dominates our weather from November through late Winter when the lake finally freezes out far enough to cut off the warm moisture supply that feeds the north wind. We grow up with a great appreciation for lake effect because we shoveled too much snow in a howling north wind as a kid not to.

We learned it at a young age because we live up north, or as the old Finns say, "up nort'." We're used to it. We dwell in the shadow and bask in the glory of Lake Superior. We know where snow comes from. And the Big Lake's effect on our lives applies to so much more than snow. We live in the land of the lake effect, up above the bridge. If it's not God's country, it's where He hangs out a lot.

The U.P. is shorthand for Upper Peninsula, that part of Michigan that looks like it should be part of Wisconsin and sometimes gets left off the Michigan map altogether. We used to be known as "stump jumpers and jack pine savages," to our southern brethren back in the day, because they assumed that we were all lumberjacks. They weren't far wrong. We, in turn, called them "sugar beaters and apple knockers" because that's what they grow in the northern part of the Lower Peninsula, which was as far south as most of us ever ventured. We're not good big city folks. But our stereotypes and labels have evolved since then.

The term Yooper has been around at least 40 years and it comes from "U.P." It's phonetic. I don't know who first coined it, but for whatever reason the term stuck, and it persists. We are not just Yoopers though. We are proud Yoopers, and the peninsula's silhouette has become an iconic image. And Yooper is always capitalized.

"Loper," for our brothers to the south, for obvious reasons, never caught on so we just call them Trolls because they live beneath the bridge. The Mackinac Bridge. It's a formidable structure and it scares some people. It's also as symbolic a link, as well as a boundary, as modern man could build. For us, it's both. And Troll is mostly a term of affection.

Our great-great-grandfathers settled this cold northern land and staked their claim along the lakeshore, deep in the woods, along the iron ranges and up into the copper country. They built their homes and planted their seed from the Falls of St. Mary and the limestone coast of the Detour Passage to the wild rice along the Menominee River, and from the Pictured Rocks to the copper hills of the Keweenaw Peninsula.

For two centuries now we've wrested our living from this harsh land with all its wild beauty. We're descended from miners and lumberjacks, trappers and fishermen. We're Finns and Swedes and Italians along with a few Frenchmen whose fathers got kicked out of Canada after their fathers got kicked out of France. We are all part Nishnabe too, at least in spirit, and we are all brothers to the earth. We're built for the weather, low to the ground and leaning into the wind. We live close to the land that we call our home, and we cherish its diversity of geology and geography, habitat and wildlife. We're proud of our individual cultures and blended heritage.

We like camps and trucks and boats and ATV's and snowmobiles. We like skis and snowshoes too. We welcome all four seasons, and we are ready for each. We revel in their passing of one into the other. Where would life's metaphors be without the seasons?

We hunt deer and bear and partridge and rabbits. We fish for trout and salmon and perch and pike, and bluegill and . . . well, we just like to fish, and our peninsula between these freshwater seas is crowded with lakes and streams and ponds in which to try your luck.

And then there's the Big Lake.

"Mother Superior" we call her with respect and even reverence. She casts her shadow across most of this land and creates her own weather year-round, but especially in the winter. Kewadin. The north wind. The winter maker. When the north wind blows across the lake we like to hunker down at camp and fire up the sauna.

And it's pronounced Sow-na (rhymes with cow and wow), not Saw-na (rhymes with ma and pa). The rest of us Yoopers learned the pleasure and comfort of sauna from the Finns, and if you throw in a bottle of peppermint schnapps you have a poor man's pharmacy. It will sooth away whatever your affliction or complaint. And nothing will betray you as an outsider faster in the U.P. than saying "saw-na." You will be corrected, ostracized, and possibly even scorned.

Ours is a sparsely populated land between three great lakes, filled with simple and honest people; a place where no one feels the need to stand out from a crowd, because it's all we can do to stand out enough from the landscape so that our friends can find us. Besides, you'd have to go pretty far on just the right day to find a crowd to stand out from.

Some people say we talk funny and we do talk slow, especially in Winter when our jaws are frozen. But we think fast enough and though we are simple folk by choice, we ain't no dummies. Never confuse measured, thoughtful, and deliberate with slow, ignorant or stupid.

We speak pretty good American, but after 200 years of living here we have developed our own vernacular which varies across the length of the peninsula. To the untrained ear we all sound like Yoopers, "Holy Wah, or yaw, eh." but a Copper Country accent is readily identifiable to someone from Trenary or Negaunee, which have their own distinctly different dialects though they are less than 50 miles apart. I can easily tell a miner from Negaunee from a farmer from Trenary, especially if they're both Finns.

Being on the border we also speak perfect Canadian, eh. And there's enough Packer fans up here (Oh yah, we love da' Packers) that we can converse with our neighbors in Wisconsin, don'tcha know. And we talk passable Minnesotan too, yah sure, you betcha, when we venture that far west.

There's also this thing we call U.P. arithmetic. It's pretty simple. We live in the land of three and a third. We are one third of the state and only three percent of the population. We are also the land of one and 104. One area code, 906, but 104 different zip codes spread across two time zones.

We are thinly spread across those 400 miles too. Most places big enough to have a post office measure their population in the hundreds, instead of thousands. There are places where the post office is the only public building in "town", and we use that term loosely.

And we all get along up here too. We have to. There are fewer opportunities up north, to be sure, but there are also fewer competitors. It's in our nature to cooperate with one another, regardless of the undertaking, because it's necessary to spread our meager resources over such a large geographic area.

More than half of the land in the U.P. is public land, either federal or state owned, or else its set aside as Commercial Forest Reserve, dedicated to forestry and open to recreation. That reality is both a blessing and a curse.

The blessing is that all this land is free for the public to use, most of it with few restrictions. Not surprisingly, the forests and fields and lakes and streams of the U.P. that help sustain us, are also our year-round playground. But CFR, or what we call "company land" pays very little in taxes and public land pays even less.

So, the curse is that as little as 20% of the land carries the entire tax burden in some counties up north. Property taxes are not any higher than anywhere else, in fact they're lower, but services are spread as thinly as the population. Because of that we've learned to fend for ourselves and to look after our neighbors. It's part of our very nature and it's embedded in our character. We're in the habit of looking out for one another as well as any strangers who come to visit.

Ronald Reagan once said that the best social program is a good job. Up north the best social program is a good neighbor. We like it that way.

For 200 years we've survived each and every effort to exploit and export our natural resources. First it was furs and then fish, then it was iron and copper and timber. And then it was our children. Kids who grow up in the U.P. do well wherever they go, and most of them have to go somewhere else to make a living. Life is lean up here and it is hard. But it's also fresh and clean and never crowded. If they're lucky like me some day they might be one of those economic ex-patriates who gets to come home and raise their kids here and then grow old here.

I'm not sure if I live in God's Country, but I know that I live in His neighborhood. I live on the finest natural harbor on Lake Superior, surrounded by the Pictured Rocks National Lakeshore, the Grand Island National Recreation Area—together, more than 80 miles of Lake Superior shoreline--the Hiawatha National Forest, the Seney National Wildlife Refuge, four national wilderness areas, three state forests and thousands of acres of company land.

So, when people ask me what my home's greatest natural resource is, I tell them that it's hard to choose. But then I tell them that it's the hospitality of my neighbors and we're proud of that. It's very much who we are.

So, be nice to the locals and you will see and feel that hospitality. Listen to them and you will avoid misfortune and have a good time.

Welcome to the U.P. Pack extra dry socks, bug dope and a sweatshirt and, oh yes, do try the whitefish.

Life's Short! Drink the Good Scotch First!

I Walk These Hills

I walk these hills every day with my dogs. The hills surround the town where I was born and where I live, and our walks give the dogs a chance to run and give me a chance to think. I've been walking these hills my whole life. They are old and they are my friends, my sanctuary in times of trouble and my playground in times of joy.

I walk these hills in the fall, in the winter and in the spring. Summers are for the lake.

I walk these hills because I find peace here and we live in a world where peace is hard to find.

I walk these hills through stands of hard maple sprinkled with cherry and yellow birch, hemlock groves and sentinel white pines, and everywhere dying beech trees.

I walk these hills with the dogs out front, measuring the miles with my staff, ten feet at a time, letting the old dog set the pace while the wolf hounds spar in the brush and wrestle at full speed.

I walk these hills with my quarter staff in hand and I notice how worn it is getting where I hold it. It is my favorite walking stick, found on the edge of a balsam thicket one day several years ago when I'd forgotten my ski pole on a weekend hike. It's a spruce sapling that died in the understory and is pencil-straight and worm-scarred. It fits me like a glove and I've used it ever since. When I die give it to a fellow wanderer and point him, or her, toward the hills.

I walk these hills everyday with my dogs and it is the highlight of their day. At noon they gather around me and stare at me expectantly. As I move around the house, they follow me and watch my every move. When I reach for my boots the happy dance starts and they gather by the door and wait for their vests. Blaze orange for all three in the fall and then fleece for the big dogs in the winter.

I walk these hills everyday with my dogs and they know the trail ahead. These are their trails, too, but no matter how many times we walk them, everything is new to them and in need of examination. Every stump they encounter and every critter track we cross gets a new sniff.

I walk these hills with my dogs and the ghosts of old friends.

French Dave lived on one of these hills--the one that bears his family's name, and where his grandfather once ran a dairy farm. I would visit him when he was dying and he would ask me "well, how are things going down there in the flat?" I think he borrowed the line from a movie but it made us both smile and always broke the awkward silence that creeps into conversations between friends when one of them is dying.

French Dave knew these hills as well as I did because he grew up wandering them as a boy. He walked these hills his whole life.

I walk these hills and I think of him and it warms my heart to know that I'm walking on the same ground where he walked and where his father walked and where his father before him walked. It keeps my connection to him strong. He's been gone 24 years this month and I still miss him.

I walk these hills on old trails once trod by dairy cows through forests that were once pastures that were once forests. I walk along old logging roads and I look at the marks we've made on the land in the 200 years we have used these hills for our own purposes. But the earth is resilient and Mother Nature has shrugged off our use and reclaimed the hills as her own.

The marks of the Nishnabe over 5,000 years are long gone. The scars of the white man are transient, especially in the high hardwoods. Seeds have sprouted, saplings have fought for light and grown into mighty trees that have died and lay rotting on the ground since we began walking these hills.

I walk these hills with my dogs and the ghosts of old friends.

Captain Dave was born and raised in these hills on a road that bears his family's name and as boys and men we wandered these hills together. Mischief and trouble mixed with wonder and joy marked our journeys of exploration.

He, too, grew up walking these hills and we shared the need to see what was over the next rise or around the next corner. We sought the holy grail of a big tree or a new vista and found the simpler wonders of nature in the process. He knew the hills well and he showed them to me.

I walk these hills now and I think about him and the miles we wandered through these forests and I miss him. He's been gone ten years this spring. I took a long walk through these hills on the day that he died and I felt his spirit walking with me.

I walk these hills with my eyes wide open. Though I've been down all these trails and roads before there is always something new that I find for the forest is ever changing. There is always something I haven't noticed before. Life is like that. Each day is like that.

I walk these hills with my dogs and at least one angel.

Saint Kewpie lived in these hills and raised her family here. She was powerful and wise. She was kind and good. She lived a humble life hunting, trapping, fishing and foraging and she had a simple philosophy. Work hard. Be strong. Respect the land. Treat everyone with dignity. Do the right thing. Help others. Do not judge.

She dug a flower from my mother's yard when they were both young women and planted it in her own yard where it bloomed faithfully every spring. Each year a single white snowbell rose from the lawn behind the garage and she'd be careful to mow around it and she always reminded me of where it came from.

I'd go up the hill to see her and no matter what troubles darkened my day, no matter what obstacle blocked my path, no matter what burden stooped my shoulders, she would get out her step stool, look me straight in the eye and give me a hug that made everything alright.

We lost her this past November. She was 93. I cherish the memory of the time we spent together. She was an angel on earth and she walks these hills with me too. Through this long dark winter I look forward to spring when the snowbells bloom.

I walk these hills with my dogs and at times I could close my eyes and my feet would still find the trail for I have a steady hand to guide me.

I walk these hills with a furrowed brow and the worry slips away with each step. The coiled spring winds down and the glass refills. I find strength and courage and patience.

I walk these hills and ponder problems and search for answers that come in small pieces from unexpected places while each mile makes the problems seem smaller and more manageable.

I walk these hills when I'm happy and I find joy in the world around me. It's there in every rock and every tree, along every ridge and down every ravine. It's there in squirrels scampering and partridge drumming, in mushrooms sprouting on rotting logs and in dried leaves swirling in the wind beneath the clattering harmony of bare branches overhead.

I walk these hills alone with my dogs and they are my solace and my strength, my cradle and my cathedral, my future and my past. These hills of my home above this lake that I love comfort me and nurture me and remind me what's important, what's worth saving and what's worth doing.

I walk these hills everyday with my dogs, with the ghosts of old friends and at least one angel, with Mother Nature and with God and so far, at least, we all seem to get along.

Life's Short! Drink the Good Scotch First!

Life's Short! Drink the Good Scotch First!

The Big Lake

Those of us who live on her shore call her Mother Superior and we do so with great reverence. She is the cold-shouldered lady to the north. She is our playground and our larder and sometimes she is our nemesis.

There are those who would assign her a masculine persona, but she is feminine. She is a summer siren, a wistful autumn muse and a stone-cold bitch when she gets her dander up. She is also maternal. She is the local face of Gaia's strength, and she holds us all to her icy bosom. Whatever you think of her she cannot be ignored.

Three hundred fifty miles from Duluth to Sault Ste. Marie, 150 miles across here in the middle of the U.P., she's 1,300 feet deep just ten miles from where I sit in this quiet little town tucked in between the green hills and the sheltered bays of the Big Lake's finest natural harbor at "les Grande Isle."

The French voyageurs who explored and then named the wonders of this coast surely must have thought they were grand and they were right. But as you make your way along the shipwreck coast from Grand Marais past the Grand Portal to Grand Island you start thinking the French needed a few more adjectives in their vocabulary. Nonetheless, they did not misuse the one they had.

We here on the north coast live smack dab in the middle of the "Pure Michigan" you see on TV. That's us, especially in the summer. But before there was "Pure Michigan" the state's tourist slogan was "the long blue edge of summer." OK, in the winter it was "Winter Wonderland," but we will get to that.

I grew up on her shore. I was weaned on her water, literally. One of my very first chores was helping my big brothers hall water from the lake before we put in the well. This was the old U.P., the still-being-electrified U.P., when people still lived in tarpaper shacks with barrel stoves and outhouses and survived. Thrived even.

The lake has something to do with that. We are hardy stock. You must be tough to lean into that bitter north wind for six months every year. Mother Superior becomes the sub-arctic in the Winter but let's tarry a little here and take the seasons in their turn.

In the spring Lake Superior is fresh and clean and cold with ice flows that sometimes shove in and out of the bay until May. Blue, winter ice can be found in the deeper caves along the Pictured Rocks and on the back side of Grand Island until June. As kids (and obviously without proper adult supervision) we would cut long poles from maple saplings and ride the pack ice around near the fish docks. The trick was to find an ice raft big enough to hold your weight, not so wobbly that it would tip over, but also not so heavy that you couldn't move it. And we would joust with the poles and try to push each other off. Yes, we got wet and cold, but no one ever drowned because we were young and invincible then.

Even as children we are taught to respect the Big Lake. We were not taught to fear her—that would not be practical when she makes up the dominant half of your world—but we were taught to respect her and to never turn our back on her for she is many things and merciless is one of those things. But we are also lake men. We like boats and fishing, and Lake Superior is our playground.

If you don't know the lake first-hand imagine a sandstone swimming pool the size that I have just described filled with water so clear you can see pebbles on the bottom in sixty feet of water, surrounded by a shoreline that's a vertical study in random combinations of pine and birch, beech and mountain ash clinging to the crumbling sandstone cliffs. The beaches are either washed gravel or a combination of pure white and purple sand that's eroded from the cliffs above over the last 10,000 years.

Imagine this crystal clear and painfully cold pool teaming with whitefish and lake trout, herring and salmon, all smaller than their better fed cousins in the warmer, lower lakes, but firmer and more flavorful than any fish you will find in the world.

Our summers on Lake Superior are defined by the hours we spend on the lake and there is no better day than a boat load of friends and dogs, a cooler full of food and drink, and a leisurely putt along the 35 miles of Grand Island shoreline. We always go east to west to enjoy the sunset behind the Channel Islands as we idle back into the harbor past the tourist park, sunburned and happy 10 hours later. There is nothing like the smell of a hundred campfires, and a hundred campfire dinners cooking, to remind you that it's summer.

When we were young and fearless we made a point to swim in the Big Lake by Memorial Day. It was an annual badge of honor for invincible teenage boys—an early test of our budding manliness. Full submersion was required but no one stayed in longer than it took to get out. Forty years later I seldom get in before the 4th of July and some years not before the music festival in August. Mother Superior is a stern mistress, so she never actually gets "warm." If a steady wind stacks the surface water up on a lee shore the lake will get up to 70 degrees, as long as you don't go too deep. Dive down ten feet, though, and it's still 45 degrees.

We baptize our children in it, and ourselves at least annually, as well as many unwary visitors each year. Of course, we remind them that it doesn't count if they don't get the top of their head wet and if they fail to do that we deem them unworthy and banish them back to the land below the bridge from whence they came, blood kin or not.

Swimming temperature in the Big Lake for the locals is anything above 50 degrees if the sun looks like it will stay out long enough to warm you back up when you get out. Sometimes we just jump in to sober up a little if the day is still young and our thirst has been great. Immersion time varies accordingly, and no one goes to the beach or boating on Lake Superior without sweatshirts and blankets.

We measure the success of our summers by the number of times we get around Grand Island and we measure the success of each trip by the number of eagles we see. I counted four active nests on the island this year, and one more on Williams Island. We often see a half dozen mature birds and that many more juveniles on a good day, fishing the surface waters from their lofty perches high above us.

Our corner of Mother Superior also has some world class snorkeling with endless underwater rock formations and many shallow wrecks to explore but I don't snorkel much anymore. I have trouble getting a mask to seal around this cheesy mustache that I wear as a sign of my gathering maturity. No, our crew likes beach hopping. I guess we're getting old. We especially like showing our lake and our island to people who have never seen it before so we can see the smiles and the awe on their face when they do. It's worth a tank of gas and a box of beer just to see that.

Grand Island has maybe 50 beaches. I say maybe because it's hard to tell sometimes where one beach starts and another begins, and some of the smaller, gravel beaches along the west shore are temporary and seasonal. Some come and go every couple of years. Most of the beaches don't have names. Neither do the dozens of waterfalls on the island. We let our guests name them and we don't keep track.

We always stop at Trout Bay and the North Light Beach for a swim (and a pee), and to socialize with like-minded friends we meet there by some combination of chance or design. Everyone keeps their eye on every weekend forecast during boating season. These beaches are never crowded but they are favorite rendezvous spots for locals. And before the day's out we will find the seclusion of "Peanut's Cove" or the waterfall by the Mather Lodge for that last swim of the day.

My favorite picture ever is one of my wife when we were courting. It was her first trip around the island and she was captivated. She's sitting at the waterline on a narrow gravel beach against a 300-foot cliff lit up by the setting sun. Her legs are in the water and she's framed by furrows of "pretty rocks." She has a hoodie on and the pouch pocket is stuffed so full that it has sagged into the water and she's grinning at me like a kid while stuffing even more rocks into it. I found out that day that her favorite things were rocks and sticks and leaves and feathers and I knew right then she was a keeper. I brought her five-gallon bucket and she has loved me ever since.

Summer along the Big Lake is brief, too brief, and in my lifetime the season has changed. June is now a spring month and September has been added to the back end of summer. Less daylight but fewer flies. My record last trip around the island is October 5. Captain Dave and I took my daughter Sam, who was going in the Navy the following week, and Dave's mom, who turned 82 that year, out on the Gull to the North Beach for a swim and a picnic.

This doesn't count the quick and dangerous crossings we made as teenagers to the island in November to hunt deer. But we were young and invincible then. My record last swim in the Big Lake, at least on purpose, is October 15.

The last boating day of the year is always special because it just might be the last nice day of summer. The mountain ash berries burst into flame and the hardwood canopy that tops the tan and purple cliffs burns orange and scarlet. That day is always too short when you're that deep into fall and it is bittersweet as you say goodbye to another U.P. summer. Come late September kayaks and pontoons and other summer boats are stored for another season while the die-hard fishermen break out foul weather gear and keep their boats trailered and handy for Cohos and Kings until the first hard frost in late October.

Fall on the Big lake is tumultuous on a good day. But when the leaves come down and the land turns gray and brown, the lake turns an even deeper shade of blue. In late October and early November she turns "Lake Superior Blue," a hue that defies my powers of description. Though squalls can come out of nowhere on a hot day and sink your boat during the summer, fall is when the lake gets angry. Even the sheltered waters of the bay are white-capped by then and the sky above is piled high with mountains of billowy white clouds. Soon, the prevailing north winds back around to the northwest and she blows a gale every week.

Lake Superior does not have enough reach to build a sea swell, so 20-foot crests that would be hundreds of feet apart on the ocean are often only 50 feet apart on the Big Lake. Ten-foot waves can sink 30-foot boats. Thirty and 40-foot waves can break iron ore freighters in half and send them to the bottom. And then there are "the sisters," three waves in succession that are significantly larger than the rest. It's phenomena that's peculiar to the Big Lake.

No one who was alive in these parts then can forget where they were on November 10, 1975, the night the Edmund Fitzgerald sank. A friend and I went to the range light in Christmas that night and stood as close to the lake as we could get, sipping whiskey and shaking our fists at the storm. We didn't stay long, and we got wet and cold, but we didn't care because we were young and stupid then.

As the cold weather sets in the storms pound the shoreline and ice coats the rocks and trees. The wet sandstone cliffs sprout pillars of ice and climbing them has become our newest winter sport. While the lake is still open across to Canada the northwest wind piles up feet of "lake effect" snow and reminds us of exactly where our water comes from and where it goes on its way to the aquifer.

And then the lake freezes. The aqua rigor mortis varies from 40 to 150 days each year, depending on the wind. There are years when the ice in the bay is not safe enough to cross either channel to the island and then there are years when you can drive your truck there. Ice fishing on the bay before the new year is rare but this year the Big Lake made ice on Christmas Day and there were shacks on it the day after. We fish until the ice in no longer safe— some years March, some years May. Some years you lose your shack. Some years you drag it off with your pickup.

    I've written a whole 'nother story about the "Long White" so of winter I will say no more. It's January and I need only look out the window to remind me of it. Ice-out is a much anticipated and heralded event each spring. One day you come down one of the hills into town and the bay is no longer white. It's blue. It's blue! It's Lake Superior Blue and spring is here at last! And the kid in you wants to go find a pole and park down by the fish docks and ride the floaties along the shore out toward the point because that's what you did in the Spring when you were young and invincible.

Life's Short! Drink the Good Scotch First!

Life's Short! Drink the Good Scotch First!

A Good Man in the Woods

My dad was a good man in the woods and I know this because as a kid I heard him described as such by the lumberjacks we worked with on the island. They were all good men in the woods themselves, so it was a common enough remark considering the time, the place, and the company we kept in those days.

My dad made firewood and did most of the handyman work for the summer residents of Grand Island in the 60's and 70's and his crew were those of his seven sons he could lay hands on in the morning. The Cleveland Cliffs Iron Company still owned the island then and descendants of the company's executives who had built cottages during its heyday as a company retreat still summered there. We made their firewood, roofed their cottages, shot a few wells and evicted a few bats.

By then the company was prime cutting the island's timber and on days when we took the barge back and forth, we usually shared it with a pair of log trucks and the cars of a couple of the "islanders" coming and going to town. Most mornings we took a boat because my dad did not like being tied to the barge's schedule, even though his cousin, John, was the captain and he would always wait for us. The barge ran back and forth all day across the narrows from the mainland to Williams Landing leaving each side as soon as it was full.

The Silvics, which is still in use, could hold two of the era's straight bodied log trucks with 16-foot beds, along with four or five automobiles and it was about 30 minutes to load, cross and unload on the other side. The boat ride was more work, and it was not that we couldn't accommodate the barge's schedule, my dad just didn't want to. He avoided it every morning that the lake would let him.

I have vivid memories of those days as an 8-year-old boy with my chin in the very bow of an old wooden boat that smelled like tarred rope and fish. We would leave the dock at dawn, round the point and run across to the island, an old green, 20-horse Evinrude getting us almost up on plane. I was always amazed to see the bottom rise sharply though the dark blue water as we crossed the drop-off and approached the beach on the other side.

My dad was at home on the island. It was his family home. It's where his people, and mine, had settled back before the Civil War. He was at home on the island and he was at home in the woods too.

Lud Carr and the other jobbers were cutting the hardwood hills up the Center Road in those days, taking old growth maple and yellow birch, with a few virgin white pine, and leaving the low-grade timber, mostly beech, behind. I remember log trucks coming across with as few as five or six logs. The timber was huge then. I was always a little scared by how low the barge would squat when they rolled off the ramp and I kept waiting for them to drive off the front and into the lake, but they never did.

Prime cutting was not good for the forest though and it's no longer used to manage hardwood, but it was common practice at the time and we took advantage of that. We cut, split and delivered a couple hundred face cord of firewood every summer, and we followed the logging crews and harvested the big pulp trees they left behind. Whether we ever had formal permission to do so or not was never mentioned because nobody really cared and, in comparison to the scale of the logging operations on the island, we took very little and only what the company didn't want.

The day always started at my great uncle Harry's place. He was the island's only year-round resident, and everyone went by his house coming and going. He had the only phone on the island and was everyone's source for news and messages. We parked the truck there and my dad always had something on it that needed fixing before we could begin the day.

On mosquito infested summer mornings, we'd use chainsaw and grub hoes to turn skid trails into roads just passable enough to get the one-ton 48 Ford flatbed we used off the road and into the woods if we put it in "crawler gear." My dad used a manually-oiled Homelite saw with a 20" bar to fell and cut up trees. It was as heavy as a cement block and I remember it being a chore for me to lug it very far. We harvested old growth beech trees, three and four feet across and, by definition, too crooked to cut a decent log from. He'd pick out a tree in the morning and drop it where we could get at it. I remember him circling each one three or four times before he made sure we were out of the way and he began to notch it.

Once it was down, my brothers and I would play in the huge tops while my dad spent a tank of gas cutting the trunk into hockey pucks. While he gassed up his saw, we'd start standing them up to split and it would take him two more tanks of gas to finish cutting the tree into 16" pieces. He'd stop then, have a slug of cold coffee and smoke a cigarette. Then he'd pick up the maul and say "well, let's see if it'll split." We'd have all the rounds stood up by then and while we threw limb wood in the truck or started a pile between two trees, he'd spend the next two hours walking around in circles swinging that maul like it was an extension of his arms, slabbing the rounds, sometimes getting two dozen pieces out of each one. He had a steel wedge for the most twisted pieces.

Some days we cut all day. Those days were hard. Some days we delivered. Those days were the best. We'd stack a row of wood across the back of the truck where a chain held the sideboards together and then throw the rest of the wood loose in front of that and off we went, boys piled up in back on top of the load. We hauled a couple cord on each trip. Most of the wood went to the cottages around the landing, but there were at least a dozen trips out to Trout Bay each summer and a couple each year to the North Light. We always stacked it for the customer, and it was carefully measured by both men before payment was rendered in cash, $10 a cord. I remember the occasional half-dollar tip us boys would get from a man we knew only as "the Judge." He always astounded us by pulling the big coin out of our ear.

Looking back today, OSHA would have put my old man in jail. The truck we used (we actually had two and they served as parts for each other) had little in the way of brakes inside mismatched and pretty smooth, hard-rubber tires with patched inner tubes. A couple of blonde kids held the load on while we drove along washed out, cliff-edge roads with no guardrails. It's amazing we all survived, but those trips on the Trout Bay Road are forever etched in my mind.

On those days we'd have our usual lunch of tinned beef on homemade bread, washed down with a spring water from a one-gallon A&W jug, at Duck Lake or on the beach in Murray's Bay and we always visited the cemetery because my dad wanted to "to check on the relatives."

I'm certain that I complained every hour of every day that I had to work as a kid, but I spent my summers on the island, and looking back I would not trade that experience for anything. It has forever shaped who I am. It gave me my work ethic and helped define those things I hold dear. And my dad was a good man in the woods because those lumberjacks said so and I looked up to them, trying my best to remain invisible while they gathered on the side of the barge near Captain John who held court in the pilot house of the Timber Queen, the small tug that pushed the barge, each morning and drank coffee and smoked and used course language and laughed about the night before while they planned the day ahead. And if I was quiet and they didn't notice me, I got to the listen.

I did not truly appreciate what being a "good man in the woods" meant until many years later when I went back to work there and got to know many good men as peers. I'm spending a lot of time in the woods again these days, a very good thing, and it's got me thinking about those days I spent working in the woods 50 and then 25 years ago.

Next to the submarine navy, I've had no other job that has affected me as much as being a lumberjack. I swung a chain saw on and off for five years and it was the hardest job I ever had. But it was also tremendously rewarding and I was in the best shape of my life. I'm a better man today for the danger we faced, the skills that I learned, and the company we kept.

A good man in the woods shows up early and is ready for whatever work he has to do that day and for whatever weather he has to do it in.

A good man in the woods has tools and spare parts for whatever might break while he's doing it too. He's prepared for that day's work, but also for whatever else the day might offer up or throw at him.

A good man in the woods can be counted on no matter what. If he says he will be there, he will be there. If he says it will be done, it will be done. He can change gears on the fly in response to the needs of the job and the course of the day.

A good man in the woods has dry gloves and a sweatshirt in his truck, an extra sandwich in his lunch box and a cold six pack in his cooler for later. He's got a fire going when you walk in for lunch on a cold winter day and he'll spray you down with bug dope on those warm spring mornings when the black flies threaten your very sanity.

A good man in the woods is not just good with a saw, but he's equally skilled with a knife and an axe, a grub hoe and a come-along. He's got a tool belt in his truck and he knows his way around a welder and a box of wrenches. If it's broke, he can fix it and he's always there to lend a hand to a friend or anyone else he comes across who needs help. He's a damn good man to have around.

A good man in the woods knows his way around and seldom needs a map. He knows this land from his work, every old logging road and two-track, but also from a lifetime of hunting and fishing and foraging for mushrooms, berries and firewood. He is a crack shot and he knows all the best fishing holes.

A good man in the woods is a trusted friend. He's always there when you need him, and he will never let you down. I have been fortunate in this life to have several friends who I can describe as "good men in the woods" and it's a level of personal respect that I aspire to someday.

Only after working in the woods for a couple of years did I truly appreciate the amount of work my dad put in every day and the wide range of skills and abilities, mostly self-taught, that he possessed. These days I think about him every time I pick up a chainsaw or try to split a gnarly beech round with a 8-pound maul. Admittedly, this is not very often anymore, but I'm still pretty good with both tools.

While I was working in the woods I spent a lot of time thinking about what made a good day in the woods and I wrote them down. I found that list the other day. They're simple and very practical concerns for anyone who spends his day remodeling the forest.

On a good day in the woods no one gets hurt and nothing breaks down. Everyone shows up and the road is in good shape. You get to the landing in the morning while the eastern sky glows crimson before the sun begins to break.

On a good day in the woods your saw is ready and you get an early start. The land is flat, the timber tall and straight, and it's a short walk through your slash to the paint line.

On a good day in the woods it's not too hot and it's not too cold. It doesn't rain or snow and the wind is light and steady. The black flies are done, and the deer flies and horse flies are still getting their wings.

On a good day in the woods your saw runs hot and the chain stays sharp. The trees fall all the way down and right where you want them to. You see all the spring poles and widow makers coming and your reflexes never fail you.

On a good day in the woods you don't bark your shin or get poked in the eye. You don't get whacked on the knuckles or whipped in the face or thumped on the head. You don't stumble and you don't fall down. Or at least not very often.

On a good day in the woods all the big pulp is marked, there isn't much pole timber and you get at least a few good logs. There's no whip or old slash to fight and no rotten snags to get in your way.

On a really good day in the woods you get a run of hard maple veneer or 8-stick hemlock to cut. These days are special and are to be savored.

On a good day in the woods you leave the landing in the morning with your gas jug juiced to the cap and come in for lunch when it's empty. There's still some coffee in your thermos, your lunch pail is full of ham sandwiches, home grown tomatoes and homemade cookies and you've an hour to recharge around a tail gate in the sun or sitting on a log next to a big fire.

On a good day in the woods you cut them down and then you cut them up, and you hardly ever pinch your saw or throw your chain. The trees hit the ground with a mighty crash, your mind is at ease and you are satisfied, even gratified, to be doing what you're doing.

On a good day in the woods the birds sing, the squirrels scold and the mice skitter beneath the leaf litter on the forest floor. You see deer in the mist as you drive across the plains at dawn and the raspy cry of sandhill cranes is the time clock you punch to begin your day, changing by the hour as the seasons progress.

On a good day in the woods everyone gathers back at the landing at the end of the day, no one is hurt and nothing is broke. You lean on old pick-up trucks and drink a few beers and talk about the day that's now done and the night that lies ahead.

You're young and you're strong. The day has been won, and you can see exactly how much work you did. It's lying there in piles. The beer is cold and you're sharing it with men you like and trust, fellow woodsman and stalwart souls who are known in these parts as good men in the woods.

Life's Short! Drink the Good Scotch First!

Life's Short! Drink the Good Scotch First!

My Father's Enemies

There is a photo in the family archive, a black and white snapshot, of my dad and his twin brother sitting on the deck of the USS Wichita, the heavy cruiser they served on in World War II. They're in fresh dungarees, long sleeves rolled up past their elbows, and both have their white hats cocked back at a jaunty angle that never was and still isn't regulation.

One is handing the other a cigarette and only the other members of their generation, all gone now, were ever certain which one was which as they were identical twins and in their prime. The caption on the photo reads "Nagasaki Harbor, Sept. 20, 1945." The war was over. They were going home. You could see it in their eyes.

They'd both joined up with three other brothers and a sister right after Pearl Harbor and had fought with their ship from the North Atlantic and the Mediterranean to the South Pacific and then north to Okinawa. In reading the ship's official history which documented 13 battle stars, they'd also made several ports of call in the Pacific that I'd get to visit 35 years later; Pearl Harbor and Guam, Manila and Subic Bay, Nagasaki and the nearby port of Sasebo where I had the good fortune to be homeported for five of the years I was in the navy on a pair of old diesel submarines.

My dad never mentioned Nagasaki during the few times I heard him talk about the war, but he was there twice that September of 1945 for a week each time, just a few weeks after the second atomic bomb flattened that city and killed and maimed a hundred thousand people. Maybe that's why he didn't talk about it.

I don't believe my dad got much in the way of liberty there or in any of those other ports during the war but knowing that he had seen the same shorelines and channels, hills and harbors that I was exploring thirty-five years later gave me a connection to him that I didn't learn to appreciate until I was much older.

By Japanese standards, Sasebo is a small town of about half a million people. It's nestled on the north end of a large, protected harbor and there is a shipyard and naval base there. It was home to a Japanese fleet during the war and the naval base is now shared by the U.S. Navy and the Japanese Maritime Self Defense Force.

When we arrived on the Darter in 1979 our crew of 75 doubled the U.S. military population on what had become, by then, a naval ordinance facility---a depot for the munitions needed by the U.S. Navy's 7th Fleet. And it was a large enough facility that it could accommodate the whole fleet which visited regularly and so Sasebo had the ubiquitous "sailor town" just off base.

I raised many a glass with my shipmates and the rest of the fleet across the Sasebo River in the Panama Bar and the Westerner, the Pub New Happy and the Blue Moon. For those of us who called

Sasebo home, we also had access to the nicer bars and private clubs frequented by our Japanese hosts, both military and civilian.

We made many friends. Japan is a wonderfully hospitable society and they still liked Americans and anything American. Some of us stayed there after our enlistments. Some of us got married there. All of us had a good time and none of us will ever forget those days.

Even in 1979 a sailor could only drink so much before he ran out of money and needed a less expensive pastime. It turned out that the local chamber of commerce had raised a club football team which played a full schedule of games against local college teams and other club squads.

The Sasebo Sarapis played junior varsity-quality football, but we were good enough post a 6-3 season record the year I got to play. The team's advantage was that they were able to recruit American sailors, ostensibly with football skills, and there were four or five of us who played on the squad.

I didn't speak good enough Japanese to play offense, but I was as big as anyone else on the field and I growled a lot, so they let me play nose tackle on defense. We all had a good time with the bonus being the formal banquet after each game. Most of the local players owned bars or restaurants and they would take turns hosting a victory dinner in the "private room" of their establishment where we reviewed the game film.

These were formal affairs for them and at any given time, there were a dozen different dishes in front of me and kimono-clad waitresses in constant motion topping off my beer, whiskey and sake. Being the best players on the team, the American sailors were always treated as guests of honor and we joined in the traditional cheer that went up as we watched each good play on a large screen projection TV. As the night wore on polite toasts of "Kampai" gave way to loud shouts of "Banzai!" which we yelled again and again until the end of the evening when we were all drunk and stupid and our hosts poured us sailors into King taxis and we were taken back to the base.

One night our host was a crew member from one of the Japanese submarines stationed at the base and our banquet that night was held at the Japanese equivalent of the VFW. I remember going down a street I did not know and being left off at a very formal looking street door which the cab driver pointed to and said "sensekan," Japanese for submarine. I buzzed and was admitted to a short hallway leading to a stair with display cases on each side going up which were filled with military gear, uniforms and other memorabilia, a good portion of it American.

It was mixed together rather randomly, as these cumulative displays tend to be in our country too; Japanese and American, war trophies and modern plaques and patches of ships from both navies that had visited Sasebo.

It was a slow, sobering climb for me up those stairs as I saw World War II-era American weapons and gear that had once been in the hands of a young marines or sailors. Each one counted a young man who didn't make it back to his girl or his family and the displays were eerily similar to those I'd seen in the U.S.—the residue of war collected from both sides of the battlefield. Still, I was unready for it and I hesitated on each step and stared at each item.

My host was there to greet me at the top of the stairs and he had watched me take in the displays. He bowed very formally when I reached him, and I returned the gesture slightly lower as he was of senior rank and he said, "Our fathers," and then he paused as he searched for his English. "once enemies."

"Hai," I responded.

"Very brave," he replied.

"Hai," I agreed.

"No more," he replied with a sweep of his hand over the whole display.

"Same team now," he grinned. "Come!" and he led me through the door and into the banquet room where our arrival raised a cheer from our teammates for our victory on the field that day.

I almost got married a couple of times in Sasebo and I'm pleased to report that both young ladies came to their senses in time to avoid what would have been a mistake. And I'm also pleased to report that I remained friends with both afterward. I was young, and I fell in love on a regular basis, but being in the navy made me transient for months at a time so all those romances were ill-fated.

The most serious one, Kuniko, lasted a couple of years during which we shared a small house halfway up Mount Yumihari that overlooked the harbor. On nights when we were in port and I had the duty on the boat she would come down for dinner and stay for the nightly movie. As luck would have it, one night we played Tora! Tora! Tora! and she sat politely through the first reel but then got increasingly upset as the scenes of the attack on Pearl Harbor played out in the second reel. She demanded to leave, and I followed her topside and tried to calm her down on the pier. She was fuming.

"Why are you watching that?" she demanded. I started a lame explanation of not knowing what movie was on the schedule while I was figuring out what a dolt I had been for not realizing that the subject matter may have upset her.

"That did not happen!" she said defiantly. "The Japanese navy did not do that!" she insisted, and I suddenly realized that she had learned a very different version of history in school. I put her in a cab and we made amends a few days later though we never spoke of it again.

I got to know her well enough that we talked about getting married and so she brought me home to meet her folks. They lived out of town in a fishing village on a small bay just past the crematorium. That detail may sound morbid, but I couldn't read any of the road signs and the chimney was one of my landmarks. It was 200 feet tall and attached to what looked like a modest temple. When I first asked what it was she couldn't find the word.

"They burn people there," she explained. "Their dead first," she added matter-of-factly. All bodies are cremated in Japan as there is no room for expansive cemeteries. Her father owned a small woodshop and lived on the property in a modern, western style house. Her mother lived in the "old house" behind her father's house. They were separated but not divorced and as was custom her father was still responsible for keeping his wife housed and fed.

Her mom was a hoot and insisted I call her "Okaa-san," mother, and we sat on tatami mats with our legs beneath a blanket around a low table and drank plum wine with her. She gave me a new pair of socks each time we went to visit, and we would bring her pear-apples and persimmons from the market.

Kuniko's father was another matter altogether. He was quiet and stern and very formal, and he eyed me suspiciously even after I made him a regular gift of a top-shelf bottle of scotch. We would sit on chairs in his living room. She would pour, and we would sip the warm whiskey from teacups. There was a small Shinto shrine in the room with a photo of a young man in a cadet style uniform. Kuniko told me only that it was her uncle and he had died.

My Japanese was in it's very early stages, a state from which it never really emerged, and he spoke no English, so Kuniko translated. He asked of my family and was impressed that I had six brothers. He told me that my father was a lucky man and I told him my dad had died just two years before. He apologized, bowed deeply, and whatever he said then needed no translation.

We talked of the ocean and of the kinds of trees that grew in America. His curiosity about me and my country was more polite than it was genuine and he always seemed detached but felt obligated to forward the conversation.

Kuniko and I helped him sometimes in his small shop. He directed me with gestures and grunted approval at my Wally Michelson-taught wood shop skills. I was a master at guiding the dumb end of the board and he saw that I understood the grain. He'd made his living with the shop since the war (which, along with the navy, was a subject we never mentioned) and he specialized in making trim and traditional sliding door frames. His two sons had been his helpers when they were young, but both had now graduated from college and had no interest in taking over the family business. Now in his late 60s, he was looking at his daughter for his legacy. And she was engaged to this American--an American who seemed competent and not overly rude or stupid, but an American just the same and one who spoke just enough Japanese to order a drink and give a cab driver directions home.

It was an awkward relationship that neither of us ever got comfortable with, but it was always polite, and it almost got friendly. Then I left for three months and when I returned the flame I once had for his daughter, and that she once had for me, had dimmed in my absence and we parted ways.

She still worked as a hostess in one of our favorite bars and we saw each other regularly. One night we were talking, and she told me that her father had decided to sell his sawmill. He couldn't run it by himself anymore. And she confessed that he had seriously considered leaving the business to the two of us when it looked like I was going to be his son-in-law.

"It was hard for him to like you," she explained, "but he was starting to. He was in the war on a ship," she added. "Cargo ship. He was sunk by American submarine. His brother drowned."

I think about her sometimes and I remember those days we spent together when I was young and in my prime. And I think about her father too and that picture of his brother. I think about my dad and his brothers and sister who went to war so long ago and who all came home. And I think about that Japanese VFW club and the relics it contained that had belonged to guys who didn't come home and of the Japanese rifle I have in my basement that my uncle brought home as a war trophy. And I think about the young soldier who had once carried it who didn't get to come home to his girl and his family either.

I have been to the Arizona Memorial in Pearl Harbor several times and I have been to the Peace Park in Nagasaki as well. In both places I was surrounded by thousands of Japanese people and in none of their eyes could I find my father's enemies.

Life's Short! Drink the Good Scotch First!

Life's Short! Drink the Good Scotch First!

The Continuing Adventures of Charlie Bear (Prologue)

I like my dog more than I like most people and, well, I like almost everybody so what does that say about my dog?

His name is Charlie Bear and, technically, he's my daughter's dog. She brought him home in her junior year of high school and used my mom's 80th birthday party as the setting for the "can I keep him" plea—cue the puppy dog eyes on both the dog and the girl. He joined the clan that day and my daughter then proceeded to do a poor job of training him before she went away to college a year later at which time I become his human.

Charlie Bear, or "CB," or sometimes just "the bear dog," is both a rare breed and the product of the shallow end of the gene pool. He comes from good stock, but the tail end of it. His momma was a pure-bred black lab, 10 years old, and his daddy was a pure-bred collie the same age. They had only two pups and I didn't see his litter mate. He is coal black like a lab and long haired like a collie with a white blaze on his chest. He thinks he's handsome and I do too.

He cut his puppy teeth on a yellow lab named Jake in the little house on Chestnut Street and spent a year learning the ropes from that good dog, one who had also protected my family and blessed our lives. Tragically, we lost Jake just a year later and Charlie Bear ruled the porch and the yard as an only dog for the next 8 years. He joined our family at a time of change. My kids grew up and moved away. I divorced and then remarried when he was still young and with that came a change in my lifestyle or, more accurately, a return to a lifestyle I had all but abandoned. And Charlie Bear walked every step of it with me. He was, and still is, my boon companion.

My one concession from my daughter had been that I got to name him, and I did so after Charlie Brown, my old friend and shipmate from the submarine navy who I had lost track of in recent years. We have since reunited and he was the best man at my wedding six years ago. And as Charlie Brown has told me more than once, "I guess you gotta like a guy a whole lot to name your dog after him." I do, so I did.

When I think of the miles we have wandered together and the adventures we've had, I knew I had to tell his story. In doing so I would tell some of my own stories or at least those written in the last ten years but not yet put down on paper.

There is no Alpha male in Charlie Bear. These days he is afforded respect by the two wolf hound pups he shares the house with and who he is training, but they defer to his age rather than to any dominant trait he may have acquired in his 11 years on the planet. He still leads the hikes, though, and instinctively knows which way I want to go, even when we're bushwhacking. As we get older he knows the way as often from memory because he's been down those trails with me before, some of them many times. He seldom rambles more than fifty yards ahead and rarely goes out of sight. Squirrels and rabbits don't interest him beyond a bark and then a half-hearted lunge in their general direction and he's always looking over his shoulder to make sure the pack is following.

There are certain words I don't speak out load at my house; walk, run, swim, truck, ride and camp. He knows these words and if I don't say them out loud he at least lets me put on my boots and load my backpack before he starts doing the "Oh boy! Oh boy! I getta go! I getta go! happy dance" in front of the door. When he was younger he would sometimes give himself seizures from the anticipation.

He's a water dog and he loves to swim. We walk the beach near the Tourist Park from March to November and he's in Lake Superior as soon as the ice is out. And the walk is definitely "all about the stick." He will fetch them until he's so tired he's dragging himself out of the lake, but in 11 years he has never brought one back. He sees no profit in that. He walks around with it in his mouth like it's the only stick on the beach until I grab a new one. Then the old one is forgotten and it's all about the new stick.

He's a boat dog, too, and has been around Grand Island more times than most of the people I know. He does not get to go fishing with me, though, and he hates that because I prepare for a day on the river just like I do for a hike. I took him fishing once down the Indian River and he went after every splash my spinner made in the stream. He would not be deterred and eventually I put away my pole and we just hiked downstream and saved the fishing for another day.

He's a snow dog and prefers the winter. We shear him every April so he can tolerate the summer heat and for three months at least he looks like a lab. As the snow melts in the spring he rides the push piles in the yard right down to the ground, preferring to lay on the cool snowbank than on the warming earth. Eventually he can be found lying on the last patch of snow, his black fur completely covering it.

We camped one winter on Hartney Lake for pike fishing and I had built a warm nest for me and the two dogs. Up out of the snow on a six-inch mat of cedar bows, I had lined the floor of my tent with a sheet of polystyrene foam and had laid out extra sleeping bags for the dogs to nest in next to me. I had also left the tent flap open on the bottom so they could come and go and when I woke up in the middle of the night Charlie was missing.

I stuck my head out of the tent and it took me awhile to spot him in out on the lake in the moonlight. He was a black silhouette fifty yards out with his head raised alertly. He may have simply been too warm in the tent, but I think he was watching the camp from a position where he could see anything coming. He's a very good guard dog.

He's also a bacon whore of the first magnitude. He loves me unconditionally, but he would leave me for you if he thought you had a piece of bacon in your pocket. And he would know if you did. After a Sunday breakfast he can smell that plate on the back of the stove from across the room and tell exactly how many pieces of bacon are still on it. And then his day gets planned around getting them all. He's right there in a good spot every time you walk through the kitchen and he looks up at the stove knowingly, and at you lovingly and patiently, as you pass by.

But he's also very social and has lots of two and four legged friends. Everybody likes Charlie Bear. We live next door to a daycare home and in the summer when the kids are out back they call to him to come over for the kind of loving and attention you can only get from a half dozen three-year olds.

He looks at me and waits until I tell him it's OK and then he runs over and lays on his back in the sun, basking in the attention and adoration of children. He shoots me a half-guilty look each time because he knows that he's cheating on me, but he doesn't really care, and neither do I.

He's also a 10-year veteran of the Grand Marais Music Festival, our annual summer vacation where, for the better part of a week, all the dogs and old hippies get to run around off their leashes. We host the musician hospitality area in the center of the festival campground (right next to the portable sauna) and Charlie Bear is recognized as the "top dog" whom all the other dogs must recognize in some fashion as they come and go by our camp. Again, it is respect for his age. All the old hippies know him too and they always stop and give him a pat on the head or a scratch behind the ear. He likes that.

We play a game every time we go out rambling. I stomp my foot and he bows and barks a challenge. I stomp again a step closer and he retreats bowing and barking. I stomp again and he attacks and gets me by the pantleg. He snarls and growls and won't let go until I stomp the other foot and then he retreats again, bobbing and weaving, bowing and barking. We can do this for hours. My wife calls it "dancing with dogs" and it's a game that always ends with the two of us rolling around on the ground or in the snow.

We've been on so many adventures and my wife has taken so many pictures of him that he had his own Facebook page for a while. But the Bear Dog doesn't pay much attention to social media these days and he didn't even notice when we stopped posting to it. You can still "like" him if you want.

He never judges me, and he always forgives me no matter what I've done or have forgotten to do. I am, and always will be, the center of his world and as he gets older I take every opportunity to let him know that he's my boy and a very good dog. That's all he wants. It's all he needs. I wish people were that easy.

I frequently remind him that he's a "four-legged, fur-bearing, flea bitten varmint" and that I love him like a brother. He would die for me. I know he would. He would die for every member of my family. The one time I saw him vent his loyal fury in my defense he cowered a dog who was twice his size. It was a swift, focused and terrible wrath that I do not ever wish to see again.

But he's getting lazy and even obstinate in his old age for he knows I cannot scold him. He has a 12-hour bladder and if it's too cold in the morning, or if it's raining, he'll go back to bed until it warms up or the rain stops. Sometimes he just ignores my command with a look that says "yeah, I heard you but I don't need to go out right now. And by the way I happen to know that there are seven pieces of bacon left up there."

He's getting fat from too much bacon and too much pilfered puppy chow. I asked the vet if I should change his diet to a senior formula and she said no. He wouldn't eat it anyway and though he looked heavier to me, he had only gained five pounds in five years.

But we've both cut back on the bacon as we try to keep up with Shadow and Murphy, the two young wolf hounds who have taken over our lives and our home and our hearts. His willingness to train them even as he tolerates their intrusion into his senior years impresses me. It's instinctive and it is keeping him young. He tolerates the playful mauling he endures as part of the game and he lets them know when they're getting too rough. They acknowledge his status and his mood by licking his chops in submission.

There's melancholy in watching a beloved dog grow old, especially when seen in daily contrast to a pair of pups learning their abilities, testing their limits and finding their place in the world. He will get the best care and comfort I can provide right up to that last day that we all dread but that we all know will come. That and my love is the least I can do.

In the meantime, Charlie Bear's story is worth telling because it's common to all humans who have been lucky enough to have been adopted by a faithful canine who seeks only their approval and their company.

So, look forward to regular installments of the Continuing Adventures of Charlie Bear, Wonder Dog of the North. He and I have been around some and we've poked our noses down a few trails and we've seen a few things that are worth remembering and telling other people about. If only he could speak. He'd tell these stories better than me.

Life's Short! Drink the Good Scotch First!

Sentenced to Matrimony

There aren't many perks that come with being the mayor of a small town.

Oh sure, there's that $50 a month salary and the never-ending opportunities I get to listen to the insightful, objective, and unvarnished concerns, complaints and opinions of my constituents while walking down the street or buying paint at the hardware, standing in the check-out line at Bob's IGA or enjoying a cold beer down at the Legion.

I also get to run city commission meetings and I've been doing that long enough that I can't recall the last time I had to use the gavel for anything other than convening and then adjourning the meeting. I sign a lot of documents and make quite a few speeches and I "hereby resolve" and I "therefore proclaim" quite a bit. And on infrequent occasions I give away keys to the city.

That's always fun. They're impressive--solid brass skeleton keys, about 8 inches long and they weigh about a pound. They're inscribed with "City of Munising" on the shaft and they have a functional bottle opener in the handle. People are always tickled by that. But they're also expensive—about $40 each—so I don't give them to just anyone. You have to be a pretty important poohbah or potentate to get one or else a resident who has devoted your life to serving the community.

One of the few benefits of being the mayor is that I get to decide who's important enough to get one and who's not. The governor didn't get one when he came to town. Neither did either of our senators or our congressman. Santa Clause gets one each year, but we make him give it back when the kids aren't looking so we can give it to him again next year. I gave one to the captain of the Coast Guard buoy tender that stopped in Munising one time and when the captain wasn't looking, I gave the chief bos'n's mate a fist full of drink chips I'd collected from all the bars in town.

I gave one to the Cabin Fever Band when they came up north to play, just because I like those boys a lot, and I also give one every year to the winner of the "Mayors' Choice Award" at the car show in September. Last year it was to the owner of a powder blue '62 T-Bird. That was a sweet ride!

Maybe the coolest part of the office, other than being called "your honor," is marrying people. In the 20 years I've had the job I've performed maybe 150 weddings. I quit counting at 100. Getting married is arguably one of the biggest days in a person's life and it's a joy to be a part of that.

I give a damn fine, and very short, civil ceremony and the couples who choose that option represent the whole spectrum of people who do not want to be married in a church. They've all got their reasons I suppose, and I don't ask. I've married a lot of my friends as well as a lot of tourists. I'm always honored that people come here to get married and I let them know that.

I've married a couple of people twice—to each other and to different people—and I let people know up front that I offer no guarantees. My first wedding was at City Hall and it was scheduled for 4 o'clock on a weekday. I didn't know the couple, but the clerk called me about 3:15 and asked if I could please come down and marry these people so they would leave. I hurried down and there were about 40 very drunk people crowding the counter area and conference room. The bride was beautiful in her wedding gown and easily the largest woman I had ever met.

The groom was resplendent in a light blue tuxedo made even more festive by the blackberry brandy he had spilled down the front of his shirt. And he was easily the thinnest man I had ever met. Every member of the wedding party was related to the bride and the groom was so drunk I could have married him to a fire hydrant, and he would have cheerfully said "I do."

I don't marry many people at City Hall and that's one of the reasons. Most often, I take my show on the road.

I remember one wedding I performed out in the sticks and I was late because I had trouble finding the address. I had the right fire number but there was no house. I was eventually flagged down by a guy who came out of what looked like a chicken coop. He was carrying a shotgun. As I got out of the truck, I noticed there were three more guys with shotguns. It was a joke, but they were real guns and they were loaded because, well, it doesn't make much sense to bring an empty shotgun to a wedding.

Only in the U.P. would this not faze a dedicated hard-working public servant and I performed the wedding outside a one-room shack with no electricity and no running water. They were a beautiful couple. It was his fifth wedding and her fourth. You get details like that when you fill out the marriage license.

I did a wedding in the canteen at the Legion last year and noted the groom was 74 and the bride was 83. He was a veteran and they both had a good sense of humor, so I mentioned to her that technically she was a "cougar."

"You're damn right I am," she laughed. "I like my men young!"

I have officiated very formal weddings with a half dozen groomsmen and bridesmaids and have worn a suit myself when necessary though these days I only promise to shave, wear deodorant and a clean shirt. I performed one formal wedding at Miner's Beach in the Pictured Rocks National Lakeshore. There were a hundred guests and a large wedding party and it was hot. By game time the temperature was 94 degrees. The best man, who was referred to as "dumb-ass" for the hour we all waited for him to get back, had forgotten the rings in town. We waited an hour.

Life's Short! Drink the Good Scotch First!

The little kids all got bored and played in the lake in their Sunday best and then they all got dirty building sandcastles. One of the groomsmen finally walked the 200 yards back to the parking lot and drug back a cooler of beer. Being one of the more important people there, I got dibs on a cool one. The best man finally returned with the rings and the ceremony went ahead as planned. They still call him dumbass.

I've never been late for a wedding, or at least they never start without me. I have started a wedding service by banging a spoon on a pan and saying "OK, everybody put down your beers and put your cigarettes out so we can get started. The groom has to be back in jail by 4 o'clock."

And something always goes wrong, so I have learned to prepare the bride for that certainty. If possible, I let her know the day before.

"Now, I know you made elaborate plans down to the smallest detail so that everything about tomorrow is perfect and special," I tell her. "So, you just forget all that right now. If anything can go wrong tomorrow, it will. But that's OK because it will still be perfect."

Most of the weddings I perform are outside so the weather is always a factor. Seldom is it the "perfect day." It usually rains and sometimes it snows.

I married a couple on the beach in Au Train one Saturday in May and the weather showed up. May is spring most of the time up north, but that day it was more like Winter. It was about 40 degrees and there was a 20-knot wind blowing right off the big lake. It was cold!

I wore a parka with a hood and had my back to the lake. The groom at least had a suit jacket on. The bride, who refused so much as a shawl, wore a very thin, very skimpy wedding gown with spaghetti straps. I could tell she was cold, and I could tell just how cold she was too. We all stuttered and got sand in our eyes and when she got to her speaking part it came out as "I d-d-d-d-do."

Then the marriage license got away from me later in the parking lot and blew across the highway, up the bank and over the snowmobile trail. I got it before it landed in the river and it was only a little worse for wear.

Most weddings are in the summer and for a few years it seemed I sacrificed just about every Saturday. I'm a little more selective now. If it's boating season I just say I'm busy. People almost always get married on Saturday in the middle of the afternoon. That makes it hard to plan anything.

I went to two weddings by boat.

My friend Joe dropped me off at Miners Beach for one ceremony halfway through a boating day. I waded ashore, performed the service and was back in the boat before my beer got warm.

I once took a boat to a wedding on the Shipwreck Cruise boat just off the East Channel Lighthouse. I arrived on the Popeye, my friend John's fishing boat, and we came alongside playing pirate music. We both wore tie-dye and John even had his AFLAC duck on his shoulder because we couldn't find a parrot. I climbed aboard the bigger boat, performed the wedding, got back on the Popeye (before my beer got warm) and we sailed off with flourish playing Barrett's Privateers by Stan Rogers as loud as we could. The groom gave me a thumbs up while the mother of the bride glared at everyone. They're still married and we're still friends.

I've also married people in the lake. I did a combined civil—Native American ceremony knee deep in the big lake at Sand Point for my friends Jill and Thomas. That one was fun. There were drums and everything. I also married a couple beneath Tannery Falls. They stood under the falls, and I stood just outside but I still got wet. That one was a little strange.

I have married people in the Winter, too, one time where Trail 8 crosses Highway 13. The bride had a veil duct-taped to her snowmobile helmet and they both had a collection of beer cans tied to the back of their sleds. They drove off triumphantly together in a cloud of 2-cycle exhaust toward their very own happily ever after.

And I've even performed one wedding in prison. It was at Camp Cusino, a minimum-security facility near Munising, that has since been torn down. It was a rather solemn affair. The groom was doing 4-10 for cocaine distribution and the bride's father also served as best man. Why, I'll never know, but after the ceremony the bride's father patted the groom on the ass and he quickly responded "please don't do that dad. I'm in prison."

I got so many calls from women wanting to marry prisoners after that, that I called the prison chaplain (he's not allowed to marry prisoners) and asked if he was giving out my phone number. He laughed and said "Oh, I don't have to do that."

Marrying people was also how I met my own wife. I was officiating at the wedding of a mutual friend and she was one of the witnesses. We were filling out the marriage license the night before and she said, "you don't look like a minister."

"That's because I'm not," I replied with a salacious wink. That made her curious enough to dance with me at the reception and my friend Captain Kate married us 18 months later. I had performed Kate's wedding a couple years before that and we've had a running joke ever since that "I married Kate, and she married me, but we're not married to each other."

Whether it's formal or so poorly planned that I had to go to the Corktown to round up some witnesses, there's always a few moments when I'm standing there with the groom and we're waiting for the bride. She is always late, and the groom is always nervous. To lighten the moment, I always share the secret of a happy marriage with the groom and I can usually get him to repeat the following after me.

"Honey, I've been thinking. I was wrong and you were right, and I should listen to you more often."

And though I always end the ceremony with the obligatory "by the authority vested in me as mayor in and for the City of Munising, County of Alger, State of Michigan, I now pronounce you husband and wife," just once I'd like to say, "by the authority vested in me, I hereby sentence you to matrimony."

I haven't yet, but one day I might.

Life's Short! Drink the Good Scotch First!

Life's Short! Drink the Good Scotch First!

Etched in Stone

A Facebook friend recently posted a picture of some initials carved into the sandstone outcropping at Miner's Beach. He was upset that someone would be so disrespectful as to deface the natural beauty of the park's landscape and he said so. Along with several other people, I agreed with him that we couldn't permit that sort of thing in the Pictured Rocks National Lakeshore, or in any of our national parks for that matter, and I posted a comment to that effect.

But I also pointed out that there were other places around here on the south shore of the big lake where people had been carving their names and initials in the soft sandstone for years and that those markings were part of our history and our cultural heritage.

Ever since we figured out what those opposable thumbs were for and got the first inklings of identity and individuality, we have been leaving our marks on stone. The first prehistoric cave drawings of animals were essentially graffiti, the paleo world's version of "Grog was here." As soon as we developed tools, we started scratching our marks into rock. Eventually, it's where we learned to write, and it helped us develop language.

I guess most of the men I know have carved their initials in a tree. Though that was a decidedly masculine thing to do in my time (girls didn't carry pocket knives when I was a kid), stone is more permanent and, regardless of your gender, whatever is carved there is meant to last. Granite and the other hard rocks of the volcanic world are not easy to carve without serious tools, some technology and a fair amount of patience. You won't find many initials or much in the way of true love pledged in any of the hard rock outcroppings to be found in the U.P. No one loves anyone that much.

Sandstone is much easier to scratch letters into and it defines the edge of our world up here on the shoreline of the Pictured Rocks and Grand Island and the coast between Au Train and Grand Marais. And we have been carving our mark in it for years.

In his book, The Face in the Rock, my friend Loren Graham tells the story of Powers of the Air and how his face came to be carved in the sandstone cliff near Scott Falls in Au Train by a French voyageur travelling with the Cass expedition in 1820. Though it's unrecognizable now, the face was clear and distinct when I was a boy and fortunately for us all, many photographs were taken of it before the wind and waves and winter ice eroded it away. It lasted as long as it did because of its location above even the largest waves crashing on the beach below it. It was a handsome face and the artist who made it, though unknown, left it as a memorial to the "Gallant 13" warriors of the Grand Island Band who died in the battle of the cavern. He etched the face of Powers of the Air so that no one would forget the story which has become a central part of local Nishnabe history.

Nearby, my family's homestead at Powell's Point is sculpted from the same assortment of sandstone formations. They rise from the lake in fractured grandeur and some formations have been split by tree roots while all are topped with all manner of trees and shrubs and other plants. In many places the stone itself is covered with moss and lichens where it's not exposed directly to the elements. Central to this very special piece of property is a prominent outcropping that we called "Indian Rock" when we were kids because of the small face that was carved in its south side. No larger than a baseball, it was just possible then to make out the eyes and nose of a face, but impossible to attribute any ethnicity to the carving. But we were kids and decided it was an Indian. I apologize to my Nishnabe friends, but this was the 60s, so we didn't call it Native American Rock. It's still there but you would have to know what it once was to recognize it as a face.

Near it and still recognizable if you trace it with your fingers is the name, "D. McCAULEY" and the date "1873." It's carved deep in capital letters six inches high and obviously took some time and quite a bit of effort. I can find no record of anyone named McCauley associated with my family, at Powell's Point or on Grand Island, but there were two important events that occurred that year.

Abraham Williams died in the spring of 1873. He was the first European settler in the Central U.P. having settled on the island in 1840. He was also my great great great grandfather. But in the summer of that year they also finished the first road from Marquette to the frontier village of Onota, then a bustling community of 700 souls located near present-day Christmas. They pushed over the ridge at Powell's Point the next year and completed the road to old Munising in 1875. Onota burned to the ground just four years later when sparks from the blast furnace caught one of the nearby houses on fire and then that quickly spread until it consumed the entire settlement.

Mr. McCauley's visit may have been for Old Abe's funeral or the disposition of his estate, as he was a man of some means, or he may have lived in Onota or had some business there. He may have come by boat or via the new road from Marquette. He may even have been a guest at the nearby Hotel Hiawatha, built and operated by the Powell family, but whatever the answer, he was either a friend of the family or was otherwise welcomed by my ancestors. Either that or he was trespassing when he spent a whole day carving his name in that rock. In any case, he felt compelled to leave his mark and he did so with flourish. His name is now a mystery forever tied to that spot.

I remember finding the initials "DG" carved in the rock face of an escarpment in the park on the other side of the bay one day many years ago. The carving looked relatively fresh. I was hiking with Captain Dave and they were his initials, but he would not claim the carving and neither of us was certain that we had even been to that particular spot before. We came up with a half dozen people with those initials but discounted them all in turn as we were equally certain that none of them were that adventurous. Another minor mystery etched in stone.

Perhaps the most prolific sandstone venue for carving is out on Five Mile Point just west of Christmas. Known to my grandparent's generation as Swimmer's Paradise, it's now known simply as Paradise and it is aptly named. A half mile of low sandstone coast eroded into caves and pools and small coves, the rock has been scrubbed smooth, or as smooth as sandstone gets, by the relentless waves of Lake Superior. For as long as anyone can remember we've been carving our names and initials in the soft stone there and there are hundreds of autographs and other works of art, a sign board that's constantly changing as new ones are added and old ones are worn away.

I never had the patience to scratch my own initials there. I started to one day 20 years ago and never finished. My kids all put their mark on the rock, but it's been awhile since I checked to see if they're still there. A Phillips screwdriver is the best tool, but any piece of pointed steel will do. Some carvings are stick-figure crude, and some are quite artistic. There is even some pretty good calligraphy. The carved letters range in size from an inch to a foot tall and over the years several pieces of art have come and gone. I recall the face of a woman etched ever so lightly one year. You could only see her from one angle, and she was beautiful. The carving lasted a few years before fading into eternity.

I do not and cannot find these carvings offensive. They are an ever-changing cultural touchstone and they do not detract from the beauty of the rock. One year some lazy people made their mark with spray paint at Paradise and that was ugly and offensive, but it all disappeared beneath the weight of a single winter's ice. I don't make it to Paradise much anymore. The road is in pretty bad shape, but I have no doubt that the tradition continues and that's a good thing.

When I started writing this story, I went back to the family homestead and climbed up on Indian Rock to make sure I'd remembered the name carved there correctly. I traced the letters, barely legible beneath the lichen, and was reminded that the crossbar of the A was an inverted chevron that made it look like a teepee and I wondered if that was why we had given it that name. As I pondered this, I noticed another carving, below it and smaller, that I had forgotten about and I bent down and traced out "LWD 1936."

In truth, it could have been "LWP," but there is no one in my family history with those initials. LWD would have been my dad and he would have been 16 years old in 1936. Even as a young man he felt obliged to leave his mark on this spot and I am very glad that he did. However humble the inscription, it is now part of his memorial. And it is fitting.

When it comes to stone carving, there is a fine line between graffiti and art, between idle doodles and deliberate memorials. But when you think of it, beneath our name etched on a stone slab is where we all end up eventually.

But I suppose we can't have people carving their name or their initials, or anything else for that matter, into the natural stone monuments that stand in many of our national parks. If we let that happen pretty soon people will be carving mountain tops into the likenesses of dead presidents and then making national parks out of them.

Life's Short! Drink the Good Scotch First!

The Long White

December. The month of the long shadows. Real Winter begins. The "long white" has descended upon the denizens of the Lake Superior shore and people get up early, put on an extra layer, take a deep breath of frosty air and start to shovel snow. And we stay at it until mid-April when we throw down our shovels with finality and say "screw it! The rest will melt."

Sure, it snows as early as October and it often stays as late as May, but that snow comes and goes and doesn't amount to much. December through March are the cold, dark, snowy months of Winter and if you don't embrace the season up north, you can survive, but you will not enjoy it very much.

For newcomers, Winter is an acquired skill and one best acquired in a hurry. It ain't for sissies. But for those of us who were born to this land, it's in our DNA. It's part of our history, our culture and our architecture, our livelihood, our diet and our way of life. We are Winter people! Grrrrr! Not Brrrrrr!

My family has lived on the south shore of Lake Superior for 180 years. Our finely-honed Winter skill set is partly genetic and partly passed down from generation to generation like a good pair of snowshoes or cross-country skis. We thrive during the Winter and take full advantage of the many things you can only do when the world is frozen.

I capitalize the "W" in Winter because for us it is a proper noun. Winter is mystical and magical in the way it wraps an already magnificent land in sparkling beauty. But the season is also respected and even feared for it will hurt you and it can even kill you if you don't pay attention.

Admittedly, our relationship to the long white changes over the course of our lives just as it changes over the course of the season. There is joy in catching that first December snowflake on your tongue, and there's indescribable joy in watching your first child do it. It's a joy that cannot be measured or purchased. And there is a sad resolve in tossing out an old snow shovel in March that has simply worn out over it's part of your lifetime shoveling snow. You discard it with remorse. It fits your hands perfectly. It was a part of you for years.

I love Winter, but it sucks.

OK, only some of it sucks.

The parts that suck mainly involve picking up snow and moving it so that you can park in your driveway and walk up your steps and your roof doesn't cave in. Dirty, frozen snowbanks and snowplow furrows suck. Salt encrusted cars and frozen door locks suck. Black ice and whiteouts and spinning helplessly down the road at 30 miles per hour sucks. Dead batteries suck. Frozen fingers jumping dead batteries suck. Three months' worth of dog turds floating to the surface of your back yard in the spring sucks.

For some of us, moving snow is our Winter employment. For all of us the relocation of 250" of snow is a part of our daily existence. Where do we put it all? Over there. It requires planning. Shoveling snow is how we start and end the day, sometimes for weeks on end.

It's such a common thread in our society that my friend, Virgil Longwalk, the "Alger County Snow Pilot," even wrote a folk song about it. You can find it on Spotify or his Facebook page. No, there are not two Virgil Longwalks.

As Mayor of a town that bills itself as the "Snowmobile Capital of the World" I wholeheartedly support both the snowmobile industry as well as the sport. It's in my job description. We didn't invent snowmobiles, but we did invent snowmobiling. In addition to being the engine of our Winter economy, it's our sport. Every other garage in town has two sleds in it and our streets have been open to snowmobiles since 1966. If you went trail riding then you brought three extra belts and a fistful of spark plugs and you covered maybe twenty-five miles. Today's sleds are like rocket ships. They're sleek and fast and 200-mile trail rides are the norm.

Snowmobiles are popular and a lot of fun, but I don't ride, mainly because I don't like going fast. Mountains of white fluffy snow also promote a false sense of safety. How can you hurt yourself in all that fluff? Yet several times each year we get reminded that a 4-inch maple sapling will stop, dead, five hundred pounds of snowmobile travelling at 50 miles an hour, but the driver will keep going.

Downhill and cross-country skiing are also popular in these parts, but I don't ski. When I strap long slippery boards onto my feet the predictable happens. I fall down and I can't get up. I used to do a lot of ice fishing but I don't have time to maintain a shack anymore. Ice climbing is all the rage around here now, but I've yet to try it.

And somehow I never learned to skate when I was young though I grew up on the lake. Kids around here live and breathe hockey beginning in October of each year. We don't have soccer moms in the U.P., we have Hockey dads. They're similar but there's a distinct difference in the vocabulary used and the volume it's used at.

Snowshoes are more my speed and I own a half a dozen pairs. For me, the Winter landscape is to be savored if only because it's so fragile and so temporary. Our favorite Winter outing includes a half dozen friends and almost that many dogs to a spot with a view of the bay or a place not accessible in the warmer months. Swamps turn into pure magic in the Winter.

We pack lawn chairs and a full picnic with at least two extra bottles of wine and we make camp when we find a spot with a lot of easy firewood. Then we build a big fire and stay until we run out of firewood or wine.

Walking out in the dark is half the adventure, especially by moonlight. The snow brightens the landscape and you can see hundreds of yards through the woods. Walking beneath a canopy of Winter-bare hard maples rattling in the wind can be eerie but it is also serenely beautiful.

Lake Superior country is known for blizzards which close highways and shut down schools for days at a time. But there are also days in Winter when the sky turns gray and the clouds are full, the heavens open up and it snows silently all night and all day, big fluffy flakes that accumulate inches per hour. The snow piles up on every twig, on every branch and on every tree until all the trees bow down in prayer and the world is hushed by the majesty of it all.

The Grand Island Ice Caves are our favorite Winter outing. The ice in the East Channel is only safe enough to walk on three out of five Winters and we could not go last Winter. But a treacherous half mile walk across sometimes iffy ice to the lighthouse is rewarded with a chance to spend a day in what's truly a "Winter Wonderland."

The wet sandstone cliffs from the lighthouse to Trout Point transform each Winter into a series of majestic pillars and caves that rival the Parthenon in their grandeur. Not too many years ago our small circle of friends were the only people who went there. I guess it's no longer a secret.

No one went last year, but the year before the ice was three feet thick in the channel and hundreds of people made the trip each day. There were twenty people (and four dogs) in our group that sunny February afternoon. We had staged a cord of wood that morning so we had a big fire, set up the buffet table and wine bar and made dozens of new friends. We always drink wine because beer freezes and whiskey makes for a hard trip back.

Fire is the essential ingredient to a successful Winter outing. It's so important that, if necessary, we will bring wood with us. But we try to make camp where we find a lot of easy dead wood to gather. And there is no such thing as too much firewood or too big a fire. It's Winter fergawdsake! It's not like you're gonna' start a forest fire. And it's our way of keeping old man Winter at bay for a few hours.

Winter is an acquired skill for those who are not born to it. Having fun in the Winter is the necessary half of surviving the season because right after you're done, you'll have to come home and shovel all the snow that fell while you were out having a good time. But it's worth it.

Life's Short! Drink the Good Scotch First!

Life's Short! Drink the Good Scotch First!

Ice Monkeys

Shawna adopted the first three one night at the Legion during the blizzard that was the 2016 Michigan Ice Fest. We hosted the festival that year and I'd taken off work early to help with the 750 climbers who made American Legion Post #131 in Munising their headquarters that week. I met my wife in the canteen and before I could order my first beer she said, "see those boys over at that table?"

I looked and nodded.

"Well go over there and give them each a drink chip and one of your "get out of jail free cards," she said.

"OK," I replied obediently, and I dug out my wallet and penned "Get out of Jail Free! (Or not) on the back of three business cards and signed them. Then I grabbed my beer, scooped up the drink chips she had ready for me and I went over and introduced myself.

Chris, Ben and Alex were from Milwaukee and after giving them each a drink chip and a card and convincing them that the sketchy looking hippie guy really was the mayor, we chatted for a beer and then I went back to the bar for another.

"They seem like nice kids," I told my wife.

"Good," she said. "I'm glad you think so cuz I invited them to come stay at our house."

It turns out they had spent the previous night in their Ford Explorer in single digit temperatures, and the night before that in a snow cave. They were cold and wet and had three more nights to look forward to. As it will with young people, their trip planning had a few gaps.

Along with the 750 climbers who were in town, there was a hockey tournament that weekend and it was still the height of the snowmobile season. There wasn't a motel room available anywhere in Alger County and the forecast said three more days of snow and blowing snow. M-28 between Munising and Marquette was already closed and people staying at the motel in Christmas were being escorted through the white-out by the state police in convoys.

"I needed you to convince them that I wasn't some crazy woman at the Legion who invited young men she didn't know home with her," she added and kissed me. I wasn't sure what I was getting myself into, but I had obviously done good.

That weekend the three of them got some simple U.P. hospitality--warm beds, hot showers, good food and cold drinks--and Shawna and I got the first three of what's grown into a dozen new friends. I had taken the rest of the week off to help staff the Ice Fest headquarters, so we laid in some supplies and just played host.

We renamed them Robbie, Chip and Ernie and I finally had to show them a you tube video of My Three Sons before they understood my cultural reference. Poor Alex became Ernie and found out that he was adopted. But they had a good time and so did we.

Between us, Shawna and I have six grown kids and we look forward to their visits home. I cook big breakfasts and Shawna makes special dinners and all the cousins come over and sometimes stay until the wee hours. Three empty bedrooms get put back into service and our home bustles with the noise and excitement of young people again, at least for a long weekend. We love it and we miss it.

Shawna's oldest son had also just moved to Oregon. She was missing him and that had a lot to do with her decision to invite these three wet strangers into our home. They were all his age. I warned them that first night that they might find a juice box and a lunchable in their back packs the next morning.

They settled right in and they went climbing every day, telling us the stories of that day's adventure each night over dinner and cocktails. They are fine young men, fun and light-hearted, and our house was filled with smiles and laughter all weekend. We invited them to come back the next year or any other time they were headed north. We told them to bring their friends and last year they did. And then they came back again this year.

Munising has hosted the Michigan Ice Festival for about 35 years. I say "about" because Bill Thomson, who organizes the event every year, can't remember exactly what year he and his friends began gathering at Sydney's Restaurant each February to plan the day's climb. Munising is the gateway to the Pictured Rocks National Lakeshore and the Grand Island National Recreation Area and the wet, sandstone cliffs that make up most of both coastlines feature the best natural ice climbing east of the Mississippi.

There are dozens of different climbs within a few miles of town with crazy sounding names like the Dryer Hose and Left Soda Straw, Sweet Mother Moses, Udder Delight and Help Me Rhonda. Some formations reach as high as two hundred feet and much of the climbing takes place over the frozen, or partially frozen, surface of Lake Superior, so their playground is framed in dramatic sub-arctic vistas.

Most ice climbers are also rock climbers and you won't find a healthier, heartier group of people anywhere. They're easy going and fun to be around and they smell better than hockey players or snowmobilers. The event attracts climbers from all over the world and features national sponsors and first-class speakers and productions. The Red Bull girls were here this year and made a real cool video with ice boats and epic climbs way out in the park.
For a taste of what it's like, search the Internet for "Michigan Ice Festival," or go to downwindsports.com/ice fest.

I do not climb, rocks or ice. In fact, I've learned that there are only two ice climbers here in town. People who come here to climb some of the world's best ice find that very odd and I can't explain it. It's like none of the people in Jackson Hole knowing how to ski. There's plenty of other things to do here in the Winter so I guess we just never thought of it.

The locals do like the spectacular ice formations and we visit many of them each Winter, especially if we can get over to the island. Instead of backpacks full of climbing gear though, we bring backpacks full of food and drink, build a big fire and just sit and admire the scenery.

I try to address the group each year and welcome them to town. Their numbers have grown to almost a thousand and they pack the Mather Auditorium each night for presentations by world class climbers. In addition to being the capital of Pure Michigan, Munising is best known for the hospitality of its citizens and I try to set a good example. It's my job. Besides, how often does a guy get to tell jokes to a thousand people in the 100 year old auditorium of his alma mater.

Ice climbing is an extreme sport and climbers look the part. In full climbing regalia, an ice climber also looks pretty well equipped for a bloody fight to the death. Crampons on each foot, spiked on the bottom and off the toe, and holding a pair of lethal looking ice axes that would make a Klingon grunt with envy, these guys climb big wet icicles that at the top are attached to crumbling sandstone cliffs and at the bottom sometimes to nothing at all. What could go wrong?

Alex and Ben couldn't make it last year, but Chris came with his girlfriend, Jessy, and brought along Grant and Lucas and a different Alex. We found room for them all and we lived vicariously again each night through the eyes of these thrill-seeking, fun-loving kids. It was an adventurous year too. Jessy fell during a climb and was injured bad enough that she couldn't climb back up and the five of them spent several hours huddled at the bottom of the cliff with an angry, open lake beneath them.

Eventually, she got to go for a helicopter ride and the boys were able to climb out after the Coast Guard plucked her off the cliff face. Talk about exciting! She got checked out at the hospital and they all got home around 3:00am with the story of their young lives to tell. They were OK because they were well equipped and well prepared and because everyone pitched in to help. Jessy was bruised but more embarrassed than hurt. I tried to cheer her up by telling her that she'd remember these four guys the rest of her life, her four knights errant who had stayed by her side when she needed them most. And then some good came of it too.

Like I said, ice climbing is an extreme sport and the Pictured Rocks cliffs are isolated back country in the winter, yet it was the first accident anyone could remember that required an organized rescue. Climbers are a tight knit bunch, and in response to that accident, Bill and his group worked with the Park staff and local Search and Rescue to create a rapid response team, trained and equipped to rescue injured or stranded climbers along the cliffs. Thankfully, they were not needed this year, but it was good to know they were ready.

Alex #2 also took a great picture of Chris near the top of Strawberry Daze and won the festival photo contest last year. His prize was some nice climbing gear and a free pass to this year's festival.

I've watched ice climbing and it's not much of a spectator sport if you're not a climber yourself. But we hosted the governor last year who came with his wife and some friends to watch the climbers and get his picture taken with a climbing helmet on and some ice behind him. He was touring the U.P. and had taken a sled dog ride that morning—Ice Fest is also the weekend of the U.P. 200 sled dog race, a qualifier for the Iditarod. One climber pointed out that he was wearing a Stormy Kromer, the ubiquitous Winter head gear of real, everyday Yoopers, but I assured him that we had people stationed in St. Ignace who were going to make him give it back before he crossed the Bridge.

He also got to meet Conrad Anker who, I'm told, is one of the most famous climbers in the world. Conrad was belaying some young climbers at the Curtains when someone mentioned that the tough looking nerd who looked like he was wearing someone else's hat was the governor of Michigan. Conrad's a formidable presence and he immediately asked the governor what he was going to do about global warming. This was not a conversation the governor was prepared to have right then, but he was surrounded by constituents holding ice axes, so he did his best to sound like he cared for five minutes all the while looking about as comfortable as a dog trying to shit a peach pit. He eventually escaped without falling down the hill.

Chris couldn't make it for this year's festival, but he was up in January to climb with his friend Patrick and we had them over for dinner one night. Alex #1 and Grant were here the weekend after that and they stayed with us again for the festival this year and they brought new guy Nick and Alex #3 with them.

Alex #2 and Lucas, Ben and new man Nate stayed up the street at the Terrace Motel, but they joined us for breakfast and dinner each day, so we had eight climbers lighting up our home. The East channel froze over early and they all got a chance to climb on Grand Island too. And they're all invited back anytime because we just like having them around.

I call them ice monkeys, a term of respect and affection, and I'm proud to call them my friends. There are times when I have very little faith in their generation, but these boys help restore my faith. They're a mix of college kids and young professionals from Milwaukee and Chicago with new ideas and fresh perspectives that more old hippies should take the time to listen to and consider. Theirs is a different world that we share.

They turned me on to some new music that isn't completely awful, "Alexa, play Trampled by Turtles," and they showed me the world they see through eyes that are not yet jaded and bitter. Their very youth softens the hard, ideological edges we all form as we get older. Hell, my dogs even like 'em.

Those of us who live up here on the North Coast never take the great natural beauty that surrounds us for granted. Indeed, it's why we live here. But what we enjoy most is sharing it with others to see the joy it puts in their eyes. It truly is a wonderland in Winter and made for adventurous young people who like to test themselves against the extremes of Mother Nature. Bless their hearts.

There is a bond that forms between people who have endured and shared sacrifice. That bond also forms between people who have shared great danger and great joy. These ice monkeys of ours have known all that already and it's a treat for us to listen to them recount it and re-live it around our dining room table on a cold February night through their stories and their jokes and their laughter.

And they really like Shawna's "so good" egg rolls.

Life's Short! Drink the Good Scotch First!

Life's Short! Drink the Good Scotch First!

Fresh from Hard Water

Ice fishing is perhaps the most civilized form of angling known to man. Two guys sitting in lawn chairs in shirt sleeves in a warm shack out on the bay with the north wind howling outside. Cold beer, snacks my cardiologist wouldn't approve of, and maybe a pint of something friendly to share. Add the "Music of Our Lives" from a tinny, transistor radio hanging from a nail and it doesn't matter whether the fish are biting or not. It's a good day.

There are many ways to get your dinner from hard water and where I come from ice fishing is serious business for most people.

There is some commercial fishing here in the Winter. Tribal fisherman set gill nets out and this year they're getting whitefish and lake trout, pike and shoepac in good numbers off Muskrat Point and in Trout Bay. The pike are huge, up to 48", but the fisherman hate them because they tear up their nets. They give the pike and the shoepac away. But they can get better than $10/pound from the restaurants for fresh trout and whitefish this time of year.

I remember one of the local restaurants when I was a kid used to proudly proclaim that "the fish that graces your plate today, last night swam in Munising Bay." That's true, at least it is for a while this Winter. They set their nets through holes in the ice that they cut with chainsaws. They push the float on the end of the net underneath the ice with a pole to the next hole they've cut and then on to the next one. Depending on how thick the ice is, setting 120 feet of net may be an all-day job.

They began fishing gill nets in Munising Bay about ten Winters ago, something that hadn't been done since the Great Depression. A judge reinterpreted a state ruling on a federal treaty and changed the tribal fishing boundaries to include the bay. It was controversial at the time. The sports fisherman didn't like it much because gill nets take everything that goes by and there were hard feelings and harsh words between men who had known each other their whole lives. There as even some vandalism reported.

But it's a big harbor on a big lake and there are still lots of fish, too, so they've learned to co-exist. Besides, only a couple tribal fisherman ever fish the bay anyway because it's cold, hard work with a hit and miss return for your effort.

A shoepac, for those not familiar, is one ugly fish. They're more properly called a burbot and they're the only freshwater cod. They're slimy, an ugly green color and they look like the front half of a bloated catfish stitched to the back half of an eel. They're positively prehistoric but their long tails are good eating. We call them the poor man's lobster, but you need a pair of needle nose plyers to skin 'em. They're so slimy and ugly I've seen people cut their line rather than touch them. They're also referred to as lawyers.

But sports fishermen, and fisherwomen, are equally serious about fishing because the bay is very productive in the winter and you can bring home dinner every night. There is no fresher or firmer catch than that taken though lake ice. And like I said, it's also a very civilized way to catch fish.

There are four types of ice fishing; running for tip-ups, bucket fishing, portable shanties and stick built shacks.

Tip-ups are used mainly on inland lakes and almost always for northern pike. Michigan allows up to three lines per person so, depending on the size of your group, you might set out a dozen tip-ups in a line. Essentially a wooden cross with a spool of line attached and a spring-loaded flag, fishing with tip-ups can be both a spectator sport and a drinking game. We set up fish camp on a point of land sticking out into a lake—on Forest Lake we use one of the islands--so you can be in the middle of the line that runs in both directions. Then we build a big fire and take turns running down the flags as they go off or we just assign the fish catching portion of the afternoon's entertainment to the younger members of the crew who are faster and need the practice. It's a very wholesome Winter activity for teen age boys.

Tip-up fishing is pretty thirsty work for grown men though, and the fishing can get entertaining as long as the beer doesn't freeze or you've made allowance for the temperature and brought whiskey. We always do. And those young fishermen turn into designated drivers when you're ready to go home. If it's an all-day event with a big crew we do a shore lunch on a tripod over our campfire, frying the first few fish that we catch. After they're filleted, "skinned and pinned," we cut them into fingers and fry them in spicy butter or oil to be eaten with chunks of sourdough bread and washed down with more beer. You know it's fresh when the fillet quivers as it hits the pan. Tip-up fishing is a very social activity and I've never done it alone.

Most ice fishing is out on the big lake though. Munising Bay ices over in late December or early January and stays frozen until somewhere between March and May. Each year is different. First ice on the bay is always the best fishing, though, and the day after the bay freezes you'll find a handful of very brave "bucket fisherman" out on the ice just off the Anna River or the city dock, sitting on one bucket and filling another with whitefish and splake.

Splake are a hybrid cross between a brook trout and a lake trout that the state plants every year in a program designed to encourage men to spend more time fishing—many hours that, as you know, "are not subtracted from a man's allotted span." Sometimes government is wise.

They say that one inch of clear, solid ice will support a man's weight. I prefer three or four inches as a minimum. Yet there are those guys who will risk their life for their dinner and head out on first ice. I am not one of them, but I did temp fate once. I was working as a reporter/editor/photographer/and the guy who goes and gets beer for the boss at the Porcupine Press and I decided to do a story on first-ice fishing. The bay froze over that week and, sure enough, the next morning I saw a single angler a hundred yards out from the mouth of the river sitting on a bucket in the sun.

Gingerly, I ventured out with my camera and my notebook, testing each step before I put any weight on that foot. When I got about fifty feet away I recognized my friend Stub and shouted the standard, internationally recognized, fisherman's greeting. "Catchin' anything?" He tipped the bucket he wasn't sitting on toward me and it was half full of whitefish.

"Nice," I said as I continued my careful pace toward him. When I got about twenty feet away he said, "that's close enough" and he held up his hand. I halted.

"How much ice we go out here?" I asked with sudden concern.

"Almost an inch and a half in some spots" he replied as he picked up his ice spud, hit water with one chop, and then slid it to me. "You can throw that in my truck when you get back to shore" he said, and we talked for a few minutes from twenty feet apart. When we were done he held up his biggest fish and I got a good picture. The story ran that week with a front-page picture of Stub holding up a big fish. I sent him a dozen copies. The next day he was out there again surrounded by twenty other guys catching fish. And I found a bag of whitefish on my porch that evening.

As the Winter wears on and the ice builds through the channels and into the open lake, the portable shanty guys push further and further out in search of bigger and better fishing. These portable rigs have gotten pretty elaborate in recent years and they range in size from something one man can drag up to big, two-man sleds you need a snowmobile to pull. They provide a windbreak and come with heaters, but they're still just a tent inside a plastic tub. Because they're so light you can't leave them over night, but their popular and portable and the preferred equipment of serious sports fishermen who go wherever the fish are biting that day. They catch a lot of fish.

My oldest brother, Mike, used to fish with his friends out on the very edge of the ice. Sometimes they'd go five miles or more north of the island on snowmobiles dragging a home-made sled with a windbreak to jig for lake trout. I never could decide if they were just too lazy to chop a hole or they liked risking their lives for their dinner. They always came back with fish though.

And then there is civilized ice fishing. If you've seen the movie 'Grumpy Old Men' you've seen the epitome of civilized ice fishing—big ice shacks arranged into neighborhoods with streets where mail gets delivered and vendors hang out in their trucks selling beer and bait. That's how they do it in Minnesota.

Lake Superior ice shacks are not like that and you can only drive your truck safely on the ice maybe one year in ten. But there are fifty shacks scattered around the bay right now. The average size fish shack is six-by-six feet, just large enough for two men. They're wood framed and usually built from scrap. There was a time when the mill gave the used belt fabric from the big paper machines to employees and almost every shack on the bay was made of that. Stout and wind proof, it was also waterproof and damn near bullet proof. There are still shacks out there made of paper mill "felt."

There are two types of shacks, those used for spearing and those for jigging. The hole in a spear shack takes up from a quarter to a third of the floor. The shack has no windows, or else it has black out curtains for good underwater visibility. Most of the spear shacks are clustered around the mouth of the river in eight to fourteen feet of water, shallow enough to see and spear whitefish, suckers and carp on the bottom.

The standard jigging shack has two to four small holes, usually in the corners, which are just big enough to land a fish. This minimizes the amount of ice you have to chop each day and it also gives you more floor space. I liked spear shacks for jigging so that I could watch the fish.

You'll notice the past tense of that last statement. Regrettably, I haven't been ice fishing in several years. The downside to having an ice shack is that it requires attention at least every other day. You have to block it up off the ice, bank the sides with snow, keep the holes chopped and the bottom chummed. I just don't have the time for that anymore and I am a lesser man for it.

The locals jig in thirty to 150 feet of water and, in addition to the bottom feeders, there are good catches of lake trout, splake and rainbow trout, herring, perch and pike, along with schools of rainbow smelt that bring in the Coho and king salmon each spring. My technique was to jig one line off the bottom for whitefish and then hook a smelt minnow through the dorsal fin and let it swim around in a wounded circle about six feet below the ice. That's why I preferred using a spear shack. I could see that minnow and anything coming in to get it. Even in deep water you can see fish thirty feet down and somedays it was like fish TV.

When you're using an ultra-light rig on a two-foot noodle rod, you have no rod tip and you're essentially fighting the fish with your fist. It's somewhere between a hoot and an ordeal if you hook a ten-pound rainbow trout that takes a half hour to land.

Hard water fishing has distinctive seasons. First ice is always best and then the fishing slows down to a steady hit and miss pace before sliding into the doldrums in late February. There are a couple weeks then when no one is catching anything. But the diehards are still there because as soon as they start catching smelt they know the salmon won't be far behind. The kings are loners, but the Coho come in schools in March and fishing then becomes an hour of boredom punctuated by 5 minutes of frantic catching, unhooking, rebaiting and getting your limit before the school moves on.

I was laid off the Winter of '96 so I went fishing every day for two straight months. After I got my kids off to school, I was in my shack where I stayed until they got out of school at three. I was there so often that some days I didn't even have to chop the hole. And I caught fish, hundreds of pounds of fish, mostly whitefish and perch. I went home every day with a bucket of fish and always had plenty extra for my family, my friends and my neighbors. A man who has fresh fish to share in Winter is wealthy and welcome everywhere he goes.

I was jigging single eggs off the bottom and I'd secured a good supply of perfectly cured salmon eggs from a guy I knew on St. Martin's Hill who was about the best fisherman I ever met. I had a month of good fishing. Come late February, however, even my magic bait failed me and I went home skunked for the first time. But I was back the next day and I caught a nice big whitefish who was spitting out smelt minnows as he flopped around on the floor of the shack. He had gorged on them. I didn't know whitefish would take a minnow, but I baited my hook with the freshest one and sent it down.

"Bam!" I had a five pounder on the second jig, a nice humpback that the commercial fisherman would call a "Number 1." And the lake kept on giving all morning. I stopped fishing before noon that day because I could fit no more fish in my bucket. For the next month I walked off the ice every day with a bucket full of 5-pound fish while everyone else caught nothing.

"What are using for bait," they'd ask.

"Minnows," I'd reply.

"Whitefish won't take minnows," they'd say.

"These ones did," I'd respond and then I'd go home with twenty pounds of fish and they'd go home with nothing.

Stubborn can be a funny thing and fisherman are good at it. They kept on fishing eggs and catching nothing for a couple more weeks before they started fishing with minnows. And then we all went home with a bucket of fish every day. It was the best year anyone could remember. That was also the year the lake froze all the way to Canada, the ice in the bay was four feet thick and the biggest selling item at the hardware store was ice auger extensions.

I caught a few nice rainbow trout that year, and a lot of herring too. They were the most impressive to watch and to catch as they came through the hole in huge schools stacked up from the bottom of the lake to the bottom of the ice.

A lake herring looks like a fat, blue-tinted whitefish, almost tuna-shaped, and the schools were so large they would cloud the hole for 30 minutes giving me time to throw everything I could think of at them. They were finicky and I kept a half-dozen rigs on the wall above the hole and something different worked every time they came through.

If I could take two fish out the school I would quit and just sit there and watch them. They swam in a slow circle and the vortex moved slowly in the direction they were going. It was like watching a tornado of fish from above. It was beautiful and even majestic.

The danger of jigging in a shack with a spearing hole, especially when two guys drinking beer are engaged in a frenzy of fishing activity in the dark, is kicking or dropping stuff down the hole. I've lost car keys and lighters, tools, my ice strainer and even fishing poles down my fish shack hole. Seldom do you get anything back but one time I did hook a pole with a random jig. Problem was, it wasn't the one I dropped in the hole. It was a nice one though and I kept it.

I didn't fish my first Winter back in the U.P. in '92 but that year did produce my favorite ice fishing story. We rented a house across the street from a guy I went to high school with and one February morning I saw him unloading his dive gear from his truck. I was curious, so I went over to give him a hand.

The temperature was in the single digits and there was ice on the lake as far as you could see. I asked him where he was diving, and why, and he said he'd gone down in a fish shack to retrieve some stuff that our friend "Fred" had dropped in the hole. I grabbed his tanks and his anchor line while he grabbed his duffel bag and we went into his garage where, framed by the irony of him hanging up wetsuit parts to dry, he told me the following story.

"You know since he retired from the mill Fred fishes all day, every day," he began. "He's got his shack off Powell's Point and it's set up nice with a recliner and a cot and a stove," he explained. "He goes out in the morning, throws two lines in the water and hides from his wife all day, fishing, drinking beer, and reading the paper."

"That sounds like a good retirement plan," I said with genuine envy.

"Well, yesterday he hooked a big one and was working it slowly off the bottom, taking his time and tiring it out. "After about a half hour he had the fish up near the ice and he saw it flash through the hole, but when he leaned over to see what it was, and how big, his reading glasses slid off his nose and fell in the hole." At this point my neighbor unzipped a pouch on his duffel and set a pair of eyeglasses down on his tool bench.

"And he had you dive though the ice for a $5 pair of cheaters," I asked in surprise.

"No, he sent me down after these" he said and plopped down a full set of dentures on the bench. I grinned waiting for the rest of the story.

"Well, the way he tells it that fish went straight back to the bottom," he explained, "and it took him another half hour to get it back up. It flashed through the hole again--the biggest rainbow trout he'd ever seen--and he said 'Holy shit!' and spit both his plates in the hole."

We laughed, and I asked him "well, did he get the fish?"

"No, he got impatient and tried to horse it up and it snapped his line," he said, "but he will get his teeth back and we both get to tell the story."

It's still winter up north, but I'm lucky enough to be eating fresh fish again. I am happy and so is my cardiologist.

Life's Short! Drink the Good Scotch First!

Life's Short! Drink the Good Scotch First!

The Chapters in my Closet

It was the last item on my bucket list of chores for the house this year. In October I got the attic insulated and the eave heaters hung. Thanks nephew Joe. In November and December, I painted the kitchen and the dining room, the front entrance, the upstairs banister, the guest bedroom and the upstairs bathroom. (I have paint left over, by the way. If you need a shade of gray, give me a call. Buying paint is a pricing and quantity conspiracy, but that's a different story).

I even cleaned the basement and got my workshop set up so I could try my hand at making walking sticks. That job had been waiting for me since we moved here in 2010. My last chore was the closet in my office/second spare bedroom, and I deliberately put it off 'til after the holidays because I had company and I knew I would need the whole room. It's a big closet, 16 feet by 6 feet, and it was busting at the seams. It's a knee wall closet, though, so the six-foot width tapers to a point about 6 feet high. The profile is a right triangle, and you have to duck your head to get in through the door and then stay crouched while you're inside.

But it contains the sum total of my life and my wife's life in paper and in photographs, in mementos and in junk, from first grade though college, through two marriages and six kids. It turned into a three-day project that proved both cathartic and melancholy.

I went through it methodically and deliberately. There was a navy pile and an old technology pile. There were boxes of old media, including VHS tapes, floppy disks and diskettes, and most of the supplies necessary for a black and white darkroom. Need any photo paper? I got some. There was everything I had ever written and saved. Then there were the boxes of "stuff" which presented the biggest challenge.

Like most of us, I've lived my life in chapters and the more important and memorable treasure and residue of those chapters ended up in boxes. Some of those boxes hadn't been opened in 35 years. There were a lot of things I'd forgotten about and even some things I didn't remember at all. I alternately chuckled and scratched my head as I unpacked and sorted each box and I also choked up quite a few times in those three days.

The good thing I found is that I've kept most of what I've written over the years and I've been writing since high school. I look forward to sharing some already published material soon, as well as working on some old story ideas I found in a notebook I started when I was working in the woods 20 years ago. It was one of several attempts I've made in my life to keep a journal. None were successful, but this one lasted six months and there's some good stuff in there.

The bad thing I found were the photos that have never been organized. I really need to do something about that. My wife is a photographer and most of her family pictures are in catalogued albums. Most of mine are in tomato boxes still in the drug store envelopes they came in, complete with negatives. Remember taking film to the store and waiting a week for pictures? That technology along with the routine amount of adult patience it required is long gone. None of those pictures ever got deleted either. I made the mistake of pulling out a few of those envelopes and looking through them. They were like random pages from my life, and I realized if I kept doing that I'd get lost in the past and I'd never finish the job at hand. That's a project for another month.

But I also found a never-used machine in my wife's half of the closet that copies photo negatives to digital. That's a project for my kids at some point in their lives. For the rest of mine, I'll live with the hard copies. With measured reluctance, I set the photos aside and just made sure they were all in labeled boxes.

I still had the technology pile to go through; computers, cell phones, old laptops and monitors, remote controls and miscellaneous hardware in a tangled pile of cables on the day bed. It would prove to be a chore. It's all dated and I'm sure I could have safely tossed all of it, but I won't. My excuse is that it's e-waste and should be recycled and the nearest place to do that is 50 miles away. But we all have a bit of hoarder in us and there's nothing wrong with this stuff. It still works. It's just old. I'm old too. I do need to check the hard drive on that old computer though and that will require making it work and finding a way to copy the important files.

I distinctly recall downloading all the word documents to a thumb drive when I got my new laptop, but then I immediately misplaced the thumb drive. It's safe in a drawer somewhere and someday I will find it, or else my kids will.

In the end I just sorted and tidied up all the cables and packed it all in boxes. When I'm a famous dead writer some historian in search of "the lost manuscripts" can team up with a smart fourth grader and a blacksmith and figure out how to extract the files from that hard drive. Yeah. That works.

Fortunately, I made paper copies of almost everything I wrote that I liked or felt was important and I kept clips from the various papers where I had honed my new-found skills as a journalist. I found some gems and nuggets in there for which I'm grateful. There were also some turds in those boxes, but turds with my by-line on them so they're part of the story. Much has been lost, though, and that's the way it goes.

I took my time with the project, sifting through the chapters of my life in my pajamas while I played old music and sipped coffee, safe in my cocoon while the north wind whipped the outside world into snowdrifts and below-zero wind chills. Some stuff got tossed, but not much, and I was able to consolidate the randomly packed boxes and milk crates into half their previous bulk. A lot of things stopped me in my tracks, sat me down and made me read them again. That slowed the process considerably.

The big box of everything I'd ever written and saved stayed out and I'm almost finished going through that. The repacked closet is still full, but I can move around in it now and I can find things. All the boxes got new labels.

Chronologically, the first chapter was my childhood though age 17. There were report cards from elementary school in there, my first bank book, a file marked "Alger County Probate Court letters" and a piece of bondo from Bub's 1970 Chevelle SS that we bounced off the guardrails on the 7-mile hill coming home from a keg party early one summer morning. Yes, I am the product of a misspent youth.

Then there were the nine years I spent in the navy followed by six years working in the Puget Sound going to school and starting my family. I collected a lot of stuff while I was in the navy and those boxes took up most of my time. I found treasure so precious it made me sigh and just hold it in my hand. I joined the navy 42 years ago. 42 years! During those nine years in navy blue I travelled a lot and each base and each boat was a different city or a different country. I was a west coast sailor, San Diego and Pearl Harbor, and I spent five of those years in Japan and the Philippines.

I found Zippo ship's lighters, copies of old deck logs, irreverent poetry, worn navigational instruments and charts, service records, medals, a hand-tailored set of gaberdine dress blues I had made in Hong Kong with dragons on the cuffs (I didn't even think about trying it on), trinkets from a half dozen different navies, foreign currency and coins from twice that many countries, swizzle sticks from bars I don't remember (I had a gin and tonic phase for a couple of those years) and of course, letters and cards from the folks back home.

I have a whole pile marked "make a copy for Charlie Brown," my old shipmate.

From my six years in Washington I kept college papers and theses, stories I'd written for the composition classes I had, clippings from the school paper and the local weeklies where I worked as a stringer, newsletters from the engineering firm where I worked, ship's patches from the aircraft carriers we worked on and trinkets from all over the world. We travelled a lot and did our job on a not-to-interfere basis with the ship's operating schedule. So, we went to where the ship was at and that often meant trapping and then launching off the deck of an aircraft carrier in a C-2 COD, but that's another story.

We also had a contract in the late 80s to test minesweepers being built in Sturgeon Bay and Marinette, Wisconsin, and because I scheduled the field work, I always put myself on those crews. That got me home every three months and those visits convinced me to return to the U.P. in 1992.

And all the addresses I've had since then, in Washington and Michigan, are each their own sub-chapter as is each job I've had since I got out of the navy 33 years ago. I found mail addressed to me at 20932 Miller Bay Road and 21875 Apollo Drive, both in Poulsbo, and at four different addresses here in Munising.

Like all Yoopers, I've done whatever I could and whatever I had to do to make a living here in the U.P. While starving as a writer and part time reporter, I've been a carpenter and a lumberjack, a security guard and a professional boy scout. I've worked with disabled veterans, the unemployed, the mentally ill and the homeless. I've busted little old ladies out of nursing homes and taught work skills to the blind. I've been a coordinator, manager, supervisor and director in fields totally unrelated to my education and the stuff I've collected from all those chapters of my life is newer, not yet faded yellow with time, not yet musty, and for the most part organized.

But with each new job or each new house things got packed into boxes, poorly labeled or not labeled at all, and some of those boxes were never unpacked. Some had been opened and poked through in search of some lost treasure or important document and then poorly repacked. Half-full boxes got mixed and consolidated with each move.

I found an old CD in one box that my friend Tom Keen made at a party at Matt's house on Blush Lake early in this century. On it my friend Dale sings Harry Chapin's All My Life's a Circle. I've always liked that song but hadn't heard it in a while. Dale has a lonesome voice and does a good cover and while I listened, I remembered that party and how many of the people who were there that weekend are gone now.

But for the first time the circle analogy seemed wrong or at least, incomplete. My life, like all our lives, is a novel, a book full of chapters, a how-to manual with dog-eared pages, a colorful story, tragic and wonderful, of well-laid plans mixed with random events, a source of physical and tangible history, recalled in vivid technicolor by the memories evoked when you take the time to go flipping through the pages.

It was good way to start the new year.

The Scar

I stared at it in the mirror when I got out of the shower. There it was. The scar. About eight inches long it was still festooned with the 22 staples that had settled at odd angles when they took off the vacuum pump bandage.

"Chicks dig scars," or so I had been told my whole life. I tried to see it as attractive, but all I could see was pain. Perhaps it was too soon.

Equally impressive were the two holes beneath it where the drain tubes had been. You could still get a pinky in each one if you tried. They told me that they would heal from the inside and that's why they hadn't stitched them up. Having holes in my chest big enough to stick your fingers into was a bit disconcerting so I quickly covered them with a large bandage. Gotta at least keep the belly button lint out.

And then I stared at the scar again. It was relatively straight and slightly purple around the edges. The incision appeared to be healing nicely but something was wrong. Something was out of place. That's when I noticed that there were actually two incisions.

The surgeon, or his helper, had started to cut at the top and had gone about an inch and then stopped. Apparently, he (or she) had decided it wasn't quite in the middle, so they had started over about a quarter inch to the right, my right, and then finished a slice about eight inches long.

I cocked my head and looked again and it still seemed a little off, not quite centered on my sternum. I wasn't sure why but this bothered me. Quality control issues set in. My opinion of my surgeon began to plummet. I mean, if I'm gonna wear this thing the rest of my life it would have been nice if it were straight and symmetrical. I had even joked with my roommate before surgery about what I could tattoo on it after it healed.

So, I stood there in my underwear, staring in the mirror, rocking my head back and forth and studying the scar some more. I thought about getting a tape measure to confirm my suspicions and that's when I noticed that my left nipple was lower than my right one.

"My God! They put me back together crooked!" I screamed to myself. "All the kids on the playground are going to call me Frankenstein!" And then I laughed loud enough that my wife heard me.

"What's so damn funny," she hollered from the bedroom.

"Never mind," I said. "I was going to ask you to bring me the tape measure, but I changed my mind. I don't need it."

And I just let that sink in as I put on my shirt and shut off the light.

Life's Short! Drink the Good Scotch First!

Life's Short! Drink the Good Scotch First!

Pussy Willows, Crows, and the Ten Dollar Hill

March is a busy month up here along the north coast, all full of lambs and lions. We learned as kids that it comes in like one and goes out like the other, or sometimes just the opposite. For weather, it's not a very reliable month though it usually starts out as ice-crusted snow, and it always ends in the mud.

It's almost early Spring in the U.P. and the longer days and sunshine bring warmer weather and an end to the bitter cold of Winter. The melting snow crusts over every night and for a couple of weeks you can scamper over the landscape without punching through. It's good weather for a walk in the woods.

March has been a lamb so far this year and I've been hiking the hardwood ridges south of town with the dogs almost every day in search of the holy grail of early spring—the first patch of dry ground, always on a south-facing hillside. But the snow is still deep in the woods. The day's thaw refreezes each night but the crust is not quite thick enough yet to support my weight. The dogs can stay up already though and they love the new-found freedom of being able to go anywhere and everywhere at full speed.

The local sled heads like to play in these hills where I hike and I'm thankful for that. The tourists seldom venture off the groomed trails, but the local boys carve the ridges and ravines along the back side of St. Martin's Hill enjoying hundreds of acres of the best riding in the area. Their play leaves me a spiderweb of packed trails to walk on without the need for snowshoes.

Lately I've been hiking in to a bald knoll on the edge of a ridge that local riders still call the Ten Dollar Hill. It's a steep, 300-foot climb from the valley floor below. I ran into my friend Dan up there the other day and he explained that it got its name from a standing offer of ten dollars between him and his friends to anyone who could conquer it on their snowmobile. Back in the day, before snowmobiles became crotch rockets, it was an epic achievement. But now it's easy.

You can hike into the back of the Ten Dollar Hill without much of a climb though and you're rewarded with a breathtaking view of the Perch Lake plain. You can't see Perch Lake or Mud Lake in the broad, flat valley below, but you can see a couple of miles across to the ridges on the other side and to the shore of Lake Superior twice that distance to the north. Because it's bare of trees and faces south and west, I'm counting on this knoll to give me my first patch of dirt and I check it with the dogs a couple of days each week, noting the firewood supply that's emerging from the slowly melting snowpack. It's the kind of spot Eeyore would pick for a day of cloud watching and it will be a nice spot for a fire and a spring picnic.

The mile-long walk to it on snowmobile trails that follow old logging roads climbs through an almost pure stand of mature hard maple with only an occasional beech and yellow birch thrown in for contrast. There is no understory in the high hills, and you can see for hundreds of yards through the trees which are growing melt rings around their trunks as the bark absorbs and then reflects the sun's warmth. The 40-degree days and 20-degree nights have just triggered the thermo-pump that gets the sap rising. We're still a week or so away from the beginning of syrup season but all over the U.P. people are readying their sugarbushes for the annual harvest.

I can hear the sap rising in the trees when I walk. The squeaks and knocks of the wood as it stretches and expands are the sounds of life returning to the land after the long white. It's a soft sound in the tree trunks and it stands in sharp contrast to the raucous serenade coming down from the branches above.

In early March the crows come back from wherever they go in November, and they all arrive at the same time. There just there one day, a whole murder of them sitting in a tree talkin' smack at each other and at you too. I noticed them last week and it was a welcome sign. You don't miss their obnoxious caws until you hear them again and realize they've been gone all the long winter.

As kids in early March we'd shovel snow from sagging snowbanks to dam up the streams of melt water that ran down the road going up the hill from our house. It was an all-day project. We'd build the dam and watch the water rise behind it until if overflowed and burst in a torrent of slush and then we'd build another one further downstream. We wouldn't go home until we were all wet and cold. But we'd arrive red faced and triumphant brandishing wet mittens and a bouquet of pussy willows for our mother to put in a mason jar on the kitchen table. They lasted for weeks and I liked the soft tickle of silk that coated the willow buds.

I loved early Spring as a lumberjack. Every day was a little longer than the day before and mornings were still cold but no longer painful. We'd start earlier and earlier each day and take advantage of the hard crust before that day's thaw and then we'd quit as soon as we began punching through. Crotch deep in crusty snow is no fun and its suicide with a chain saw. But each afternoon we saw a little more of the forest floor and we lived for the day when we could shed our Winter layers of snow pants and insulated saw boots and enjoy the freedom of denim and leather again.

I used to take an empty water jug in the woods on those early spring mornings and fill it with sap from the butt of the first big maple I cut. If the trunk were laying at an angle it would pour a steady stream and you could fill a half gallon jug in a few minutes. It's still my definition of refreshing. By lunch we'd be working in shirt sleeves, and it would still be warm enough when we quit to linger over a tailgate for a beer while we made plans for Friday night.

My walks in early spring are solitary outings with only the dogs for company. I'm usually scouting new hikes for the crew. I like to walk the hills around the bay for the views that you only get when the leaves are down. These hills are too inhospitable in the Winter to explore because of the deep snow and icy north winds. They're also a tough climb on snowshoes. But the steep slopes are the first to melt in the spring and the lure of dirt beneath my boots after months of ice and snow is hard to resist.

When I was a kid I wandered and played on most of these hills, and I revisit my childhood haunts every spring. One hike takes me to the "bear tree," an old beech who's smooth, muscle like bark, was scarred many years ago by a bear hugging his way up it in the fall after beech nuts. The scratches have turned into scars in the smooth bark and the span of his claws is greater than my fingers spread wide. He was a big bear and I visit his tree every spring.

Beech trees are also the perfect surface on which to proclaim your undying love for your sweetheart with a jack knife. I know dozens of mature beech--centurions I call them--along the tops of these hills where youthful love has been pledged in wood for the last 100 years. Some of these trees I have given names to, and some are signposts with dozens of sets of names and initials, hearts and arrows.

Alas, they are all dead or dying from an invasive combination of fungus and beetle that has swept the U.P. over the last decade. It's like when the Dutch Elm disease took all the Elm trees in the 60's. They're just now starting to come back. So it will be with the beech. At least one generation, perhaps two, will not know them as part of our forest. Here's hoping that some of the love proclaimed on their dying trunks survives.

I have another hike on the Brown's Addition side of the bay that takes me up where the old ski jump used to be. Ski jumping was big in the early 1900s and Munising had the perfect hills for it. Before my time there were a half dozen jumps in town, the landing for one being Cherry Street which rises steeply before it dead ends against the bottom of the hill. I've seen pictures.

The biggest one they ever built was also the last one standing and we used to play on it before they tore it down in the late 70's.

There is an open spot in the trees above it where I go and have a fire in early March. It overlooks the bay and the whole town. I can see the fish docks and the ball field where I used to play little league, the range lights and the mill, the single stoplight and dear old Mather High. I like the view from up there of this humble, hard-working little town dotted with chimneys and church steeples and nestled snug between the hills and the harbor. My home.

When the snow crusts hard enough to walk on I follow the snowmobile trail at the end of Five Mile Point Road out to Paradise. So named because it's a swimmer's paradise in summer, the low sandstone shoreline is coated with mountains of ice in Winter and the pack ice on the lake still floes north as far as the eye can see. I hike the two miles of shore ice back to Buckshot Bay on frozen dunes of hard pack with blow holes that look like mini-volcanos that you can slide down inside of and poke around in. The still ice-covered cliffs of Grand Island, with the Channel Islands in the foreground, are the perfect backdrop for a leisurely afternoon jaunt in the warm sun. The dogs and I are never in a hurry.

Once I'm back around the point there's a lakefront lot for sale that has been cleared for a homesite. There's always a dry spot along the shore and I have a little fire there and take in the view. It's mostly ice and it reminds me that it's still Winter. But there's usually a patch of dry grass and a log to sit on there. The dogs and I have lunch and then we roll around in the grass and sometimes we nap in the warm sun. Real spring is still a month off, but it's coming, and we can feel it in our bones.

Postscript: We walked in to the Ten Dollar Hill yesterday on a hard pack of snow covered by six inches of fresh powder. It's still early March. There are lions about yet and spring will come when she is damn good and ready.

Life's Short! Drink the Good Scotch First!

Wandering in the Winter Woods

I officially have a hobby. It's my first. Writing is not really a hobby. It's more like a calling, a passion, a need that must be satisfied. My new hobby is making walking sticks, quarterstaffs, from dead, worm-eaten balsam saplings that I find in the woods. I've used one of these sticks while hiking for several years now without paying much attention to the intricate designs carved into the wood by grubs. Then I found a really nice one while deer hunting last fall and that got me started.

I've done some research and found that the cambium layer on these trees is eaten by a couple of different species of pine beetle larvae. From what I can tell, instead of killing the tree, they infest trees that have already died. I find the raw material for my new hobby in balsam thickets and for every twenty dead saplings I find with the bark sloughed off, only one will have worm scars on it. So just finding them is a treasure hunt that gets me out in the woods for an afternoon a couple of days each week.

The snow in the woods is deep this year and I tried taking the dogs with me on my first few outings after Winter set in, but even the long-legged wolf hounds struggled to get around and Charlie Bear just lay down as soon as we climbed over the snowbank on the Trout Lake Road.

"Nope," he told me with a glance. "I'm too old, I'm too fat and my legs ain't long enough for this foolishness. I'll wait here." His favorite Winter pastime is to lay down in the snow anyway, so he kept an eye on us that day and we didn't go far. Since then, "fetching sticks" has become a solitary pursuit for me and I've come to appreciate the time alone.

Someone once said that solitude is a wonderful thing if you have peace of mind and something definite to do. I'm a stranger to solitude. I have never enjoyed spending too much time alone. After all, it's not something I have much experience with having grown up with ten brothers and sisters and then going straight into the submarine navy. Hell, I'm not even sure what to do with the privacy that I have most of the time.

But I'm learning to embrace solitude in my old age and I have recently regained my peace of mind. And wandering around in the woods looking for sticks gives me something definite to do. Finding these sticks in the winter is much harder than it was last fall. I can't cover nearly as much ground and an afternoon on snowshoes will wear a man out. But Winter does give me access to parts of the swamp that I couldn't get to otherwise so I'm out there twice a week. It's a great workout and it gives me bragging rights with my cardiologist.

"Yep, Doc, I had oatmeal for breakfast this morning with bark and twigs in it and then I did three miles on snowshoes" I report and wait beamingly for a nod of approval. He loves it.

I was a big fan of "Survivorman" and the other outdoor survival shows on TV. Not that I learned anything. I watched them and shook my head at their stupidity while telling myself that no self-respecting Yooper would ever get lost in the woods for a week with only a ball point pen and three corn chips to survive on. And I suppose I could get a fire started rubbing two sticks together, but it's just easier if you bring matches.

Winter is no time to go unprepared into the woods, even if it's only for a few hours. I always carry a knife and a compass with me, and I take my daypack if I'm going further than shouting distance from camp. In addition to lunch and a thermos of coffee, it always has the following supplies: a multi-tool, first aid kit, snowshoe repair parts and extra bindings, rain poncho, head lamp, dry sweatshirt and chook, a zip lock bag of matches, straps and cordage, a bottle of vitamin water, a fistful of beef sticks, string cheese and granola bars and, of course, a small flask of whiskey in case I get bit by a snow snake. Being prepared is worth the fifteen extra pounds on my back. I also carry a Japanese trim saw and snippers for cutting the saplings and trimming the branches.

I've come to relish these solitary Winter outings. The north woods are dormant this time of year but definitely not lifeless. Though I see and hear little in the way of company, maybe a glimpse of a raven soaring overhead or the machine gun tapping of a pileated woodpecker in the distance, there are other signs of life. There are lots of rabbit runs, little piles of pinecone parts left by hungry squirrels and the occasional deer track. Most of the herd around camp has left though. They've migrated down the Whitefish River valley in search of better forage and snow that's not quite so deep.

There's also sign from a pair of bobcats working the area, a female and her kitten, and at least one fox, and I saw otter tracks the other day. They're distinctive in how they slide through the deep snow. I found the fox den on a hillside near camp and I'll put a game camera on it this spring to see what our new neighbor is up to.

I've been working the swamps around Trout Lake near camp, so I am frequently serenaded by the three dozen trumpeter swans who Winter there. The lake stays open on both sides of the culvert that runs under the road that crosses the lake and the swans take advantage of the open water. People stop there and feed them, and we've taken great pains to educate folks on what not to give them. No store-bought bread please. Cracked corn from the feed mill in Trenary is best and we keep a stash at camp for that purpose. The swans have become conditioned to these handouts now and though they're still wary of humans, they've come to trust the people who feed them. They sound off every time someone stops to do that and take pictures.

They're so used to me that I can bring my dogs with me when I walk down from camp during deer season to feed them. To the dogs they've become part of the landscape and the swans know I bring food. There are only four cygnets this year, a very low number for a dozen breeding pairs and that worries me. But I will know when spring is really here when they're gone--flown off to the other lakes in the area for courtship and procreation.

I use an old pair of Alaskan snowshoes that I inherited from Captain Dave for these Winter outings and I finally broke down and bought new bindings for them the other day. My old neoprene three-strap bindings were beyond repair. I had salvaged them from my bear paws when I got too heavy for those shoes and I did get 25 years out of them so I can't complain.

The key to snowshoeing is to not be in a hurry. In addition to wearing yourself out, step on or "stick" a snowshoe and you'll find yourself face down in the snow and it's really hard to get back up. I try to avoid that and taking my time is half the reason I'm there in the first place.

Balsam grows in a variety of terrain from bogs to upland hardwoods, alone or in mixed stands with cedar, tamarack, and spruce. Left to their own devices they grow as a thicket and then thin themselves out as they mature and form a canopy. This creates my harvest of dead saplings in the understory and I've had my best luck along the edges of these thickets where the balsam borders and mixes with stands of aspen and ash.

Blowdowns are especially productive, but there is no pattern or key to where I find wormwood. When I do find them, I usually find more than one though and judging from the size and patterns of the etchings, there are at least three different types of larvae that feed on the dead trees. I cannot explain the feeling I get when I find a good one, especially after a couple hours of searching. Each one is a small joy for me and if I pack out a half dozen sticks at the end of the day, I feel lucky.

But it's the search itself where I find my reward. There is an underlying hush to the deep snow in a conifer swamp that amplifies what few sounds I do hear or make myself. Every footfall and each breath I take is clear and distinct. A clump of snow falling and rattling the branches beneath it will often startle me, but then it will reassure me.

It's a landscape and soundscape that fosters a gentle mindfulness, invites quiet reflection and allows serenity to seep in and soothe a man's soul.

I'm learning to like the solitude I find on these hikes in the Winter woods. My objective is clear and my goal is tangible and achievable. I am well equipped and prepared for the task at hand. There are no man-made distractions and my prize is something that is delicate and beautiful, decorated by some of God's most humble creatures. It's something which mother nature is done with and has cast off. It has no value other than what I give it.

This apparent contradiction does not bother me. It comforts and reassures me, and it gives me purpose. It reminds me of what's truly important. Real treasure has no monetary value. That's the secret. On the other hand, I'm hoping the tourists will give me $50 for each one of my walking sticks. After all, they're pretty cool.

Life's Short! Drink the Good Scotch First!

The Warm Smile of Early Spring

I put my snowshoes away today. It was finally time. I took them with me on a stick fetching expedition yesterday, but I didn't need them. Though it was afternoon, the snowpack was still crusty enough for me to walk on top. That freedom was a bonus on what was already going to be a good day.

There's still plenty of snow up here on the north coast and it will linger through the rest of April, but I shouldn't need my snowshoes anymore. My next trip into the woods will be opening day of trout season at the end of the month and even then, I won't stray far from camp.

I put my scoop and my shovel away too. Let it snow. I'm not moving the white stuff around anymore. Nope. Don't have to. It will melt. And both my wife and I have four-wheel drive. So, go on, let it snow. I did leave the broom out front though, sticking out of the big snowbank next to the truck because there's at least a few more mornings when I'll need it to sweep windshields.

But it's spring at last, or at least it's early spring. No robins yet, but the crows are back, and the deer have come out of the swamp to graze on whatever they can find on the bare shoulders of the highway. There's nothing green there yet, but deer can't afford to be too picky this time of year. They'll eat whatever they find. They look pretty good for the Winter we had.

That makes my morning commute a little more interesting though. I'm on the road at dawn and these days my head is on a swivel from tree line to tree line. The roadkill ratio is climbing fast for deer and racoons and I saw my first dead skunk today. Each day I see at least one fresh carcass covered with ravens. However sad, it is but another sign of spring.

It's also that time of year when you measure each patch of brown or bare ground you see with a calibrated eye to see if it's any larger than it was the day before. And you gaze achingly at the first bare hillsides and long to be up there soaking up the spring sun, but you can't get there without fighting crotch deep snow and, well, like I said, I put my snowshoes away today.

It's that time of year when as kids, we'd finally have a bare patch of playground big enough to dig a marble pot with our heel, usually in the gravel, and freeze our fingers playing those first few games of the season; cat's eyes and purees, with equal amounts of mud, stuffed in the front pockets of our corduroys coming in from recess if it had been a good day. Just mud if it had not. Fortunes changed fast in the 4th grade.

It's not quite that time of year, but it's getting close to the time when as a boy I'd be working on the farm with my dad. I remember days when he'd park the tractor and take his lunch on the south side of the barn and then curl up in the sun and have a short nap in the dry grass. It's not quite that time of year yet, but it's getting close.

Though the lake is still frozen as far as you can see here in Munising, Marquette Harbor is open, and my eyes were dazzled, and my heart lifted, coming over the Shiras Hill the other day after work. The sun was shining, and the lake was a stunning shade of blue all the way to the horizon. After six months of nothing but white and gray, it was a welcome sight. Below me I saw the Michipicoten inbound to the ore dock in the upper harbor for its first load of the season, gray hull, white deck house and self-unloader making her easy to identify. She's one of the older Lakers and it was postcard moment that I captured only with my mind's eye. But that was a good place to put it.

The trucks of a half dozen fishermen were parked at the mouth of the Carp River when I went by, and I'd seen similar gatherings at the mouth of both the Au Train and Rock River that morning on my way into work. Spring ice fishing is a social sport. Ice shacks have been put away for the year and fisherman congregate around river mouths and fish in groups, using yesterday's holes that no longer freeze over at night.

They're getting a few coho salmon and rainbow trout and they stand together on the slowly thinning ice, sipping coffee or drinking beer depending on the time of day, and talking about fishing and doing it in a boat soon while they wait on the next run.

Trout Lake near camp is open now too and all the swans have left for the season, their place taken by migrating gaggles of geese and rafts of ducks. The pileated woodpeckers have been busy all winter and now that it's spring they've begun singing while they fly, advertising for a mate. They look like red-tipped darts zipping through the canopy. I hear their trilling when I'm in the woods and I automatically look up to see if I can spot them.

The blue jays are getting more vocal now too and even the chickadees have burst into song in anticipation of the coming warmth. I haven't seen any sand hill cranes yet, but I long for their primeval cries overhead. Then it will be spring, and it won't be long. The world outside is waking up and making noise. Mother Nature's seasonal symphony is building toward a full orchestra with choir.

We came upon a young and very thin racoon the other day. He was moving slowly, no doubt cursing groundhogs under his breath, and he had stopped and was sitting on a push pile snowbank on the switch road down at Munising Junction. He looked at us while the dogs and I looked back at him. I'm glad we were in the truck as I'm sure that, had we come upon him while we were walking, the dogs would have introduced themselves with spring-like enthusiasm and the encounter would have ended badly for all of us. He did not look happy and his prospects for a meal were slim. The nearest garbage can was a half mile away, but at least he was headed in the right direction.

Life's Short! Drink the Good Scotch First!

The temperature is climbing into the 40s each afternoon now and when the sun is out, I can leave the back door open for a few hours to air out the house. Mornings are still frosty, though, and the temperature swing has the hard maples pumping sap upward. All across the U.P., the sugarbush fires are burning through the night and into the morning producing their annual river of syrup.

I've had several chances to surf the crusty snowpack with my dogs so far this spring. Scamper I guess is the right word. The warm sun makes the deep snow sag and grow heavy with its own melt water, and it refreezes overnight. On cold days I get to wander anywhere and everywhere in the woods and the dogs and I have been doing just that every day.

Shadow and Murphy are frisky in their canine youth, and they race full tilt, chasing each other over the hardwood hills where we walk just south of town. We've been hiking the ridges to hilltops I haven't seen in years and the wolf hounds prance and spar in earnest and at a dead run. Even Charlie Bear, the elder dog, has more bounce in his step these days and he barks with the joy of just being outside in the woods with me and the pups.

It's warming up more each day and the snow is getting punchy. By mid-day that freedom to wander disappears and most everyone has put their snowmobiles away for the year, so I don't have those trails to walk on anymore.

We're stuck on muddy backroads for a couple of weeks and the inside of my truck looks it. Mud season beckons and with it the urge to get dry dirt beneath my heels again. But I will not put away my winter boots quite yet. They'll stay handy for the rest of April.

But Spring fever has set in. The longer days have lightened my step too and every day I see more people out walking and talking and shaking off the Winter blues. As the snowbanks melt, the clogged arteries that are the city's streets have begun to widen back toward the curbs that disappeared in November. There's even a swarm of kids up the block who've dug their bicycles out of the garages and sheds where they've sat idle all Winter.

There's not much blacktop to ride on yet, so they sit on their bikes in a circle, cold hands and rosy cheeks, one foot up on a pedal ready to go. Some days they park their bikes in a heap and play king of the hill on the icy snowbanks that still decorate everyone's yard. It's almost spring.

The next milestone of the season is the day the ice goes out. It will happen overnight. One morning half the bay will be open, and the sun will twinkle across open water for the first time in months. Then the rafts of ice will ebb and flow with the changing winds until they disappear altogether in mid-May. Only then will it truly be spring, the spring of wildflowers and morel mushrooms, two track roads and brook trout streams. The spring when boats come out of storage and everyone aims at the first day that's warm enough for shorts and t-shirts and a ride around the island.

For now, though, the promise of spring is enough. Days with the temperature above freezing are enough. Warm sunshine is enough. Rain instead of snow is enough. May the ice pack rot and recede and the snowbanks melt gradually and not flood my basement this year. May the earth warm slowly and thaw. May my deck and my patio reappear, along with the driveway and the sidewalk. May my windshield be clear in the morning.

Let me rake and sweep away sand and salt and the residue of another Winter. Let me banish my shovel and my scoop, my roof rake and my ice scraper, to the back shed and the basement. Let me haul out my gravel rake and my garden hoe, my spade and my wheelbarrow. Let me move brush and leaves and dirt instead of snow.

I want to scratch in the dirt and wander in the woods without the need for Winter boots and gloves, warm hat or heavy clothes. I want to wear tennis shoes and then sandals. I want to walk barefoot on the beach . . . .

But I'm getting ahead of myself. I always do. I can't help it. Early spring is here and with it comes the satisfaction of having survived another Winter, along with the anticipation of the warmer days that lie ahead. The world is turning once again towards the summer and we're all along for the ride. That prospect alone will bring a smile to a man's face and warmth to his Winter-bitten soul.

Life's Short! Drink the Good Scotch First!

Spring in the Valley of the Left-Handed Echo (from the Continuing Adventures of Charlie Bear)

Charlie Bear always rides shotgun when we head out in the woods. He likes to see where we're going, and he recognizes many of our destinations long before we get to where we're headed.

He was already snarfing up the window with excitement by the time I coasted off the pavement of the Buckhorn Road onto the Doe Lake Road. You don't turn there at Kentucky Corner. You go straight and the pavement turns.

His nose was in the wind before I got the window rolled down all the way and I was fairly sure he knew where we were going before we even got past the Twin Lakes. He'd been there before. Every spring of his life. By the time we turned onto the two-track that led to our camp site he was dancing a fidget there on the front seat.

It was a fine spring morning, already 50 degrees, sunny and most of the snow had melted. There was just enough left that I didn't have to buy ice for the coolers. It was the last Friday in April, the day before the opening day of trout season and we were on our way to fish camp.

The Explorer was packed to the ceiling with camping gear and coolers and, despite the Bear Dog's impatience, I idled along the ridge that runs above Beaver Creek. That muddy stream was living up to its name that spring as it was more a series of ponds than a creek that ran a mile or so south from Stump Lake to its confluence with the Big Indian River.

As I took in the view through the still bare hardwoods I made a mental note to tell Edgar that the beaver were back in this neck of the woods but I quickly realized that he already knew that. He's been trapping this valley for almost 50 years and he was the last one to harvest the beaver from these ponds. We idled on and Charlie began to whine. There was no doubt now where we were going, and he was anxious to get out of the truck. We slid through the saddle notch to the top of the ridge and a few minutes later we turned into the small clearing that looks out over the river.

We'd been camping on this bluff overlooking this bend of the river every opening day since 1994. We did it in honor of French Dave who had died that winter. He had started the fish camp tradition on the back side of Hike Lake back in the late 70s. I was away during those years and missed out on those stories, but I was assured that first spring that this new campsite was easier, if only because you didn't have to put all your gear into a little boat and row it across an icy lake.

The Bear Dog jumped over my lap as I opened the door.

"All right dammit, you get out first," I scolded him without anger and without fault. I was excited as he was. It had been a long Winter and the snow had stayed late. Just two weeks before we weren't even sure we could make it into camp for opening day. But spring was finally here and while Charlie marked the perimeter of the small clearing we'd call home for the next three days I stood on the bluff and took in the view.

Below me was a floodplain where the river came in from the north and goosenecked to the west forming three ponds before disappearing out of site around a low ridge to the south. I shouted the traditional "Yoho!" and was gratified to hear it bounce off the low hills on the far side of the valley and then echo down the river to my left. We had named the valley that first year and it had become tradition to greet the spring from the bluff when we arrived. As if in response to my shout a bald eagle lifted off from its perch on a dead stub near the far pond, made a couple of lazy circles and disappeared downriver. It was going to be a good day.

Neither Charlie Bear nor I had slept much the night before. I had spent hours carefully packing totes and staging our camping gear near the door, so he knew what was coming. That morning as I loaded the truck he did the happy dance in the driveway to the point of getting in my way, so I opened the door and he took his rightful place in the passenger seat, relieved that he wasn't being left behind.

I always got to camp first. The rest of the gang would be along that afternoon and the camp building could wait for them. This morning belonged to me and Charlie and our annual opening day hike. With the dog prancing in circles I shouldered my backpack, preloaded for a half-day outing, grabbed my walking stick and off we went. Charlie knew the route and he led me through the ruins of the old lumber camp across the road and down the hill toward Half Moon Lake.

"Half-a-Brain Lake" we called it and you could just see it through the trees from our campsite. There was still ice around the back edge, but I knew Charlie Bear would take his first swim of the year when we got there. He can't help himself. He's a water dog. When we reached the canoe launch he walked into the water up to his belly and, as is his habit, he just laid down until only his head was showing. I swear he sighed in contentment.

Ducks were scattered in small groups here and there and across the lake a pair of trumpeter swans glided elegantly together in courtship, their necks intertwined and bobbing gracefully. I watched in quiet wonder at the beauty of their dance but felt a twinge of guilt for intruding on their intimacy.

I whistled, and the Bear Dog crawled out of the lake, considerably heavier than when he went in. After giving him time to shake off the excess water I headed for the railroad grade that skirted the edge of the lake. Charlie immediately bounded into the lead.

The forest floor was still bare but in two weeks this ground would be carpeted in trout lilies and dog tooth violets, trailing arbutus and Dutchmen's britches. For now, though, the only signs of new life were the red maple flowers and aspen and birch catkins that had already grown fuzzy with seed. They'd play hell with my allergies by Sunday but for now they just softened the canopy above me.

Where the grade reached the edge of the lake it disappeared into a thicket of balsam that was impassable without considerable scratching and eye pokes, so we left it behind and began climbing the ridge that separates Half Moon and Lyon Lakes from the "potholes," Rock Lake and Hike Lake, which would bring anglers by our camp all weekend in search of brook trout.

As I climbed higher the mixed hardwood forest gave way to a stand of white birch and the ground was littered with curled sheets of paper bark and I gathered some up for our first fire. It was too early for mushrooms, but I struck gold in a thick patch of wintergreen that the deer had overlooked in the fall. In no time I added a couple of handfuls of the sweet red berries to a pocket on my pack, popped a couple in my mouth and resumed my climb.

The Bear Dog had stopped at the crest of the ridge and was waiting for me impatiently as I covered the last fifty yards between us. He never went too far ahead but he always walked a long point, doubling back to check on me every time I got out of sight. When I topped the hill, he went off again at a trot. Either instinct or memory told him that I wanted to stay on the crest of the ridge and that was the path he set for us.

On we walked through the mature white birch with its understory of white pine saplings. It was easy going and before long we reached that magic spot where you could see all four lakes. I stopped and dropped my pack and pulled out a cold drink and some jerky. Charlie appeared out of nowhere beside me. It was too early for lunch, but a snack was in order and he was rewarded with his share of the dried beef. I sat on a log and he rolled on the ground in the warm sun and our spirits soaked in the silence.

There is a sweet, rotten smell to a hardwood forest in springtime. It's mostly just the presence of natural smells that you notice after months of no odors that are not man-made. It's the smell of decay and of rebirth as the earth absorbs the nutrients of last fall's leaf litter and transforms it into mushrooms and ferns, leaves and flowers. I leaned back against a tree and just let the day wash over me.

I don't how long we sat there. Time had lost all meaning. I may have dozed. But before long Charlie got up and began prancing and wagging his tail, his way of telling me it was time to move on. So, on we went along the top of the ridge until we were right above Hike Lake where I surprised him by veering right and heading downhill. It took him no time to find the lead again and we headed for the original fish camp just up from the shore.

The clearing where French Dave and the crew had camped so many years ago was overgrown and almost unrecognizable from the pictures I had seen. The fire pit, unused for more than 20 years, was just visible and the trail down to the remnants of the dock they had built there was equally faded. We did not linger. I had no memories of this place and my annual pilgrimage here was done only to honor those friends who had camped there as several of them were now gone.

We circled around and picked up the road that separates Hike Lake from its unnamed sister pond and we followed it back toward camp a mile or so away. Halfway back we took the turn-off to the M-Bridge and headed down to the bend in the river where our echoes land. It's shallow there where a wooden trestle from a timber spur used to cross but there is no evidence of the structure other than the earthen embankment on either side.

Why it was called the M-Bridge I never knew but I guess not much thought went into naming things that were meant to be temporary. As Charlie Bear waded and drank, I decided that the bridge they built before that one was probably called the L-Bridge and the one after it was the N-bridge. Lumberjacks in those days had few romantic notions.

Our detour complete, we ambled along the familiar two-track back toward camp stopping at Rock Lake to sit on a large boulder and split the ham and cheese sandwich I had brought for our lunch. There was no wind and the surface of the lake was a mirror that etched a perfect watery twin of every white birch tree that lined the far shore and the hill behind it.

The sun was high by now, so we didn't stay long. It was a short walk from there up the road to our camp site and when we arrived we were still alone, so we paused only long enough to drop a fistful of birch bark into the fire pit and then we headed down the shoulder of the hill toward the river valley below.

We got to the bottom where Beaver Creek flows into the Indian River only to find a large and well-maintained beaver dam at the confluence of the two streams. There was a new lodge in the middle and all the aspen along the riverbank had been felled, pell mell, making it impossible to approach the shore without navigating an obstacle course. The residents had dropped trees as big as ten inches in diameter and they were scattered like pick-up sticks. We sat quietly for a while and, sure enough, we got to watch a family of beavers hard at work patching and expanding their rather impressive dam to hold back the spring freshets.

Charlie Bear has never had much interest in the other critters in the forest and he too was content just to sit and watch, for a few minutes anyway, before letting me know it was time to move on again. As we began to move we were finally noticed and we heard the distinctive slap of a beaver tail as we made our way along the riverbank.

Life's Short! Drink the Good Scotch First!

We were picking our way through the tag alder on our way toward the ponds you can see from the bluff above when we heard the primal cries of sand hill cranes in flight. They were getting closer and in a moment the pair was overhead, winging their way down river looking for a nest site, anxious to get on with the important business of procreation. Their cry is a sound that I cannot reproduce, and I cannot describe, but it raises the hair on my arm whenever I hear it and I like to think that it's the same sound that pterodactyls made. Both of us looked up and watched them fly over.

"Look, Mr. Bear. The Sandies are back," I said but he ignored me as we both watched the pair fly out of sight. When we reached the first pond I heard car doors and laughter coming from the camp site up on the bluff and I immediately answered the "Yoho" that echoed down from above. Fish camp is less and less about fishing and more and more about trying out new gear and new toys and I did not want to be down range in case someone had gotten a new gun and a fresh box of bullets for Christmas.

So, we crossed the flood plain to the base of the bluff and as we broke out into the clearing at the bottom of the hill Charlie bear barked a challenge and we did the dog dance for five minutes. We lunged and parried and barked and laughed in play before rolling around on the ground in a heap of mutual bliss.

That afternoon we circled the wagons and made camp. We hauled three truckloads of dry maple and another of dinosaur bones—hundred-year-old white pine stumps heavy with crystalized pitch that later that night would give us a Viking fire that you could see from the space station.

A dozen old friends were there and we showed off new toys and camping gear and leaned on pick-up trucks, drank beer, and caught each other up on the life we had lived since we saw each other last. The Bear Dog reacquainted himself with his old mates and some new ones and they reestablished pecking orders and integrated the new pups into the pack.

We roasted a hind quarter of venison for dinner that night and feasted on it and smoked fish, very old cheese and fresh bread. As the sun went down we gathered around the fire drinking beer and passing around the good whiskey while we told stories, sang songs and toasted our departed friends until late into the night.

French Dave was honored as friend and camp patriarch and we heard the story again about the Blue Moon over Grand Island and recalled his penchant for cutting his house in half with a chain saw every October to remodel it, a project he never got around to finishing before spring.

We spoke longingly of Keener and the leprechaun that lived in him, his music and his humor and the quiet grace that marked his time with us on earth.

And we remembered the time Gravity Jack fell down the hill when Captain Dave was taking a picture of me cutting down the big tamarack at the bottom that obscured our view. I still have the picture of the tree falling with Jack tumbling through the frame on his way down the hill.

And we laughed at the time Captain Dave baptized Jack further down river during a fall canoe trip. He'd already fallen in the river trying to get back into the canoe when Dave decided that as long as he has already wet he might as well be saved too. I still have the old bottle I found that day.

With laughter mixed with sadness we recounted the many and sundry exploits of the reverend Captain Dave, Gentleman Adventurer, with whom we had all had the honor and pleasure of wandering with through the hills and valleys, streams and lakes of this very special place we call home.

The whiskey was warm and the fire was bright as the memories swirled around us like ghosts on that bluff overlooking the Valley of the Left-Handed Echo. It was spring and we'd all survived another Winter.

I awoke later that night alone in my tent. I'd left the flap open so that Charlie Bear could come and go, and he was not there with me. I poked my head out and in the light of a full moon I saw his black silhouette sitting on the edge of the bluff near the dying embers of the fire. He was home and looking out over his world. So, I gathered my sleeping bag around me and joined him in his vigil and we sat there together in the dark listening to the whippoorwills in the trees above and the peepers in the swamp below as we watched the moonbeams dance across the water on the distant ponds.

And we were both content.

Life's Short! Drink the Good Scotch First!

Trilliums and Trout

> *"I fish because I love to. Because I love the environs where trout are found, which are invariably beautiful, and hate the environs where crowds of people are found, which are invariably ugly."*
> -----Robert Traver

I am very much in agreement with the U.P.'s foremost author, jurist and fisherman and I will add that I also like the company that trout keep; beavers and otters, turtles and frogs.

There is no outing I approach with greater anticipation than a day in pursuit of the noble speckled trout. I used to go brook trout fishing only once a year--every Father's Day. It was the only day that I could seem to find the time. Now, I make sure I get at least one day on each of half dozen streams I visit each year and for that I consider myself lucky.

I confess, I am a river fisherman and a rocky, winding U.P. stream, along with the hike through the woods to get to it and back, are my neighborhood of choice in early summer. They are not, as a rule, the most productive brook trout streams in my neck of the woods, but they are the most beautiful and for me, the most serene. And they're usually good for my limit of 8" to 12" native trout and that's just enough for a meal.

In truth, the best brook trout fishing in the U.P. is not pleasant at all. The biggest fish are found in the most inaccessible of the many swampy rivers that crisscross the two watersheds on the peninsula; slow-moving, bottomless quagmires of loon shit overhung with impenetrable tag alder where the world smells of disturbed rot and the air swarms with the full arsenal of buzzing, biting creatures.

No, I prefer a stream that starts in the hardwoods and drops 50-100 feet per mile, swift and rocky bottomed with gravel races and deep holes on each bend. These are the environs that I prefer, and I'll take fewer and smaller fish as penalty for the cool breeze that always accompanies me downriver.

Now, if you're a fly fisherman you should probably stop reading right now for I am a blasphemer. I use spinners and worms by choice and of necessity as only one of the rivers I fish would give you enough room for a back cast. I have yet to encounter a fly fisherman on any of the streams that I haunt. In fact, I've yet to encounter another fisherman. There just isn't room for fly casting though and, besides, the fish that I'm after are working class trout who prefer a fat worm on a flashy gold plate for their dinner.

Opening Day on the last Saturday in April is still a sacred holiday in the U.P. and we all spend a long weekend at fish camp. We all buy a license. Someone always brings a boat and between the six of us we might scare up two rods, a tackle box, a hand net and a fresh box of crawlers, but that's about as far as it goes. The boat stays in the truck, and we seldom leave camp, so the fish are pretty safe from us. Besides, the water's still too high for "crick fishin'" in April anyway. Some years, it's still frozen. Late May and all of June are best for stream fishing, before the dry season begins in mid-summer when the fish migrate to the swampy stretches of river downstream. I will not chase them there, but some guys do.

The whole world is green up north in June—a thousand shades of green! New leaves and shoots explode from the canopy to the forest floor that's sprinkled with a dozen different kinds of wildflowers. Verdant is the right word for it and its warm balm for a winter-bitten soul. It's the north country reborn and these days, as often as I can steal the day, I fish one of the rivers that I know and last Sunday was one of those days.

It was hot for early June, and I made my way down the embankment and into the cool shade by the river's edge where I was greeted by a gentle breeze whispering out of the man-high culvert that takes the river beneath the county road where I had parked my truck. I was immediately refreshed and then abruptly swarmed with a million buzzing, biting beasties who had also sought refuge there from the heat of the day.

I always have a fresh can of DEET in the web pocket of the cooler/creel/oversize man purse that I carry, and I applied it liberally to my neck and hair and hat and wrists, as well as to the backs of my hands where the deer flies like to bite guys who smell like fish. While the lingering cloud held the bugs at bay, I speared a fat worm on a new gold spinner with a red bead and flicked it into the deep hole on the downside of the culvert. Before I'd made one crank on my reel I had a feisty little trout on the run and I quickly hauled him in. It was going to be a good day.

He was under-size, so I carefully unhooked him and slid him back into the river. You usually get the biggest trout on the first cast out of any hole big enough to hold more than one fish and the biggest fish in this hole wasn't legal, so I rebaited my hook and headed downstream through the ankle-deep rapids.

The first half of the stream is shallow and fast, and as I walked slowly downstream I tossed my line into those riffs ahead of me that looked deep enough to hold a trout. Every cast gave me a fish and they were all so small I pinched down the barb on my hook to make them easier to release. The bigger fish were further down-stream and I eased into the journey. It was just before noon and I had the whole day.

I know this stream from the winter as well as the summer. We snowshoe down the river valley to an old cedar grove between the upland hardwoods and the tag alder and red willow in the bottom of the valley. With a group of friends and a bottle of wine we have a fire and enjoy an afternoon beneath the padded comfort of the snow-draped trees near the black water of the swollen stream, coated here and there with ice. But in the summer this stream is for private enjoyment because brook trout fishing, for me at least, is a very solitary pursuit. It's just meant to be.

Before long I came to the first good, deep hole beneath the root ball of a giant yellow birch that anchors that chunk of riverbank to the shore. I rehooked my spinner with a fresh, gold #10 tru-turn, speared another fat worm and flipped the spinner sidearm beneath the overhanging branches to the top of the hole, letting out just enough line to reach the dark water, but not quite enough to snag a root. I held the prize in the stream for a moment and was quickly rewarded with a steady tug. I let him take it and turn it before I set the hook, working him upstream just far enough to clear the roots and then I held on and took his measure. He was a keeper alright, so I coaxed him into the shallows before I flipped him up on the bank and pounced on him with the urgency that only a brook trout fisherman can understand.

I thwacked the ten-inch native trout on the noggin with a stick and added him to the ice pack and two cold beers that occupied my little cooler. I smiled at the thought of fresh brook trout for dinner, untangled my rig from the sweet grass on the bank, rebaited my hook and headed downstream for the next hole.

The solace that comes from meandering slowly down a cold, clear, stream on a warm, sunny day in June can only be improved by the joy of catching your limit of the prettiest, feistiest and tastiest fish that God ever put on the planet. There is no shortage of poetry or prose written about fishing and the many lines penned about brook trout and "the environs where they're found" are for me the most languid and tranquil of all. You cannot be tense or bitter on a trout stream. You cannot be pompous, vain, or arrogant. You cannot be sad. These things are not allowed because they are simply not possible.

You're driven instead to reflection and mindfulness. All your senses are engaged; the firm crunch of the gravel beneath your boot, the chorus of birds in the forest singing in ragged harmony with the babble of the stream, the scent of the sweetgrass and buttercups on the riverbank, the twinkle of the rippling waters in the sun and the cool breeze on your neck. And there is, of course, the taste of cold beer or warm whiskey on your tongue.

After landing a second keeper and then losing a nice one on the next two holes, I came to take-a-break rock and put my pole and my cooler on the large rock in the middle of the stream while I rinsed the worm dirt off my hands in the swift current that flowed over a stepped sandstone shelf. I cracked a beer and gnawed on a beef stick while I sat on the smaller of the two large rocks that marked the middle of a stretch too shallow to have any good fishin' holes.

I resisted the urge I always have when I get to this spot to climb out of the river and search the old pine stumps for the bottle of brandy I stashed there on a winter hike several years before. It's a game that I play with the future in honor of the past.

Captain Dave was fond of stashing bottles of good brandy in hidey-holes on our regular hikes to places we knew we would go back to some-day. I was with him several times when we found a bottle that he (or he and I) had stashed several years before and I'm still looking for old brandy whenever I hike the hills and valleys we used to wander together. I stash them now in his memory and hope that some future day they will be found by me or my friends or the next hiker this way. I reckon a sealed pint bottle will last a hundred years, maybe, and I'd stashed one in that valley one winter and one spring I went looking for it with no luck. The valley looks different from the river in the summer than it does from the bank in the winter, but I know just about where we were that day. . .

As my mind wandered back over the years and the trails I saw the shadow of a large bird cross the stream, but it was gone before I could look up. Raven, vulture or eagle I reckoned by the size and then decided it was an eagle because that best suited my reverie. You get that kind of license when you're fishing for brook trout.

With one cold beer and two fat trout in my cooler I shouldered my pack and continued my quest downstream. The fish were where I thought they'd be but a few of my best holes were fouled with fresh windfalls and there was evidence of wind shear all up and down the valley. We had a big blow last November. Some of the uprooted trees were already starting to change the course of the river and I found a new hole for every one that I could no longer fish. The changes were fitting I thought, a physical metaphor for something spiritual yet so very tangible and necessary. We're all heading downriver in one way or another and we all end up in the sea at the end.

On a new hole formed from an uprooted cedar, I hooked another keeper and a little further down on my favorite hole I had the best moment of the day. I'd left the bale open on my reel and floated my spinner half the length of the long deep pool formed by an abandoned beaver dam. Just as I stopped the spinner with a crank he hit hard and doubled my rod over, but I had him! I kept my rod tip high and eased him up stream slowly to tire him out and a minute later he was flopping in the grass, fourteen inches of black and orange splendor!

If you have never battled and landed a 14" native brook trout in a clear stream on a sunny day in June you have missed a preview of the promised land, or at least what my idea of heaven looks like. And there is no smile as warm and as genuine as the one that nobody sees. Smiling, I added him to the trio in the cooler. I caught one last fish at the confluence of a side stream just before the valley flattens out and the swamp begins, and I hiked up the slope to the old logging road that would take me out to the highway.

A rusty bridge made from an old log truck bed crosses that little spring-fed stream and there I took my rest from the day's labor. The second beer came out along with the small flask of whiskey I always carry, and some crackers and cheese made for my lunch. It was a mile back to the county road and my legs were tired for being several hours in waders. I needed to rest and recharge.

I lingered lost in thought yet content to let my mind wander wherever it wished. The forest floor was carpeted in trilliums, each with three soft green leaves and three pure white petals. They were good company and I spent a full half hour contemplating a cherry burl in a tree down the slope from the one I was leaning against.

Three seemed the right number for the occasion and I ate and drank and sipped the whiskey while I listened to the wild. I smelled the earth's essence and I drank in her musky scents. These moments are too few and they are meant to be savored. This I did for more than an hour while the trilliums danced and sighed, and trees grew up around me.

The shadows had begun to lengthen when I pulled myself to my feet and began the slow uphill hike back to the road. The old logging road I was on was sun dappled and appealing—the kind of trail you had to follow, and my footsteps were deliberate and unhurried. As we rose into the hardwoods the native trilliums gave way to a sea of forget-me-nots. All along my route, brake ferns unfolded into vases on either side of the trail that was covered in knee high raspberry bushes. Birds sang. Bees buzzed and the forest went about it's business as if I was not there.

Just before I reached the road there is a clearing where the extra sun makes everything even more plush, so I stopped and turned around to revel for a moment longer in my solitude. As if to punctuate the moment and the afternoon I heard a car rattle by on the road above me. So, with a prayer of thanks and a promise to return, I finished my climb to the county road that would take me back to the highway that would carry me back to town and into those environs where crowds of people are found.

But I was having brook trout for dinner.

Life's Short! Drink the Good Scotch First!

Life's Short! Drink the Good Scotch First!

Hanley Field
(From the Continuing Adventures of Charlie Bear)

Our last run at the airport this year was on Veteran's Day. Winter had stolen in across the lake the night before on the back of a northwest wind and the air was cold and crisp. We'd gotten a foot of snow overnight and I had to put the truck in four-wheel drive and power my way through the snowplow furrow on the edge of Highway 13 to get into the field where I was still pushing snow with my bumper.

It was a bright and sunny morning and the dogs were anxious and snarfing up the windows with wet noses. A couple of snowmobiles had run the edge of the field, so the wolf hounds didn't have to break trail as they bolted down the tree line, but Charlie Bear did not follow them as he normally would. Instead, he just waded through the deep snow out into the middle of the field and lay down. He is a snow dog and he likes nothing better than to just burrow down into it.

We didn't go very far that last day as the snowmobile tracks weren't packed tight enough to carry my weight and the snow was just deep enough that I wanted snowshoes. As the wolf hounds ran, I took in the broad expanse of sky that comes with a flat field a mile long. The blanket of white on the ground sparkled beneath a blue sky full of "mare's tails and mackerel scales," high cirrus clouds that held the promise of more snow. The field was edged in gray branches and there was no sign of life in the sky or on the ground.

I'd been running the dogs here almost every day since early June when our other haunts, the bike trail and the beach, began filling up with tourists. The dogs run free when we walk and they're friendly, but they're curious too, and between them they're 260 pounds of shaggy looking hound, with a smaller old fat sidekick tagging along behind. They can be intimidating when they run up and introduce themselves and I've seen Murphy lift girls clear up off the ground with his nose. For that reason alone, we try to avoid people.

So, Hanley Field became our daily destination for the rest of the summer and fall and we usually had the place to ourselves when we got there just before lunch.

The grass airstrip occupies the southern two thirds of the field and runs north and south parallel with the highway and separated from it for most of its length by a dozen rows of mature red pine, future telephone poles of America. On our daily hike we usually boxed the north end of the field which was bordered east and west by young hardwood and left to native groundcover.

The north end drops off Scaffold Hill sloping down about 200 feet through a mature and dying beech forest. When the trees are bare you can look out over the canopy and see the hills around town and even catch a glimpse of Lake Superior. This gives us about 20 acres to roam and to run and the dogs just love it. It's the highlight of their day. It's also been known to lower my blood pressure, raise my spirits and brighten my outlook on life.

The whole area had been a potato farm at one time and the surrounding forest is a mix of maple, cherry and yellow birch and even some young beech trees that have so far survived the blight. Mixed in along the edge are sugar plums and pin cherries, and as the forest grew, the trees there had as much room to grow sideways into the field as they did to grow up, so the tree line is gently reticulated with long overhanging branches forming little alcoves of soft moss, grass and princess pine--a hundred shady corners.

The field and the forest were a thousand shades of June-green that first day I ran the dogs there. All the wide-open space made them nervous at first, but they figured it out and were soon carving long arcs in the field at full gallop and in hot pursuit of each other. Just to watch them run made each day worth the price of admission.

I kept them relatively close while I walked the perimeter chewing on sour weed while my old friend Charlie Bear trotted along behind me, stopping every so often for a satisfying roll in the grass. Here and there along the tree line we found patches of blueberries and high bush blackberries and the plain itself is a mix of native grasses and goldenrod, ferns and brakes mixed in with strawberries, blackberries and sour grass.

By July we were wandering out into the field in search of wild strawberries for which I had to fight the dogs and the competition was fierce. They like strawberries. They're also closer to the ground than I am, and they soon developed a nose for berries, and I learned to let them take the lead.

Each patch we found brought back a faded memory of another summer day 50 years ago and a pile of barefoot kids in the backseat of our red '55 Pontiac, blue-eyed, tow heads sticking out every window, looking for wild strawberries at the airport. We never found enough to take home and make into jam, but we always found enough to convince my dad to stop and let us kids out to pick and eat.

From this Fourth of July through the end of September the dogs and I snacked on handfuls of berries every day we went walking, taking whatever was ripe and following the seasons. And it was a bountiful year.

We shared that first day at the airport with a pair of juvenile eagles. They were honing the fine art of aerial combat and I got to watch them go at it most of the summer. They seemed to belong there. They were joined a few weeks later by what looked like a young peregrine falcon and then a couple of red tail hawks, all testing their new wings on the updrafts at the north edge of the field.

On warm days I brought a pail of water for the dogs and they'd politely take turns lapping up the bucket after our half-hour walk. Some days we sauntered. Other days we strolled. Some days we ambled and on Fridays we just moseyed. We were never in a hurry. Some days we lingered for another half hour, sprawled out on the grass in the shade of the tree line.

Beginning in mid-August we shared the airport with a siege of nine sand hill cranes, always in two groups of six and three. I'm not sure if they were too old to breed, or not old enough, but they were there every day. They ran flapping and squawking into the air as soon as I let the dogs out and the first couple of times the hounds gave chase. It didn't take the dogs long to figure out that two big wings beat four long legs every time, though, and after a while they ignored them. The cranes just walked the other way when we arrived like people crossing the street to avoid a neighbor they didn't like.

By early August I was picking sugar plums which I shared by bending down a branch to dog height and letting them browse. They got as many leaves as they did berries, but they didn't seem to mind. A week later we were all grazing at the blueberry patches along our route. There were so many that every few days I picked an extra pint to take home for my morning oatmeal.

I took a certain dietary satisfaction from knowing that the berries I picked and ate there every morning were as wholesome a snack as you could find on this earth and I made sure I got two, if not three, handfuls each day. It was the best year for blueberries I've ever seen, and I've picked a few berries in my time.

By mid-August the field was knee high and blanketed with the white flowers of low-bush blackberries. The ferns and brakes were almost waist high and the dogs used them for cover as they stalked each other. Dragonflies filled the air and the hounds gave chase until Shadow caught one. I'm guessing that dragonflies don't taste very good.

Then one day they mowed the airstrip and then the rest of the field, a process that took one man on a tractor a full week to finish. Gone were the ferns and goldenrod and blackberry flowers and left behind was a field of stubble that soon buzzed and swarmed with grasshoppers that rose in small clouds ahead of the dogs when they ran. The cranes feasted and were joined in turn by blackbirds, ravens and crows. For the rest of the summer I turned the corner in joyful anticipation of what manner of winged companion would join us for that day's walk.

September brought me blackberries and the unexpected treat of beech nuts that were easy to pick from the low branches sticking out into the field. I ate blackberries until early October and for the rest of that month I shucked and ate beech nuts as I walked along, slicing the triangular shaped shell with my thumbnail and carefully picking out the tiny kernel of goodness inside. We harvested half a pail one day with a tarp and a long stick and I roasted them at 350 degrees for 10 minutes. They tasted even better roasted than they did raw, but after they cooled the shells got almost too hard to pierce with a thumbnail. I left a tub of them sitting on the table at camp this deer season. Emergency rations.

My last harvest at the airport was a little bundle of wild sage that I picked in late October for a friend of mine on the Tribal Council. There's a small patch near the north entrance to the field and I made sure it had gone to seed before I took it.

October was glorious this year at Hanley Field!

It was warm, and on most days the southern sky was a staircase of billowy white clouds climbing into the stratosphere. Eeyore would have approved. The burnished hues of late summer had given way to the visual chorus of fall and the air was thick with the sweet, rotten smell of another year's growth moldering on the ground. But as Robert Frost would remind us, "nothing gold can stay."

One day the cranes were gone. And then the eagles. And then the crows. And then the sadness came.

It always happens as the fall colors pass their peak. The days shorten and the shadows lengthen. Autumn's glory fades. The cold north wind strips the orange and scarlet from the trees leaving only gray skeletons behind. As fall stretched on toward November, the skies darkened, the branches rattled, and the rains came. Cold rain. The days of light breezes were gone. I added layers and had to fight the wind either coming or going.

When the trees began to dance, and the leaves began to swirl, a sweet melancholy came over me each day as I walked. The dogs noticed and stayed close. It's a seasonal affliction, I confess, and it gets worse each year. I wallowed in it, though, and I poked at it like a sore tooth. I did not want that last fall day to come and go.

I wanted the world to stop turning, the season to stand still. I wanted the sweet smell of the good earth to linger a while longer. I wanted the cranes to stay for just a few more days. I wanted one more walk through the rustle of dry leaves. I wanted to marvel once more at a stack of thunder clouds, taste one more sweet breath of autumn air, and savor one more golden sunset. I wanted one more south wind.

I wanted old dogs to roll in the grass and be reborn as young pups.

But the world kept turning and the shadows grew longer. And the snow came, and then the cold. I was on the road for a few days after that last trip to Hanley Field, so the dogs missed a couple of walks. It stayed cold and the snow continued to fall and pile up before our next outing; a leisurely jaunt down the switch road to Munising Junction. It's about a mile round-trip and the railroad plows the road all Winter.

The air was cold and clean that day and the trees were heavy with snow. The sky was slate gray and filled with heavy, silent snowflakes. The land lay hushed. There was no scent in the air. No odors. No smells. Nothing.

Snow has no scent and that season's growth, so heavy and rich just a few days before, now lay compressed and frozen, sealed beneath the heavy blanket of white and saving its aromas for spring. The snowbanks were already shoulder high, and the deep snow in the woods kept the dogs from wandering too far. The wolf hounds took the measure of their new trail, sparring at a gallop and remembering the road from last year. With them as my guide I walked into the long white of another Winter in silent appreciation of the seasonal grandeur while my old friend Charlie Bear trotted behind, stopping every so often for a satisfying roll in the snow.

Life's Short! Drink the Good Scotch First!

Sentinels

I've been running the dogs down the switch road to Munising Junction this Winter and as I walk behind them, I catch glimpses of a pair of big white pine trees a hundred yards apart on a ridge about a quarter mile away. They crown above the bare hardwood canopy and they tease me and beckon to me as I walk along.

I may go after them this Winter on snowshoes, or I may wait until spring, but either way I will go find them and say hello. I can't help myself. I like big trees and I'll go out of my way to meet a new one up close and personal. I've even been known to set off on a compass bearing and make a day-long hike with friends in search of a big tree that I've spotted in the distance.

"Sentinels" I call these big pines. Some are left over from the days when large tracts of the U.P. were covered by white pine forests and others have grown up in the century since we finished clear cutting those stands of old growth timber. I'm acquainted with many of them in this neck of the woods and some I have known my whole life. I'm always in search of them and I'm fixing the position of these two by eye as I walk. I can see them from several spots along the road and I've also found an old two-track that heads off in that general direction. The proverbial road less travelled.

Along with these big pines, I'm also on a first name basis with some old growth hardwoods around here; maple and yellow birch trees mostly, but also a few beech and a couple American Elm that live here in town. I call them "centurions" because almost all of them have grown up in the hundred years since we cut all the virgin timber down.

The hills around the harbor are steep and have never been cut and never will be. From the toe to the crest they are covered in the last of the old growth maple and beech. Here there are still dozens of mature trees of each species. The biggest maple I knew blew down last fall. It was twisted like a licorice stick and was tucked in a stand of big hemlock trees on the back side of one of the hills that overlook the bay.

The biggest yellow birch I know stands on a widow's peak between two waterfall canyons right here in the city limits. It's about three feet across which is big for a yellow birch. From downstream the escarpment resembles a skull carved into the sandstone with the tree growing out of the bridge of the nose. The two small "eye socket" canyons are connected by a natural tunnel directly beneath the tree and if you live around here you should have figured out where it's at by now. It was my backyard and playground when I was growing up.

There's one particular white birch tree on Grand Island that, though relatively small by big tree standards, is impressive because of where it grows and in which direction. We'll take a boat ride some day and I will show it to you.

Michigan has a Big Tree Registry. Google those four words and you'll find it easy enough. I carry string with me and have measured the circumference of the biggest trees I know but still have not a found a state record. I will keep looking.

All the big beech trees on the hills around the harbor are dying from the blight, including several whose smooth gray bark I carved my name into long ago. The two big elm I mentioned survived the Dutch Elm disease 60 years ago. One stands alongside the Tribal Center in the old Lincoln School, and the other on the corner of Chocolay and Maple Streets, one block east of Elm Avenue, which for some reason seems an odd place for an elm tree to stand.

Speaking of big hardwoods, there's a hidden ravine on the west side of the bay, behind the Hillside Party store, where the city has built a bike trail. This little valley somehow escaped the ax and saw a hundred years ago, and it contains a couple dozen centurions that also managed to escape my attention as a young man.

The big maples there have burled trunks and lean in toward the center of the ravine, and because of that, their canopies are twisted and beautifully grotesque. The trail is graveled and hand-cycle accessible, and it rises at a shallow grade for more than a mile to the top of the hill and back. It's a truly enjoyable hike for people of all abilities.

But the sentinels, the big pines, are special! They stand head and shoulders above the hardwood canopy and each one is exceptional and unique.

Unlike the Christmas tree shape of the balsam and spruce, the rounded profile of the cedar and hemlock, or the neat and thin crown of the red pine, the white pine tops have irregular shapes that are sculpted by the wind. Their large branches are brittle with pitch and because they stick up above the canopy, they often break off in our frequent gales. These kings of the forest also get dibs on lightning strikes up there. I see in these sentinel tree-tops what others see in clouds.

Now, before you get the wrong idea, I am not an "environmentalist" by any means, though I do cherish our natural environment. And I have been known to hug these old trees with affection and to give them size perspective in a photo. But I was also a lumberjack for five years and those sentinels and centurions looked just as good to me, at a different time and in a very different way, as a deck of 12' logs at the landing.

In fact, the biggest tree I ever felled was one of those sentinels. It was a little better than four foot in diameter and I had a 20-inch bar on my saw. I had to notch it from both sides and then bore cut it through the notch in order too fell it. It landed with a tremendous crash that I could feel through by boots. But that's another story, or a series of stories. In the end I am a proponent of the wise use of our planet. It's the only one we have. And I believe in sustainable forestry even when that involves cutting down mature trees.

Life's Short! Drink the Good Scotch First!

The sentinels left over from the great primordial forest that once covered this peninsula were either too small when the land was cut over, or else were tucked into odd creases in the topography, places the lumberjacks couldn't get to or where they couldn't get the logs out. These were often steep hillsides, isolated high ground in swamps and the sandstone escarpment that makes up most of the coastline around here.

The sentinel I've known the longest rises in front of a rock formation at the family homestead at Powell's Point and towers 50 feet above it. It was big when I was a kid and would climb through its lowest boughs that swept the top of the rock and sit, bare feet dangling off the edge. I'd look out through the big branches at the fish tugs coming in the channel and around the point after a day out on the lake. Each tug had its own flock of gulls and the pirate in me would splash cannon shot around each boat. That tree has grown slowly in the 50 years since those summers so long ago.

There's a photograph on the interpretive sign at nearby Quarry Park, taken from the lake, of the Powell homestead and fishery built beside and below this rock. It's unmistakable in the photo, but with no white pine standing in front of it. There's a motor launch and a sailboat at the dock in this picture so my best guess is that it was taken around 1920, the year my dad was born, so that tree has grown there in our two lifetimes. I look forward to showing it to my grandsons.

I remember early mornings as a boy launching a boat beneath this rock and riding across to the island with my brothers and my dad to make firewood for the summer residents. Looking back across the bay to the eastern shore where we lived, I could see a half dozen sentinels sticking up from the hardwood canopy well back from the shore. I made up my mind that I would find all those trees and climb them for the view and in the autumns of my adolescence, I went looking for them. And I did find them. Sort of.

Over the course of the next few hunting seasons I found six different white pines growing on ridges whose tops stuck out of the canopy, but I never got to climb them. It's not that I didn't excel at climbing trees. What young boy growing up in the woods does not? But the first branch was 60 feet from the ground and the trunks were way too big to bear hug that far. I had no rope I could throw that high, so I sat at the base of each of those trees, shared a baloney sandwich with my dog, and imagined what the view was like from up there.

They logged those two sections above County Road H-58 when I was in my 20s and those trees were harvested. I noticed they were gone one summer when I was home on leave from the navy. But at least I had found them and gotten to know them. Forty years later a single sentinel has managed to poke its way through the canopy on that side of the bay and when I'm on the lake I try to triangulate its location. I doubt that I will go after it, though, as it looks to be on private property.

To walk in a stand of mature, old growth pines is humbling and it brings peace to the most troubled soul. They're not outsized and overbearing like the redwoods and Douglas Fir out west. But they will slow you down, no matter what speed you're used to, and they will make you pause for at least a moment and look up. They make you want to whisper.

There are two well-known stands left in Michigan, Hartwick Pines near Grayling and Estivant Pines in Copper Harbor. They're both worth the drive and the walk. The largest stand I know of around here is on a lost ridge between the main river and an unnamed tributary down the Laughing Whitefish River Valley. There's a dozen or so down there. A couple are five feet across. You'll need a guide to find them, though, some tall waterproof boots and extra wine. I might be available that day.

The greatest density of these sentinels is, not surprisingly, along the rugged sandstone cliffs that make up most of the Lake Superior shoreline around here. As a rule, they're not as big as their brothers who stand in better soil further inland, but their crowns are wonderfully sculpted from having to cling to the crumbling rock and bend into the north wind.

Perhaps the most famous sentinel on this stretch of coast is the one on top of Chapel Rock. The earliest sketches of this sandstone pillar from the early 1700's show this tree and it has changed little in 300 years. As juvenile delinquents we used to monkey climb the tap root that connects the tree to the cliff behind it and through which it's lifeblood flows. The park service strongly frowns on that sort of adolescent foolishness these days. The tree's remaining roots clasp the top of the almost bare sandstone pillar like talons. They put Chapel Rock on the back of a quarter last year, part of the National Park collection.

The sentinels at Pictured Rocks and along the shores of Grand Island are often adorned with bald eagles who roost in their topmost branches and fish the clear shallow waters at the base of the cliffs. There are several nests along the shore, a couple of which have been active for many years. We measure a good day on the lake by the number of eagles we see.

What a thing to be an eagle!

Imagine opening your eyes for the first time to the view from atop a hundred-foot tree clinging to the edge of a 200-foot cliff leaning out over the brilliant blue waters of Lake Superior. How could you not want to learn how to fly?

Some 200 years ago there was a man named Autumn Duck, who was chief of the Grand Island Band of Chippewa Indians. He had a wife whose name was Sound of the Wind in the Trees. Their son was Little Duck who became Powers of the Air. My friend Loren has written about them. My friend Virgil sings a song for her.

If you stand on the shore of this lake near these sandstone cliffs beneath these magnificent white pines and pay attention, you will understand why a baby girl would be given such a name.

When you listen to these sentinels, even in the lightest air, you can hear them whisper just like that old Johnny Horton song. With a gentle breeze they sigh and sway and sing and dance, and their song is an ancient and peaceful tune of lofty heights and endless time.

In groups along the rocky coast their tune is more wistful and tentative as the wind off the lake backs and veers. There are many voices along the shore. As the breeze freshens there are harmonies that rise to a chorus that blend into the laughter of the waves below. When the wind gusts, it becomes a symphony that stirs the blood and touches the soul.

Add the warmth of the setting sun on your face, a shimmering bar of light across the water, and the pure, sweet scent of the Northwind and you have a feast for the senses. No extra charge.

Of course, the experience is made that much more enjoyable with a swallow of warm whiskey washed down with an ice-cold beer near a roaring fire on the beach surrounded by friends of the old and good variety. There is a place I know. . .

It's early April now and we still have lots of snow, but I've decided to put my snowshoes away for the year. We're in the thaw-freeze cycle that gets the sap rising, in trees and in dogs and in men, and the snowpack has started to crust over. I tried it the other day, but I punched through. It's not yet sturdy enough to take my weight and may not get there this year. Let it melt. I'll put off finding those two sentinels until spring is finally here, and I can walk softly on the forest floor and once again feel the good earth beneath my feet.

Life's Short! Drink the Good Scotch First!

Life's Short! Drink the Good Scotch First!

That'll be Two Dollars

Gunsmoke was the only TV show my dad watched besides the news. He was a no-nonsense kind of guy and Matt Dillon was his kind of hero. You did not interrupt the old man when Matt Dillon was dispensing justice in Dodge City on Thursday nights.

Matt Dillon was also my roommate for the 11 days I was in the hospital. Festus, Doc and Miss Kitty were there too, along with Rowdy Yates, Lucas McCain and the Barclays, Paladin, Roy Rogers and the Cartwrights and I have to tell you right now that if you don't recognize those names, you really won't get much out of the rest of this story.

The TV is ubiquitous in the hospital, a place where you spend a lot of time waiting. They're on in every patient room, waiting room and hallway alcove wide enough to park a guy in a wheelchair while he waited for a "procedure."

Now the term "procedure" in a hospital is the ultimate euphemism. I had dozens of procedures while I was there. All of them were different and none of them were pleasant. They were all necessary but at best, they were an interruption from the important business of doing nothing and an inconvenience as well. At worst, they hurt. But that's another story.

Even though I had plenty to read and lots of visitors, I still watched a lot of TV, mainly because I was on a four-hour blood draw schedule for most of my stay. I calculated that I was down about a quart and a half by the time I got out. Add to that the quiet terror that accumulates over six days and gathers every night while you're waiting for surgery, and you'll understand why sleep was so elusive. So, I watched a lot of TV.

The hospital gets about 60 channels including the local affiliates for the major networks. They also offered the full spectrum of cable news channels so you could pick and choose your own personal combination of real and fake news. For some reason there were also three soccer channels along with all the major shopping channels, religion channels, a few nature and history channels, and a couple different Division III college football rerun channels.

I swear I watched the Salamanders from Southeast North Dakota Community College beat the Charging Chippies from West Suburban Memphis Tech four times. Same score each time.

What saved me was the "old cowboy TV show channel." I watched it all day and all night. I re-lived whole portions of my childhood in 11 days. I binge watched episodes of Gunsmoke. I rode back and forth to my procedures, tall in my wheelchair saddle, whistling the theme song from Rawhide or singing "have gun will travel, read the card of the man."

My nurses and transporters all thought I was a little odd, but I assured them that the urge to entertain is strong within me and singing and whistling also helped keep at bay the fear that lurks down deep inside of all patients waiting for heart surgery. The nurses understood that explanation and they always smiled and we're angels. The transporters kept their heads down and said, "yeah, gunfighters, OK" as they checked their text messages to see if they could get the patient on the seventh floor to X-Ray and back before they had to come back to get me.

TV drama was so much simpler in the 60's. There was no gray. Life was as black and white as the medium itself. There were good guys and bad guys and the cause was always obvious and just. The story was told simply, and justice was done in less than an hour. There were no social or moral ambiguities. There were few loose ends either and the two-part episode was rare.

Toward the end of the decade producers did start to slip in a little nuance. Good guys sometimes did bad things but, helped by the perseverance of decent guys like Lucas McCain and Little Joe Cartwright (who always seemed to have a lot of extra time on their hands) they eventually saw the light just before the episode reached its tidy conclusion. And sometimes bad guys secretly had good hearts (even though they had killed twenty men) and put away their guns and went straight or otherwise saw the error of their ways at the very end of the episode, usually just before they died of lead poisoning.

Because the episodes were from the 60s when we all got fewer than three channels, I didn't see many of these shows until they were reruns in the 70s and 80s. They didn't interest me then so most of the episodes were new to me. I watched these shows and was comforted. They helped me get whatever sleep I did manage.

Gunsmoke was my favorite. Matt Dillon was the epitome of strength, courage, justice and what an even-tempered American man should look like. He never got excited. I watched so many episodes I went through two sidekicks (Chester and Festus) and several supporting actors; Quint and Thad and Newly. Doc was always handy. He rubbed his chin, stayed up all night tending good guys and bad guys, never made a wrong prognosis and whatever procedure he was called upon to do, it cost two dollars.

Miss Kitty was innocent, kind and warm-hearted even though she ran a saloon and a brothel. Drinking beer and whiskey in the middle of the day was pretty much everyone's pastime when they weren't out righting wrongs. It was what people did back then and it was considered wholesome family entertainment. And you couldn't get through two episodes where Miss Kitty didn't befall some peril from which Matt had to rescue her.

Festus always mooched a beer, called Doc an "old scutter" and spent most of his time getting into all manner of complicated side plot troubles, usually with one of his colorful relatives. But he proved his merit when the chips were down and he was always right there after Matt had dispatched the bad guy.

Life's Short! Drink the Good Scotch First!

And for the fastest gun in the territory, Matt Dillon sure got shot a lot. Seven or eight times at least during the 11 days I was in the hospital. But he always got his man in the end. He either shot him in "a fair fight," felled him with one mighty blow from his righteous fist or just stared him into giving up or doing the right thing. And then he bought Festus and Doc and Miss Kitty a beer to end the show.

Matt Dillon was my roommate while I was in the hospital. He was a good roommate too. As I contemplated my mortality, up close and personal, he made me think about my dad because he was one of the two men the old man would watch on TV. Walter Cronkite was the other.

My dad trusted Walter Cronkite to tell him exactly what was going on in the world. If he heard it on the CBS Evening News then, by God, it was so. No fake news here. And you knew what he had reported was so on that particular day because at the end of the broadcast Walter always reassured us that "that's the way it is" and then he would remind every one of the date.

And then on Thursday nights my dad would stay up and watch Matt Dillon. The characters would be introduced, the very thin plot line carefully laid out, the injustice exposed and the stage set for the gunfight or fist fight necessary to vanquish the bad guys. Someone always had to go to town.

And, in the end, we were reminded of just what was right and what was wrong and why good guys were good guys and bad guys weren't.

Then Matt and Festus, Doc and Miss Kitty would go have a beer at the Long Branch and my old man would go to bed. And for 11 days so did I, though no one ever did offer me a beer.

Life's Short! Drink the Good Scotch First!

Life's Short! Drink the Good Scotch First!

These Scars on the Land

At the earliest edge of my childhood memory is a spring day on Powell's Point in the field near our house. The melting snow had receded toward the tree line and I was exploring the dry grass that had been flattened and compressed by the weight of the winter snow.

There I discovered treasure in the form of toys abandoned in the fall whose shapes were plain beneath the matted grass--a baseball and a toy truck, a broken BB gun and a battleship made from blocks of wood with big nails for turret guns.

A winter's blanket of snow does that in the U.P. Everything short of woody shrubs is crushed by the weight of 200+ inches of snow revealing not just childhood treasures in the Spring, but all the marks that we have left on the land in the 300 years since we settled this peninsula.

Early Spring is the best time to find and ponder these scars that we have made. It's also the best time to find the artifacts that we've left behind as we exploited the peninsula's resources and did our best to turn virgin forest land into fertile farmland with very limited success.

I confess that the last Saturday in April, the opening weekend of trout season in Michigan, is no longer about fishing for me. It's still a camp weekend with the boys and dogs, but time once spent shivering in a boat on Hike or Rock Lake and not catching fish is these days spent busting through the last of the snowpack down back roads we haven't had access to since deer season. We go looking for and finding the traces of those who came before us.

Wherever you go in the U.P. there is no shortage of the "trace" left behind by our ancestors—the trace that self-proclaimed environmentalists would decry as sacrilegious. I'm with them in being good stewards of our planet and no one I hang out with would ever leave trash behind in the woods or deliberately damage the land. But we do leave our mark. After all, we are the apex species on Earth and in most cases we can't help ourselves.

So, this notion that we should use the land while leaving no trace of that use, other than footprints, seems silly to me. All animals leave their mark. We're all familiar with them. How often do we see trees with the bark shredded by dominant bucks and others girdled by hungry porcupines? How common are piles of wood chips at the base of a dead stub, courtesy of our pileated woodpecker friends, or whole valleys flooded and logged by beavers?

These are the places where we hang out and play and if I come upon an old fire scar and maybe a pole wedged between two trees in my ramblings I'm not offended. I'm reassured. Someone else has been here--two, four, maybe ten years ago. They spent the night. It's looks like a good spot to camp. And it's proof that I'm not lost.

Old railroad grades are probably the most common scar you see in the woods. These timber spurs were often put in for only a single winter. Once all the trees within the working distance of a horse drawn sleigh were harvested, they pulled the rails, plates and spikes, left the ties and abandoned the line.

I used to fish the Silver Creek up the Rock River Canyon and the hill country between those two streams has a system of railroad grades that looks like branches coming off a tree limb where they ran a spur up each ravine to get the logs out. There is great irony and symbolism in those old scars being one of the dominant feature in what is now a federal Wilderness Area.

And then there were the camps. First came the lumber camps which moved with the timber spurs chasing the tree line. Because they were so temporary, little remains of them save cellar pits and outhouse holes.

Then the CCC Camps were built and young men from all walks of life were employed building great public works projects like the infrastructure for our national parks. The Seney Wildlife Refuge, thirty miles east of town, is 100,000 acres of man-made wetland and prime waterfowl habitat, part of which is also a federal Wilderness Area.

Some of these camps, Evelyn and Au Train here in Alger County, saw extended use as German POW camps during World War II. The prisoners were put to work in the woods replacing the young men who had all gone off to war. Whether intentional or not, the CCC was instrumental to the war effort as it trained hundreds of thousands of men from all across this country to work hard as a team while they endured harsh conditions and primitive facilities. It proved to be good training for soldiers.

All these camps were dismantled after the war, but as they were more permanent than the logging camps, much more of their trace remains—more holes and a great deal of cement foundation and flatwork. Camp Kentucky on the Buckhorn Road used to be a favorite mushroom hunting spot for me in the spring and among the ruins is a moss-covered concrete floor maybe 20x40 feet in size with a short, poured wall on three sides. I've always assumed it was the kitchen and dining hall for the camp.

Now it's a perfect spot to sit on a warm spring day while the dogs roam the site and leave their "mark" on everything vertical. There are bottle dumps near these camps too, but few have any worthwhile treasure as the sites just aren't old enough.

Then there are the old farmsteads, hunting camps and trapping cabins scattered all over the north. We did our best to make this land into farm country and we do grow some corn and hay, a few of potatoes and cows, but 200 years after we started, more than 90% of the peninsula is still forest land and thousands of these structures were abandoned and left for nature to reclaim. The trapper's cabin on the East branch of the Whitefish River is still there, but on my last visit the mice and porcupines had taken over. It still had a stove and a serviceable pipe, and there was dry firewood inside, and it would provide shelter in a pinch. But it smelled pretty bad so we had our fire outside that day.

I was "gone fishing" once many years ago and had set out on a compass bearing to find a small trout stream that flowed into the east side of the Au Train Basin. I had a pretty good topo map, a backpack full of food and drink, and the whole day to play. I found the stream sure enough, but I didn't catch any fish. But I also found a very old log cabin. The roof had collapsed but all four walls were intact as was the doorway which made a perfect seat. I thought at first it was a trapper's shack or a hunting camp but there was a mature lilac in bloom and two large apple trees in the dooryard. I took my lunch there that day and explored the clearing and the cabin without much luck while I wondered who had lived in such a lonely spot so many years ago.

I could not find it again on a bet and I had no camera so I took no pictures. But I can still see it in my mind's eye moldering away in that little man-made clearing deep in the dark forest. It was peaceful there but lonely and it humbled me. It also brought me an hour of quiet joy and I think about it every time I smell lilac.

Most of the artifacts that I find in the spring when you can see every wrinkle in the earth started out as trash. Cast off by some surveyor or trapper, hunter, logger or camper, each piece would still be trash save for the splendid isolation in which it is found. The treasure you find wandering around in the woods is much like beauty because it's definitely in the eye of the beholder. A steel gas can or the leaf spring from an old logging truck, a piece of chain or an axe head lost in the fall with the handle long since rotted off might not seem like treasure to you, but it's treasure to me. Perhaps not valuable enough to take home, but treasure nonetheless and sometimes even art.

We were cutting one summer down the Baker Grade by Kingston Lake when I found a gray, fluted two-gallon gas can sitting on an old white pine stump. The top of the stump had mossed over and the moss had grown halfway up the sides of the can. It might have been left behind because it leaked, but I like to believe it had been misplaced and forgotten. I left my saw gas and oil and my water jug next to it, so I got to come back and look at it a half-dozen times that morning. But I never touched it. I didn't want to disturb it. That afternoon I chased the paint across the road and never saw it again.

Speaking of trace, I cut a couple hundred acres of hardwood down that old road and I amused myself by cutting unique limb formations I'd find in the tops of trees I had cut down. In my mind I formed the Maple Knee Furniture Company and I was going to be rich. I called it that instead of the Maple Crotch Furniture Company for obvious reasons and I must have left 50 three and four legged crotches up on the stumps of the trees they had been cut from. I was going to go back and get them and make bar stools and end tables but when I tried to peel the bark off one I gave up on the idea. So much for finding my fortune. I left them all right there in the woods, standing on those stumps. One day I'll go back and see how many I can find, but it has been 20 years.

You find the strangest things when you're working in the woods. In an old log landing off the Perch Lake Road there's a maple tree with a single leaf spring grown into it. It's about three feet long and the tree has completely grown around it and it sticks out on both sides. I've seen trees grow around and through a variety of things, but what makes this so unique is that it's twenty feet off the ground.

Trees grow from their tops so it did not start out near the ground and rise to that height. And there is no crotch where the spring is. Someone climbed up on something—maybe the broken-down truck the spring came from--sawed a notch in that tree and stuck that spring in there. Lumberjack art.

Car parts and even whole cars and trucks are not uncommon in the woods around here and they're always a special treat when you come across one unexpectedly. I always try to figure the trajectory it took to get to its final resting place, a not so easy task when there's no sign of a road and it's resting in the middle of a 50-year-old stand of timber. It died there one day and that's where they left it. Each one rusts and erodes ever so slowly and becomes its own mini ecosystem as it ages. And at least you know the age, the make and the model of this particular piece of junk, I mean artifact.

We were hiking the beach near the Anna River one summer day when my friend Matt found a six-foot length of hand forged chain. It was near a large block of cement embedded in the sand, so we reasoned it was part of the log boom that held in the huge rafts of pulp logs they once used at the paper mill next door. He took it home and hung it on the gazebo by the fire pit at his house in Steuben. He left it behind when he moved to North Dakota and the last time I was there it had fallen on the ground and was partially covered by the tall grass.

Glass bottles are the most durable artifact you'll find in the woods and identifying old bottle and can dumps is an art itself. The cans always float to the surface and rust into the leaf litter making the bottles underneath them hard to find. I've found more than one stash of bottles by shuffling my feet and kicking them. I have a small but cherished collection. My best one came from an unplanned pee stop while canoeing down the Indian River one cool October day. It was a terrible place to get out of a canoe, but we had to go so we managed to scramble through the tea bushes and up the bank. For my efforts I got a four-ounce medicine bottle from the Manistique Pharmacy with a beautiful blue tint. Some river hog's cough syrup from a spring log drive a hundred years ago. For his efforts my partner Jack fell in the river trying to get back into the canoe and was Baptized as an afterthought.

I have to admit I've also found my share of plastic containers in my travels too, especially in areas that are still logged on a regular basis. Two-gallon oil jugs seem to be the most common. But even these are brittle and wasting away in the leaf litter. I pick them up if I have room in my pack.

The greatest treasure that I have ever found was on an early spring day when we were cutting pulp near the headwaters of the Miner's River. We were finally out of our snow gear and back in leather boots after a long winter. The silhouette was unmistakable beneath the matted leaf litter. It was a hand-made, double-bitted, Kelly Brothers axe head and it immediately became one of my most prized possessions and favorite tools. I cleaned it up, shaved and hand-fitted a new hickory handle for it and it started a new life on the wood pile at camp. It was a sweet tool and a true piece of art.

I lost it somewhere near camp several years later. Either that, or someone else wanted it more than me. I like to think that I lost it though, that I set it down one fall day and it fell over and got covered by the falling leaves. I guess you just have to be an old lumberjack from the U.P. to appreciate that loss. But I am comforted by the possibility that it may turn up on some future spring day and become another man's treasure. I hope whoever finds it cherishes it as much as I did.

Life's Short! Drink the Good Scotch First!

Life's Short! Drink the Good Scotch First!

Speed of Arrival

Unless you were in the submarine navy, know celestial navigation or are otherwise interested in the arithmetic of a sphere, you may not enjoy or appreciate this story. I wrote it about three years ago and decided then it was too much "you had to be there" for the general public. I've revised it some, but it still might not appeal to you. This story is for my friend Charlie Brown, retired Chief Quartermaster, United States Navy, submariner extraordinaire, Pilot Major of the Western Sea, international nice guy and the last of the big spenders. And it's for the rest of those steely eyed killers who punched holes in the Western Pacific with me when we were young men.

When it comes right down to it, life is all about your perspective, really. It's about your point of view, the mind's eye and the scale you use to gauge whatever you're doing or wherever you're going. Perspective is where you stand and how you measure the world you pass through. It's affected by your height and your weight, your income, your speed, your salary and your relative horsepower. It's colored by your IQ and your GPA, your net worth and your life expectancy. And it's as much about miles per gallon as it is about miles per hour.

Call it your speed of arrival and a long time ago when I was a very young man in the Navy on the other side of the planet, a crusty old chief petty officer taught me to measure it differently using two antiquated and very British yardsticks; one for distance and one for time. But that's the essence of it isn't it? Distance and time and how you measure both.

It was the spring of '79 and I was a young and tender 3rd class petty officer, crow and single chevron still stiff on the left arm of my dungaree shirt, assigned to the navigation department of the USS Darter (SS-576). The Darter was a diesel submarine, an old girl, outclassed and outdated, but she was a good boat with a fine crew and we were crossing the "big pond" on a transit from San Diego to Tokyo by way of Pearl Harbor.

You'll have to forgive a certain amount of submarine terminology in this story. At a minimum you need to know that diesel-electric submarines had three modes of operation; submerged on the battery, submerged on the snorkel and surfaced. Like our World War II predecessors, we made long transits on the surface because it was more fuel efficient as well as being faster.

All the old diesel boats are gone now, at least in the U.S. Navy, and the sleek, tear-dropped shaped nuke boats that my son serves in are just the reverse; they're faster submerged and they don't have to care about fuel efficiency. But that's a different discussion and one completely unnecessary to this tale.

It was a grand time for me, a magic time. An ocean crossing to a distant land! I was 19 years old and off on my first big adventure.

We were making a surface transit and were somewhere near the International dateline, but we were in no hurry as the Navy was using us as a target of opportunity. Once a day we'd get the order to submerge inside of an imaginary box in the middle of the ocean and they'd send out P-3 Orion submarine hunting aircraft to look for us. We'd play at that game for several hours and then we'd surface and charge batteries on our merry way to the next imaginary box where we'd repeat the process the next day with another airplane and crew.

An ocean transit, for us at least, was a long, slow voyage and there were many quiet hours spent standing watches and marking time in a vessel that never sleeps. At any one time, day or night, half the crew of 80-odd souls were awake and on watch or else passing the time playing poker or acey-deucy, reading, or engaged in idle conversation. These hours of quiet discourse were the grease of our social existence at sea. A good storyteller or a man with much experience was valued in your watch section and, taken as a whole, we were an odd lot and our subject matter was diverse and eclectic.

Of course, you ran the risk of being paired on watch with shallow companions or even running out of things to talk about. But you also had the time and opportunity to thoroughly plumb the depths of serious subjects and complex ideas.

I had qualified as Quartermaster of the Watch on my way to Pearl Harbor and it happened on the evening watch one night as we plodded deliberately west. I had just shot evening stars, reduced the sight and updated the ship's position. Once plotted, I had calculated the course and speed necessary to reach our next rendezvous point on time. Picking up the microphone for the 7MC ship's control circuit I reported to the bridge.

"Bridge, Quartermaster, based on a current celestial fix, we are on track, 19 miles ahead of PIM, SOA required to arrive at Point Oscar on time, 8 knots. Recommend reducing speed to 8 knots."

"Quartermaster, Bridge aye," came the immediate response from the Officer of the Deck on the bridge 30 feet above me.

"Helm, Bridge, All ahead two thirds."

"All ahead two thirds Helm aye" answered the helmsman on the other side of the control room at the diving station. As he spun the annunciator, and was answered, he reported "Bridge, Helm, answers All ahead two thirds."

"Helm, Bridge aye."

"Maneuvering, Bridge, Make turns for 8 knots."

"Make turns for 8 knots, Bridge, Maneuvering aye."

I watched the pit log above my chart table as the electricians in the Maneuvering Room slowed the speed of the electric motors on the two shafts to an RPM calculated to drive the boat at 8 knots on the surface. Then came the final exchange.

"Bridge, Maneuvering, making turns for 8 knots."

"Maneuvering, Bridge, aye," and the watch section settled back into its slow routine of quiet conversation.

Our "PIM" was our Path of Intended Movement and it was an imaginary box that followed us along our track so the navy could find us if we ever got lost or if they needed us for something important which wasn't very often. It was also so we didn't run into anyone else. It's a big ocean, but we shared transit lanes with other vessels coming and going and it was still possible for ships and boats to go bump in the night. That sort of thing is hard on the boat and looks bad on the captain's resume.

So our PIM was where we were at. Point "Oscar" was where we were going. And our SOA, our Speed of Arrival, the essence of this story, was how fast we needed to go in order to get there on time.

I thrived on this new existence. Though young and relatively inexperienced, I was already a competent navigator and had earned the trust of the Captain and the officers I stood watch with. And I was proud of the important role I had onboard. Later in life during the retelling of many a sea story I'd wave my hand with flourish, take a sip of whisky, and declare "no, I wasn't the Captain, but I told the Captain where to go and, by God, that's where we went!"

The sun had just set, the control room was illuminated by red night lights and the watch had settled into a comfortable routine. Aside from me and the helmsman, there were four other watch standers in the centermost of the boat's seven water tight compartments.

The auxiliaryman sat at the trim and drain manifold that moved water in and out and around the boat. He'd have been a busy guy had the boat been submerged, but on the surface he had very little to do and was absent-mindedly shining the large brass manifold.

At the aft end of the control room were the radioman of the watch who was busy sending and receiving the day's message traffic and the sonarman of the watch who, on the surface, also had absolutely nothing to do. He was sitting in the hatch that led to the crew's mess chatting with the night baker who was loading the oven with cinnamon rolls.

Rounding out and leading the watch section was the Chief of the Watch who would have also been busy had we been underwater but on the surface his job was to keep everyone engaged in some meaningful activity if only to keep us all awake. And he liked to talk.

"How fast is that in country miles?" he barked at me from across the compartment in the Blue Ridge accent that betrayed his roots. He was a chief engineman, a diesel mechanic and a lifer. A small man, thin and wiry, he was built for the inside of a submarine engine room and he was considered a good sailor, a good shipmate and a terror on liberty, but that's another story. His world onboard was valves and pistons, cylinders and lube oil. It was all real and all steel. There was nothing abstract about it. He measured tolerance and precision, efficiency and performance by hundreds of horsepower down to thousandths of an inch. And he was also fond of reminding anyone who cared to listen that he was from "West by God! Virginia."

Before I could answer he rephrased the question. "What's the difference between a knot and a country mile?"

"If you mean the difference between a nautical mile and a statute mile, it's 240 yards," I said, certain that he already knew that. He had a habit of asking younger crew members questions he already knew the answer to.

"So we're going about 9 country miles per hour," I added.

"Whyze it different?" he asked. "Why do we use bigger miles at sea than we do on land?"

I knew the math, but I really didn't know why nautical miles were 2,000 yards and statute miles, or "country miles" as he put it, were 1,760 yards. But I thought for a minute and took a stab at an explanation.

"I think it makes the math easier," I began. "The world is 24,900 'country' miles' in circumference east to west, a little less north to south, and for the purpose of navigation it's divided up into 360 degrees of longitude east-west, and 180 degrees of latitude north-south.

For longitude, think of an orange with 360 segments. For latitude, think of straight parallel lines from top to bottom." My mind had reached back to my schooling and I was warming to the lesson, eager to demonstrate how smart I was.

This was 1979 and we only had a few calculators on board. But I pulled out the one I had—about the size of a paperback novel--and started tapping the keys.

"You take 24,900 statute miles times 1,760 yards and you get 43,824,000 yards divided by 2,000 to give you 21,912 nautical miles. I'm not sure who figured it out, but nautical miles are supposed to make it easier to measure both distance and time."

For distance you use the latitude scale on the chart and every degree equals approximately 60 miles." And again I did the math for him.

"21,912 divided by 360 degrees equals about 60.8 miles. Close enough for open ocean navigation. And every degree of latitude as well as longitude is subdivided into 60 minutes. A minute of latitude is approximately equal to one nautical mile. You measure distance on the latitude scale of the chart" and I took out my dividers and showed him on the bottom contour chart that was taped to my plotter.

"How come you can't use the longitude scale to measure distance?" he asked and this time I was certain that he didn't know the answer.

"Because lines of latitude are equidistant." I answered. "They're the same distance apart at the equator as they are at the poles. Lines of longitude on a Mercator projection chart all come together at the poles. Remember the orange?" I asked, hoping he wouldn't ask me who Mercator was and why his charts did that.

"You could measure distance using the longitude scale accurately at the equator, but the distance between those lines decreases to nothing at the poles." He was listening intently now so I moved in for the kill. "You do, however, measure time using longitude," I continued.

"Time?" he asked. "Howz that?"

"There are degrees and minutes of latitude and longitude, but those are linear measurements—they measure distance. But for longitude, every degree of distance also equals four minutes of time."

I had him.

"The world completes one revolution every 24 hours so there are 24 hours in the day and, consequently, 24 time zones on the planet."

He understood that.

"So every degree of longitude is also equal to four minutes of time. If the sun sets here at 8:00pm then one degree of longitude west of here it sets four minutes later, two degrees west, eight minutes later and so on for the remaining 358 degrees of longitude." Again I did the math which he understood but the concept seemed to escape him.

"24 hours x 60 minutes equals 1,440 minutes in a day. 360 degrees of longitude times four minutes of time per degree also equals 1,440 minutes. Four minutes per degree either way."

"Is that at the equator or at the pole," he asked.

Doesn't matter," I said. "The earth turns at a constant speed, but relatively speaking, the closer you are to the pole, the slower you're moving. Time is relative chief. If you stood directly at the pole you would be in all 24 time zones at the same time."

"Eight knots then, nine miles per hour" he said as he walked back to his seat on the other side of the periscope stand scratching his head. "Minutes and miles," I heard him mutter to himself as he pondered this new perspective.

A while later while I was calculating the time of moonset and sunrise for the oncoming watch, he hollered across the compartment, "Well then, what's 8 knots in furlongs per fortnight?" And he grinned at me.

"I'm not sure," I admitted. "How long is a furlong? Neither of us knew.

"Well how fast is that in fathoms per fortnight then?" he offered as a substitute.

Fathoms per fortnight, aye, wait," I answered and I bent to my calculator.

"Eight knots times 2,000 yards is 16,000 yards times 3 feet per yard is 48,000 feet divided by 6 feet in a fathom equals 8,000 fathoms per hour."

Twenty-four hours in a day times 14 days in a fortnight equals 336 hours times 8,000 fathoms equals 2,688,000 fathoms per fortnight SOA required," I blurted out rather proudly just as the navigator stepped into the control room.

"Feels like we should be going a little faster than that DJ," he said without blinking as he walked by on his way to the mess deck for coffee and a sticky bun before he took the watch on the bridge.

"You get stars tonight," he asked going by.

"Yes sir." I replied sharply. "Good fix. On track, ahead of PIM, making turns for 8 knots. Warm and dry on the bridge. Moon will be up 'til just before sunrise."

"Very well," was his reply as he continued aft.

"The Brits are using meters these days," the chief offered from across the compartment. "Canadians too. They say the math is easier."

"I suppose so," was my reply. "Easy is a pretty relative term though chief."

By now the rest of the oncoming watch began to stir and pass through the control room on their way aft for coffee and then forward to the torpedo room for a smoke before they went on watch. I finished the last few entries in the ship's log as the boat plodded slowly on the surface toward the infinite horizon. The next morning we reset the calendar as we crossed the dateline and entered the Realm of the Golden Dragon.

We all have numbers that are significant to us. Lucky numbers. Recurring numbers. Numbers that mark special occasions or add up to something important. And we all have different yardsticks we measure our world and our lives by.

I have several numbers that have meaning to me, but 2,688,000 has never been one of them. It's just not handy. No one ever says "I'm thinking of a number between one and three million." But It reminds me of a time when I was much smarter than I am now, a time when I knew just about everything. Now it seems that the more I learn the less I really know.

One night recently, some 35 years later, I sat at the Legion canteen and shared a glass of red wine with an old friend, a retired judge. He had been the navigator on a destroyer in the 1950s where he had learned the fine art of celestial navigation in the North Atlantic. We mixed our wine with our stories while a glorious sunset lit up the hills across the bay.

He recalled what a thrill it had given him as a young man to measure the angle of a few stars, mark an exact moment in time, do a little arithmetic, and know precisely where you were on the planet. And then we had another glass of wine and lamented the fact that this marvelous and unique skill we both had once was now obsolete, replaced by a billion cheap cell phones.

I guess your perspective is reflected in the sum of your experience, the breadth of your knowledge and the depth of your passion. Sometimes it can even be found in the height of your stupidity and it's almost always the length that you'll go to or else the number of times you will try something before you finally succeed or decide to give up.

Perspective is what creates that teachable moment whose clarity often lasts for just a few precious seconds. It's sometimes there, unexpectedly, in the midnight hour and it can linger throughout life's longest day. Eventually, it gets measured by the best years of our lives.

It's about going places and growing old. It's about all those things and more. When it comes right down to it, it's what you really need in order to get to where you're going and it's how you measure your progress toward wherever that is, right up to the very end itself.

It's your speed of arrival and it's unique and very personal. 2,688,000 fathoms per fortnight is a really big number, but it's not very fast. I've always liked the yardstick though. And I use it whenever I can which is not very often.

Life's Short! Drink the Good Scotch First!

Life's Short! Drink the Good Scotch First!

I'll Take the Dirt Road

Given the option I'll take the dirt road every time. Sawyer Brown can come too. If it gets me where I need to go then I'm turning off the highway right here even if it will take a little longer. Or a lot longer. Sometimes how long it takes to get there isn't very important.

Living in the Central U.P. makes the dirt road a popular option for getting around. Here in Alger County we are both blessed and cursed with an abundance of public land and fences and gates are rare. Sixty per cent of the county is state or federal forest land or else national park, wildlife refuge, wilderness or national recreation area. Another 20% of it is commercial forest reserve, or CFR.

The blessing for us is that 80% of the county is open to the public. We can use it for hunting, fishing, hiking, foraging and even firewood cutting--almost anything we need to get or want to do in the woods within reason. There are actually fewer restrictions on "company land" than on state or federal land—the few gates you do find belong to Uncle Sam--and law enforcement on all of it is pretty much limited to fish and game regulations.

The curse is that the 20% of the land that is privately owned generates all of the tax base available to pay for the maintenance and emergency services on the other 80%. We locals learn to fend for ourselves when out in the woods where we're relatively unhindered by law enforcement activity and frequently beyond the reach of search and rescue, let alone EMS.

Paved state and county highways are few in the U.P. but they're all connected with a solid system of improved gravel roads that were originally built to access the peninsula's timber. These roads are now maintained (a term I use loosely) by the county road commissions or the U.S. Forest Service, the largest landowner in the Alger County. They're everyday arteries though and relatively speaking, they see a lot of traffic.

When you turn off the highway to take that dirt road, your speed automatically slows to 25 and the windows on the truck come down so the dogs can put their muzzles in the wind. My blood pressure has been known to drop by ten points when I make that turn and my outlook on life tends to improve significantly as well. When your tires hit the gravel it's also the traditional time to stop and make sure the cooler in the back is stowed properly and isn't overfull.

These unpaved primary roads are named by the county and numbered by the Forest Service and most of them are on the map. They're wide enough for two-way traffic and they were built when gravel was cheap and government at all levels still had funding and equipment to take care of them. They are also multi-use, so you share the road with ATV's, dirt bikes, mountain bikes and sometimes even horses. Most are not plowed in the winter, and many become designated snowmobile trails.

Branching off these gravel roads is a whole other system of dirt roads maintained to varying degrees depending on where they go and who is using them. For these roads "maintained" can mean anything from "it ain't been graded yet this year" to "the last guy down it cleared the windfalls" to "hell, that washed out in '96." These are single lane roads for the most part and oncoming traffic usually turns into a social event, depending upon how much room there is to go around and how well you know the people you're getting out of the way for.

Many of these roads will take you to one of the hundreds of rivers and streams, ponds and lakes that define the U.P. landscape and the most heavily travelled ones usually lead to someone's camp or else to their deer blind. Some have hand-made signs. All are seasonal.

And then there are the two tracks—a pair of wheel ruts with grass or groundcover growing between the ruts--heading off through the trees and over the hill. The taller the grass the more enticing that road becomes because it's not used often and may not have seen a tire track in months. There is great beauty and treasure down these roads as often as there is misery and pain.

Like most U.P. words, "two-track" is both a noun and a verb.

Two-Track (n.) a two-rutted road with foliage growing between the ruts.

Two-Track (v.) to drive down an overgrown road or trail in a truck with a friend, two dogs, a chainsaw, shotgun and/or fishing poles and a cooler full of beer enroute to an uncertain destination with an unknown ETA.

Two-tracking is usually a two-person sport and it's important that neither of you have to be anywhere before dark because you're not entirely sure where you're going, and you may not get there at all. There is risk and we've all spent a night in the woods around a fire next to a broke or stuck truck nursing the last beers in the cooler. The second most important thing is making sure you have enough beer for however long it takes to get to wherever you end up.

There are equal amounts of luck and skill that go in to a successful two-track adventure and the threshold for success is pretty low. Running out of beer is third on the list.

"Well, at least we didn't break down or get stuck."

Sometimes these dirt roads and two-tracks can go on for miles and then eventually come out somewhere.

"So that's where this road comes out at!" is a good thing to hear when you're almost out of beer and haven't recognized any of the scenery for a couple of hours. More often than not, though, they peter out and dead end at an old and abandoned log landing. But that ain't a bad thing because it's usually a good spot to water the ferns and get rid of your extra bullets.

Life's Short! Drink the Good Scotch First!

All of these roads were built in the middle of the last century to get the timber out. They were prime-cutting the hardwood then and using the first generation of skidders, forwarders and log trucks to move it to the mills. But these roads were built over and alongside an even older network of temporary rail spurs put in between 1870 and 1920 to harvest the virgin white pine that once covered this peninsula. You know when the road you're on follows one of these old grades because the roadbed is flat and smooth, the puddles are hard bottomed, and the turns are long graceful arcs.

And you know when you cross these grades, driving or on foot, because the natural ripple of ridges and ravines has a straight, man-made scar across it 12-14 feet wide that will last until the next ice age. These grades are often game trails too and we hunt them in the fall. For our crew, they're also frequent hiking destinations but that is the subject of another story.

Two-tracking is a favorite weekend or even an after-work activity and we Yoopers have a dozen excuses for idling away an afternoon putzing aimlessly and undisturbed through the countryside. Oh, and not bothering anyone while we're at it either, thank you very much!

First, we're usually hunting for something we don't really need; mushrooms in the spring, partridge in the fall, firewood year-round, saplings for tomato stakes, blackberries or raspberries, cherry burls or cedar poles, new hunting spots or forgotten brook trout streams. All become that day's Holy Grail. There's always something in the woods that needs lookin' for but doesn't necessarily need finding. There are some essential supplies and equipment for proper two-tracking too.

First, you need a truck. Then at least one good friend and two dogs, just in case you get into a survival situation that requires a good friend and two dogs. Two tracking is also pretty thirsty work so a cooler full of beer is a must. Four-wheel drive comes in handy as well as a chainsaw. Add a shotgun or a fishing pole for looks, an orange hat or two and a few sandwiches and your set for the day.

Some trips are planned days in advance and have some dubious or contrived destination or purpose.

"I saw where a nice dry maple came down on that road where I had my bow stand last year down the Stillman grade. We should go make it into wood for camp before the woodpeckers get it. I need to get in there next week to bait anyway and it's blocking the road." And then two beers worth of plans are carefully laid for Saturday afternoon.

Others start at a bar with "give us one more and then a box of roadies. Let's take the Hunt Club Road back and see if Joe has his trailer set up by the river yet." And out the door you go after that beer. Throw some John Prine or Guy Clark in the jukebox and you might make it home before dark. By the way, if I have to explain what a "roadie" is, never mind. But they come in various flavors and they're also called "road pops." They come in multiples of six and you don't need a bag.

Alger County is also famous for a variety of saloons and restaurants located out in the woods and connected by the network of roads that I've been talking about. They're all about two beers apart and handy spots to call for help if stopping there for one-too-many has derailed the day's outing.

"Honey, can you pick us up at the Buckhorn? Truck is acting funny. Won't go down the road straight. I'll buy you dinner. Please!"

The Buckhorn is a real place, and a real nice place, and so is the Bear Trap and the Jack Pine, the Boot Lake Bar and the Tanglewood. Good food, cold beer, good friends gathered watching squirrels in the bird feeder—the kind of stuff that gives a Sunday afternoon in October it's grace.

But "two trackin'" is mostly an action verb where I come from and a pastime fit for three seasons. There is nothing more beautiful or compelling than a two-rut road, grass knee high in the middle, that you've never explored and you now have the time to see where it goes. It draws you in and pulls you down it and you have to follow it to see where it might lead.

Ironically, though you seldom see any other traffic on these roads, if you're near an active logging operation the vehicle coming at you might be carrying fifty tons of hardwood pulp and it's best to stay out of their way. But you're ready for that because loggers will rearrange the forest furniture in ways you can't help but notice. Some people find logging ugly and destructive, unnecessary and harmful to the environment. Those people are idiots.

My only regret about logging (and this from a former lumberjack) is that loggers cut down ancient pulp trees near the road, left over from the prime-cutting days, that had served as my landmarks for many years. Remember, we're off the map at this point. It's tough to pick your way down an old road you barely remember after a logging crew has just remodeled the neighborhood.

When you do encounter a fellow two-tracker, you usually know them and that's worth stopping, stretching the dogs and leaning on the bed of a pick-up truck for two beer's worth of nothing serious but also nothing quite so important and enjoyable.

In the fall that two-track has a canopy of orange and scarlet that may stretch along the grade for a mile in each direction making a private and very lineal cathedral. Two tracking is a good Sunday activity. Being nearer to nature is being nearer to God and no matter what you believe in that's a good thing.

I have been fortunate to have travelled a lot when I was younger yet there is much of this country and of this planet that I would still like to see. But if I were to see no more of it beyond all the two-track roads in Alger County that I have not yet explored then I will die a happy man. And it will take the rest of my life. That's part of the blessing.

Life's Short! Drink the Good Scotch First!

    Many of these roads we travel I have known my whole life and driving on them or walking them with a shotgun cradled in my arms and a happy dog out front brings an overwhelming nostalgia. This is the space in which I have lived the best days of my life. These roads are old friends. They're my home and the place I'd rather be.

    And then there are others—a still countless number—that I've yet to explore. Some I may have just noticed because they've recently been opened up by a logging operation. Others I have driven by a hundred times and still haven't found time to see where they go. There are just too many for what I expect will be the time I got left on earth and that's part of the blessing too.

    Yup, I'll take the dirt road.

Life's Short! Drink the Good Scotch First!

Life's Short! Drink the Good Scotch First!

The Bear Dog and the Wolf Hounds
(From the Continuing Adventures of Charlie Bear)

Charlie Bear was quite contentedly staring down his 10th birthday when she came into his life. A confirmed bachelor, he hadn't had another dog in the house since Jake died eight years before. He had a good and an easy life too. He ate well and had a nice bed right by his humans, another one in the living room and even a padded eyeballin' seat in the dining room where he could keep his eye on the front steps and the yard, the driveway and the street out front.

His dish was always full, and he never lacked for fresh water. Bacon was plentiful and he enjoyed a spot beneath the dining room table at meals. He had a big back yard, little kids next door to play with when he went out, and he was happy to sleep most of the day as long as he got to go for a ride in the truck with me when I came home from work. He lived to hike with us on weekends and he's always been a boat dog. He got to go swimming a lot and was allowed to sleep on the couch when we went to camp.

Yup, he had it good and he got along with the other dogs too. He had a lot of four legged friends, and they were always welcome in his home when their humans came to visit. But she was different, and he didn't quite know what to make of her on that cold November day when she came into his life.

Shadow was ten weeks old, a gangly bundle of legs and knees and paws, and already tall enough to look the old lab/collie in the eye. Charlie Bear gave her a low growl and a suspicious sniff when they met. She cowed in submission. Then he promptly ignored her and went back to his day bed in the living room. She was scared, away from her littermates and hesitant after a two-day ride from Indianapolis with a layover at my daughter's house where she got to meet and spend the night with her two dogs. At first, she wouldn't leave my wife's side and she insisted on the security of her lap. Slowly, she began to explore her new home and she sought out and soon commanded the attention of the older dog.

Charlie Bear did his best to ignore her at first. He's pretty social though and after a few days it became obvious she was staying. Pretty soon he tolerated her advances. Before long he began to play with her, and his life changed. Over the course of the next year she became his boon companion and he became the center of her new world.

Winter came and they kept each other occupied all day while my wife and I were at work. Charlie Bear lived for Winter and Shadow followed him outside into the snow. Without his heavy coat she got cold quickly, and we bought her the first of two fleece jackets that she would quickly outgrow. She liked to chew and that cost me the spindles on the dining room chairs and a couple of sandals. That led to a never-ending succession of chew toys and bones that would decorate every square foot of floor space in the house.

Shadow rarely barked but she stared at the world though the most beautiful, soulful brown eyes framed in long gray fur. On both me and Charlie Bear she used what I can only describe as feminine guile to get her way. And he became her mentor. She learned fast and found her place in the family as she continued to learn her place in the world. And over the course of those months Charlie Bear got a new lease on life. No more sleeping all day. No more life of ease and senior citizen bachelor dog sloth. His day was driven by what quickly grew to 110 pounds of gray brindled energy with feet as big as canoe paddles.

By spring she towered over the old dog, but she still followed him like the dutiful puppy that she was and that's how she learned to swim. She followed him right into the lake after a stick and the first time she found water over her head she disappeared for a moment and bobbed back up and was swimming, long legs and big feet moving her right along. Wolf hounds are not water dogs by nature, and she was so lean that her head barely stayed above the surface.

But she was bound to follow Charlie Bear and he is a water dog, swimming in the big lake from ice-out in the spring until slush coats the lake in November. And he taught her that it's all about the stick. This stick and then that stick. And then that stick over there. You fetch them and you chew them, but you never bring them back. There is always another and he will throw them all day long.

Shadow and Charlie Bear swam together, they ran together, and when they wrestled Charlie always took the prone position and fended her off from below. They'd wrestle for hours until he got tired, or she got too aggressive and he'd give her a little growl, or a nip and she'd stop instantly. Then he'd make his way to one of his beds and she'd follow him. Once he got comfortable, she'd lay down beside him, her long, spindly legs sticking out, straight up or at odd angles. She had to be touching him. By mid-summer he could walk underneath her. But he was still the boss and his approval was necessary to her. She would not eat until he ate first, and she would not lie down until he did so. They were an odd-looking pair, Mutt and Jeff different, but they were inseparable.

And then late that summer Murphy came to live with us. He was 8 weeks of black brindled male wolfhound who was skittish and uncertain. Shadow was curious and befriended him. Charlie Bear disliked him from that first day and kept waiting for him to go away but he didn't. So, he ignored him. A third dog in the house gave the Bear Dog a break at first. The gangly pup found a more willing playmate in Shadow and she dutifully gave him her time. They would wrestle and Charlie Bear would watch and then they'd both come over to lick his chops and seek his approval. Shadow received it, but not Murphy. He'd get a growl and a snap that was serious but with no real heat in it.

This confused the young dog at first, but he quickly learned his place in the pack and as he grew Charlie Bear made sure to remind

Life's Short! Drink the Good Scotch First!

him that he was the third dog in the pecking order, and at the bottom of the food chain. Murphy accepted this as puppies do and it was as if they both knew that it was only a matter of time.

But the pup was persistent, and he wore down the old dog with sheer affection. He sought his approval constantly and came back again and again licking the old dog's chops in submission--pack behavior that I had never seen before. Charlie eventually came to accept the boisterous newcomer and less and less often felt compelled to remind him who was in charge. The pack had now formed and there was harmony in our house.

And I learned how wolf hounds hunt and fight by watching Shadow teach Murphy how to stalk and then attack the old dog from both ends as a team. Charlie was willing prey and did an admirable job of fighting them off 'til they reached a point where he'd let them know that he'd had enough.

Murphy never followed Charlie like Shadow had so he never learned to swim as a pup and he still won't. His game is to stalk the other two from the shallows and wait for one of them to fetch the stick and then pounce and try to take it away. Then there's be a lot of running up and down the beach with at least two dogs with a mouthful of the same stick.

Murphy grew fast and went through three sizes of fleece jackets that winter. My wife would not give him Shadow's hand-me-downs because they were pink. He got green, then black and red, then blue. By spring he was as tall as Shadow and by late summer an inch taller and 130 pounds.

But he's kind of a special needs dog. He's brash and assertive and has always got some mischief in his eye, yet he whines a lot and he's skittish around some people. Puppies scare him and he's only just now starting to figure out that he's the biggest dog in the county.

Shadow has become his mate and he has since bonded with the older dog too. Without any challenge or conflict that I saw, Murphy become the alpha male one day. It's as if Charlie Bear said "go ahead, it's your turn now. I'll follow." Dogs have an ego I'm sure but not the sin of pride and Charlie Bear willingly gave up the lead and retired again.

Murphy leads the hikes now and like Charlie Bear used to, he walks a long point. He will try to choose our path, but he lacks the older dog's instinct and experience in that regard. He's always doubling back to find that we've taken the other fork in the trail. But he will learn, and his instincts will adapt to his experience.

He is especially solicitous of Charlie Bear and will often go lie down next to him. Charlie is 12 now and he may see one more Winter. I think Murphy knows that his time is short. Shadow continues to seek his approval and for now, they have become a family and they do everything together.

Irish wolf hounds are an ancient breed. They're majestic animals, with a commanding presence. They are good natured, but they were originally bred to hunt and to fight. They are a match for a wolf, but they were also trained for war and could take a man off a horse. They retain that size and those skills and watching them run and spar is like royal canine choreography. They duel like two skilled swordsmen. It's almost regal and it's a joy to watch.

Shadow is quicker and can out-parry Murphy for three or four moves but then she's overpowered by the bigger, stronger dog. She's like a rapier to his saber. When he gets too rough, she will seek refuge at my side, and I've been taken down by the pair of them when she does that. I've learned to plant my walking stick in front of me when they come at me full speed.

They do this whenever we hike and the Bear Dog is content to trot along behind me on the trail and keep an eye on them, lest they pounce on him in their play. Sometimes they'll go by us at a full gallop and trip him, something they're very good at, and he'll stay down and give them a couple of rounds of what for. When he's had enough, he lets them know, and then he gets slowly to his feet.

He's a little stiff legged these days and his gate is somewhere between a shuffle and a waddle. I've learned to slow down and let him set the pace. His muzzle is gray and he's getting portly, but he keeps up. I have to lift him into the truck now though and I dread the day when I will have to lift him out too.He won't quit though and he won't be left at home. It would kill him to be left behind. He had some trouble keeping up this Winter. He'd just lay down in the snow until I turned around and called him. My wife told me that I should start bringing a sled so he could ride in it when he got tired. One day I might have to. I suppose I could hook the sled up to one or both wolf hounds but I'm pretty sure that would be a little more excitement than any of us need.

But it never came to that. He made it through another Winter and we're all looking forward to his annual spring trim. It will take five pounds of collie fur off him and for the summer at least he will look like a lab.

The wolf hounds have stirred the puppy in the old Bear Dog, and they have also brought companionship and purpose to his senior years. It's hard sometimes to watch the contrast between the young dogs in their prime and the old dog's slow decline. But the waxing and waning of youth and old age are as inevitable as the turning of the tide and the changing of the seasons. In dogs and in men.

I am grateful that Charlie Bear will have the warmth and reassurance of their company into his final days. Dogs look after each other and packs protect their elders. They will let me know when his end is getting near. For his sake and for mine, I hope that won't be any time soon.

Life's Short! Drink the Good Scotch First!

Down Below

When I was a young child, somewhere between the earliest edge of my memory and the first grade, I became familiar with a place that was referred to in adult conversation as "down below."

"Your Uncle Truman moved down below after the war," or "his brother told him he could stay with him if he found a job down below."

I did not know then that "down below" was the entire lower peninsula of Michigan. To a young boy it was simply a place that was not here where we were.

For generations many parts of my rather large and extended family worked and lived down below and, from time to time, they came home to visit their parents, their brothers and sisters, and their uncles and aunts. I only got to know many of my cousins because of these brief summer visits, first cousins I still don't really know well, but who looked a lot like me and who share roots on Grand Island. Even now as I near my 60th birthday I only see them on rare occasions, usually funerals and then burials in the family cemetery in Murray's Bay.

That young child knew only that there were two places in the world, home, where we lived in the U.P., and "down below" where our relatives lived. And I knew that you had to cross a bridge to get there. A very big bridge. And the relatives who lived down below had "good jobs" and they would not have gone down below if there had been any good jobs in the U.P. To me, down below seemed like a nice place.

As I grew older and learned my geography, I came to realize that down below was the lower peninsula and "down below" was, of course, down below the straits in my parents' days and down below the bridge in my youth, and I still have relatives in Marlette and Alpena.

When I was a young child, somewhere between the earliest edge of my memory and the realization that Santa Clause was not real, I also received a rudimentary religious education at the Munising Baptist Church. The church had a classic fire and brimstone preacher at the time and the tone with which he described everyone's probable if not eventual fate in life—certain and eternal damnation—forever soured me on organized religion, but it did force me to assess my faith later in life.

In his eyes, though, there was a slim chance, a very slim chance, and that only through pious behavior and regular attendance at church, that you could actually get into heaven. More likely, since you were an unworthy sinner, you were going "down below" to rot in hell for eternity.

You can understand the confusion that this created in an impressionable and precocious five-year-old. Apparently, many of my uncles and aunts were already in hell because that's where the work was. They had good jobs there. And their children had been born there!

On one hand, I was relieved that I didn't live down below, and it somehow made being poor in the U.P. a little more tolerable. On the other hand, it had me second guessing the cousins I saw every other summer. They seemed pretty normal.

And it scared me because my own attendance at church and Sunday school was spotty at best. I still live with the social scars of having no butterfly stickers in my Sunday School book, given for showing up on three consecutive Sundays to have the crap scared out of you by an old man who didn't even know my cousins.

So, I took to playing hooky with my older brothers and sisters on Sunday morning and learned the joy of an unescorted adventure in town. We didn't get to town much when I was young so even the few blocks between the church and my grandma's house were undiscovered country in need of exploration.

In hindsight, I think that this peculiar combination of social, economic and religious instruction I received during those most impressionable years got me to question everything for the rest of my life, especially authority figures, and it also made me the nonconformist sunovabitch that I am today.

I never made it down below as a child and I was 33 years old the first time I crossed the Mackinac Bridge. Up until then, that had been my claim to fame. I'd been around the world three times but had never been to Michigan's lower peninsula. I had just moved back to the U.P. after nine years in the Navy and six more years of working for a defense contractor out west while I went to school and had children. I had to go to Lansing for something and that first time the bridge terrified me, much more than my natural fear of man-made heights, and I got to thinking about those Sunday mornings at the edge of my memory.

The Mackinac Bridge is a formidable structure. I travel downstate several times a year these days and though I still don't like the bridge, it doesn't scare me anymore. I still don't let myself get in a position where I might have to stop on it, and I never look down through the grates. There are trolls down there. Which gets me to thinking about apple knockers and stump jumpers.

Today the citizens of the two peninsulas refer to each other as trolls and Yoopers (Yooper is always capitalized). Yooper obviously comes from "the U.P." No one in Michigan ever calls it the upper peninsula. And trolls are trolls, of course, because they live below the bridge. Both are terms of affection most of the time.

Before they built the bridge (it opened in in '57, two years before I was born), people in the U.P. were referred to as stump jumpers because of the popular belief that we were all lumberjacks. And those who dwelled in the lower peninsula were referred to as apple knockers or sugar beaters because those were the two dominant crops grown there. Yoopers who migrated down below would seldom go to "the city," but would find work and settle in more rural areas where they were more comfortable.

In truth, most of the lower peninsula is also rural and is much like the U.P., especially in pinkie land (think mitten), Grand Traverse and the Leelanau peninsula. Most of our relatives who moved down below found jobs and raised their families in the thumb (think mitten again). Ironically, I've been to Leelanau County many times, but have yet to visit Alpena or Marlette.

The U.P. is a land of blessings and curses. It's a blessing that we are so thinly spread across such a beautiful chunk of the great outdoors, but the curse is that steady work that pays the bills is hard to find, and the largest part of each generation is forced to leave to find that illusive "good job." Some get to stay here and some, like me, are lucky enough to get to come back.

Back when I was a starving reporter, I interviewed Gene Holmquist at the Trenary Feed Mill for a story about why Trenary and the U.P. were so special. He reminded me that the U.P. has always been a source of exports to the rest of the state and nation. First it was fur and then fish, and then copper and iron ore and then timber. And for the last 100 years it has been our kids.

Economic expatriates from the U.P. have spread all over the state and all over the land. Employers love them because they're inherently honest and conditioned to working hard. Living "up north" is a challenge and it starts young. Life is harder up here because of the geography, the weather and the economy. Yoopers are tough and resourceful, but they're also fun-loving and good to be around.

Even when they're forced to live in that land down below.

Life's Short! Drink the Good Scotch First!

Life's Short! Drink the Good Scotch First!

Fire and Water, Earth and Sky

It's been said that the most pleasing sight to the human eye is firelight, and if you've spent any time around a campfire, I think you'd be inclined to agree with that statement.

It's also been said that the most soothing sound to the human ear is moving water, be it the lapping of waves, the gurgle of a rocky stream, the spray of a waterfall or the gentle patter of rain on a porch roof. Moving water might also rank second on my list of pleasing things to look at too.

I'm not sure who said these things or if there is any empirical evidence to support either statement, but I do know there are volumes of literary arguments in their favor, and in a very personal way, I know them as self-evident truths. I like fire. I do. I can think of no more productive and enjoyable use of my time than tending a campfire, a simple and humble labor that is both a skill and an art, as well as a basketful of metaphors. We are safe around a fire. We are comfortable and at rest.

I like to work a fire using a heavy poker to rake and flatten the coals and reposition burning logs so the fire burns evenly and produces as much heat and light as possible. A well-tended fire makes very little smoke. And even for summer fires up north, the quantity of heat that a fire produces is just as important as the quality of light it provides.

There's no place I'd rather be than standing on the shore of the big lake around a campfire with my feet firmly planted on the earth, leaning on the ram's head handle of my four-foot fire poker and basking in the glow of the setting sun or the twinkle of the stars in the sky. I have been tending fires up here by the big lake my whole life and I'm getting rather good at it in my old age.

I'm also kind of particular about my firewood and there is no such thing as too much wood. Captain Dave taught me that. You can either build a bigger fire or have a fire that burns longer into the night, or both. And fires just go better near water whether it's falling down, gliding by, or rolling in. All are music to my ears.

The patter of the rain, the ripple of a stream and the lapping of waves are very different sounds. Rain dances in rhythm. Streams trickle and chatter. Waves swish and swash as they advance and retreat relentlessly. The metaphors are different too. Rain as the giver of life and life as a journey downstream to the sea or a voyage across that sea. One calls for shelter. The other two require a boat. But all three sounds are soothing, and a fire goes nicely with all three.

We are drawn to fire and water for primal reasons and we seek out and enjoy close proximity to both. I could stare into the heart of a fire for hours and be content to do no more. Some of the most enjoyable and meaningful moments in my life have taken place around a fire on a riverbank or on a beach, beneath a waterfall or just under a tight roof on a rainy night.

I recall one drizzling, wind-swept autumn day just a few years ago and our first weekend trip to camp that fall. I got there first as usual, and it was a chilly October afternoon, so I built a fire in the airtight stove we use as our primary heat source. By the time I had stowed my gear and the supplies I had brought for the weekend, and emptied and reset a half dozen mouse traps, the fire was roaring behind the tempered glass. I was in no hurry. After all, I was at camp. So, I found some fresh ice to drown in some leftover scotch and just sat in the rocking chair near the stove watching the flames dance while I listened to the rain on the roof and the wind in the trees.

It had been a difficult week and save for an occasional long sip of whiskey I sat almost motionless for more than an hour. I was at peace. Or at least at rest. The dogs seemed to understand and as anxious as they were for a run, all three found a spot on a couch and left me to my reverie.

I'm not sure that I solved any problems that day or did much in the way of productive or creative thinking, but it didn't matter. All was right with the world, at least at that moment, and I savored a sliver of the inner peace that we all seek, but so very rarely find. I was as happy as a wet dog on a warm couch at camp.

Winter fires are a no holds barred affair with our crew. With the ground covered in snow it's impossible for a fire to get out of hand so we lay on as much wood as we can find and just let it rip. Gotta' keep warm you know, and there are Winter spirits to banish, or at least torment. Our winter hikes center on a lunch spot that gets us out of the wind and where there's lots of easy firewood handy.

The Miner's River Valley is one of our favorite spots. You don't have to go far from the highway to find solitude in the thick stand of cedar along the riverbank there. It's a rocky stream and the black water churns around boulders turned into mushroom caps by the fresh snow. A fire of crackling cedar is a special treat, but it burns fast, and we've exhausted the easy firewood around our usual spots, so we haven't been there in a couple of winters. There is a pint of above average brandy stashed in the hollow of a tree down in that valley, but I'm afraid that I have forgotten the exact location. You're welcome to it if you happen to find it. I left it there for Captain Dave.

For many years Dave and I and others had a tradition of a year-end fire at Tannery Falls on the weekend between Christmas and New Year's Day. A bunch of us would take a torch-lit hike around and through the adjoining Twin Falls canyon and then gather in the open cave behind Tannery Falls which by late December had already grown its annual column of ice. These "Wolfpack" parties lasted only as long as the firewood held out so some years we'd hike the rim of the 'scarp in late fall to scavenge as much dead wood as we could find and throw it down below where we'd drag it into the cave for later use.

Life's Short! Drink the Good Scotch First!

The year we put the roof over Dave's trailer we packed several cardboard boxes full of lumber scrap like Jenga blocks, duct taped them securely and tossed them over the rim. Then we walked in and stashed them underneath a log near the falls along with a dozen bottles of cheap wine. That year's party came after a heavy snowfall and whenever the fire died down and the wine bottles ran empty Dave would go over and kick the snow under the log and a box of firewood would fall out. Then he'd kick the snow under another log and a couple bottles of wine would fall out. It was a good trick and the party went late while the fire painted us as grotesque silhouettes on the cavern walls. For several more hours the music of our laughter echoed off the sandstone and blended with the gentle rush of the waterfall shrouded in its pillar of ice.

When I was still a practicing juvenile delinquent, in that very same part of town, we had spring fires at the mouth of Washington Creek during smelting season. Back then the Rainbow Smelt ran up all the local rivers to spawn each spring just after the frogs started singing in the swamps. "Going smelting" was license for teenage boys to stay out all night, drink beer and do some sparking and spooning with whatever girls had managed to convince their parents that they were after fish too.

We strutted and scratched like young dogs in springtime and flirted with the girls around a fire on the beach at the mouth of the river while serious fisherman came and went, shining lights in the water and dipping the first few fish headed upstream. There again, the party only lasted as long as the firewood held out because April evenings are cold on the shore of the big lake. But we had the year's first raft of driftwood scattered on the beach so we stayed warm and waited for later that night when the river ran so black with fish you swore you could walk across the stream on their backs. A single dip then would get you all you wanted, and we'd all walk home at dawn, happy and weary, smokey-eyed and tired, toting buckets of proof that we really had been fishing all night.

For years we spent the opening day of trout season camping on a bluff that overlooks some ponds on a bend of the Indian River. The fish had little to fear from our crew and the event was more a celebration of spring. We would gather truckloads of ancient pine stumps, thick with pitch, and build a beacon fire that you could see from the space station while the moon smiled down on the river that meandered through the valley below. Though we could not hear it from our camp, we could see the stream and we could feel its presence. I have written about this place before.

Summer fires are best on the beach whenever possible, the closer to the water's edge the better. You're not allowed to have a fire on any of the beaches in the park, but there are plenty of other spots along the lake that are just as nice or better. We have fires at the city's tourist park when friends are camping there, or on the "Mayor's Beach" which stretches from the campground west to the range lights in Christmas.

Life's Short! Drink the Good Scotch First!

I call it the Mayor's Beach because, well, I'm the Mayor and I named it. I used to make sure I was the first one to walk it each spring to get dibs on the driftwood and as I walked my dogs, I'd also pick up whatever trash had come ashore as the ice moved out. There was never much, but I do have a basket full of gill net floats and other treasured flotsam from that beach and others.

I'm proud of the fact that there are no rules on the city's beach. None. You can do whatever you want. Dogs allowed! You can drive on it, build a fire anywhere you like and burn up all the driftwood you can find. The lake will replenish it with the next storm. And dogs can roam free without need of a leash, chase sticks and swim. For the most part, people behave and clean up after themselves and the number of dogs that hang out there makes everyone a better dog owner. This is as it should be and no further restriction, prohibition or regulation is required.

There used to be a big after-party on the beach at the Front Range Light just around the corner from there every 4th of July. It would get going right after the bars closed several nights in a row and last until dawn. Someone always brought a truckload of wood so we had a big fire. It was always a destination for me when I was home on leave and the bonus was that I could walk the beach most of the way back to town at sunrise. I'm too old to stay up all night anymore and a lot of the beach between Christmas and town is gone now with Mother Superior at record high levels.

I've had more than a few fires on Grand Island and the beach in Murray's Bay holds 50 years' worth of summer memories. Peanut's Cove on the west side is my favorite spot for a fire but now that the island is a National Recreation Area there are rules out there too, about fires and dogs on the beach.

The three best nights I've ever spent outdoors were camping on the beach during a boat trip Pat and Joe and I took one summer from Munising to Copper Harbor. We spent 14 hours in the boat the first day only to find that the spot near Skanee where we had expected to spend the night was actually a swamp. With a little luck we found sanctuary on an exposed stretch of coast on the east side of the Abbaye Peninsula. It was labeled "Finnlander Bay" on our chart but was no more than a shallow bight on the backside of the headland. It was the perfect spot though. It had a sandy anchorage and a nice beach full of driftwood. The wind was from the west and that put us in the lee, so we hauled our gear ashore and pitched our tents.

It turned out to be someone's camp, though it looked deserted or at least unused for a couple of summers judging from the trees down across the waste-high grass that was growing in the road that led inland. There was a fire pit, a pile of wood and an outhouse built for a man who was at least six inches taller than any of us. It was a warm night and we built a small but cheery fire, had a swim, and cooked our supper on the coals. Then we just sat on a white birch log with our toes in the sand watching the boat ride lightly at anchor.

We were taking turns getting each other beers when the horizon turned golden and the full moon came up in the channel between the Huron Mountains and the Huron Islands. It shimmered across the rippled surface of the lake and bathed the evening in an almost heavenly glow. I have a picture of that moonrise in a book that we made of our voyage, but I don't need to look at it to remember. I can just close my eyes. That scene is forever etched in my mind. But remind me some time and I'll show you the picture.

We resupplied at the store in Lac Labelle and camped the next night at the mouth of the Montreal River just east of Bete Grise, which is French for "Grey Beast." It gets its name from the nightly fog that creeps out of the swamp behind the beach in the summer and gathers along the base of the cliffs to the east. The lowest of the three waterfalls on the Montreal River is a stepped cascade that falls directly into the lake in a small cove with a deep hole that offered protected anchorage for our 20-foot boat. We pitched our tents on the beach and made our cook fire and watched the mist crawl out of the swamp and over the sand and then linger long enough to filter the sun as it went down over the Keweenaw Peninsula.

All that night the splash of the waterfall sang in perfect harmony with the slap of the waves and we stayed up late talking and laughing, drinking beer and wondering if we were keeping the bears away from the acre of thimbleberries that covered the hill just above our camp. We had side stepped plenty of sign while picking berries that afternoon.

That trip was cut short after a harrowing passage around Keweenaw Point the next day. After 3 hours of fighting ten-foot waves we pulled into Copper Harbor and trailered the boat down to Joe's camp at a place called Little America just south of the West Portage entry. On a boulder strewn beach that last night, we built a Viking Fire out of logs to commemorate our journey and watched the flames swirl skyward in a vortex as the whitecaps from the northwest pounded the rocky shore. We washed down warm whiskey with cold beer and sang and hollered a lot, went sauna three times, and slept like tired voyageurs that night.

The best campfires are the ones surrounded by all your friends. And more is always better, with firewood and with friends. Our biggest outdoor gathering each summer is at the music festival in Grand Marais in mid-August. Beneath the shade of a matched and interlocking pair of 100-year-old maple trees we set up a pickin' tent and a kitchen that feeds 50 friends and we cook around a firepit that gathers a hundred people every night for music.

The wonderful thing about fires is that the bigger they are, the larger the circle they make. The larger the circle, the more people you can gather around. After 25 festivals our campsite has become the "extra festival staff and musician hospitality, free food and drink in the middle of the night, are these your kids and have you seen any meteors yet area" and the fire never goes out for a week full of music and laughter, good times and old friends.

Unless there's a stiff north wind—when the roar of the waves echoes off the hills behind town--you have to walk over a rise behind our campfire to hear the lake out beyond the dunes. But it is reassuring sound and it's another reason that Grand Marais is that "one particular harbor" that Jimmy Buffett sings about.

Perhaps my fondest campfire memory was a spearfishing trip we took one warm September evening, maybe 20 years ago. We fished from Williams Landing down the west side of Murray's Bay to the cemetery and had a tub full of whitefish for our effort. But a breeze came up after midnight that rippled the surface of the lake and ended our fishing, so we pushed the boat ashore on Muskrat Point and built a fire on the end of the spit. Luckily, we had thought to bring extra beer.

We found a pile of driftwood sticks that had been tumbled in the lake and bleached by the sun and turned them into a fire that burned clean and bright while the waves coursed through and sifted the pea gravel on the beach. It was a warm night with a new moon beneath the twinkling slash of the Milky Way above us. You could see the lights of town across the bay some three miles distant and there was no other sound but the ripple of the waves and our voices.

The moment was perfect. It could not get any better than that, and then it did. Slowly but steadily the sky to the north lit up with curtains of green and then purple and the northern lights danced around the pole star over the tombolo for an hour or more and reminded us of why we live where we live.

For most of my life I have tended a fire near this lake. I have stared into the flames and let the sound of the surf on the sand rock my troubled soul toward peace. Many times, I have found it. I've built and tended fires on this lake and along the rivers that flow into it with my father and with my son. With my brothers and with my sisters. With my neighbors and with my friends. With classmates and shipmates and third and fourth cousins, and with people that I just happened to meet.

When I die I'd like a Viking funeral, just so you all know. Lay me down one last time on top of a big stack of firewood in an old wooden boat, set it ablaze and cast it adrift at sunset in a south wind on Lake Superior. Play some appropriate music of your choosing. Ashokan's Farewell or Garnett Rogers' Farewell to Music would be good. I've always liked fiddle tunes. Old Blue Eyes, the Summer Wind, or something by John Prine would be nice, too. Then have another big fire on the beach with plenty of adult beverages for everybody and stay out until the sun comes up in the morning.

Life's Short! Drink the Good Scotch First!

Dear John

I remember telling people that I had to write this story down before I could turn the page and move on, but I kept putting it off and I was beginning to think I'd gotten away with my procrastination. After all, it has been three months. But I didn't.

The first story I wrote in my convalescence was about the scar on my chest and the second one was about the old cowboys that got me through 11 days in the hospital. In that story I mentioned my nurses several times, but they deserve so much more than honorable mention. I think I met twenty. Some cared for me for several days, some for a single shift. They were all angels.

The story I have avoided telling was the story of the surgery itself and my recovery, especially that first night in the ICU. It was traumatic. However common open-heart surgery has become its still pretty serious business. As the days and weeks went by and my life returned to normal, I guess I just chose to put that chapter of my life away without even trying to get it down on paper. But it came up again last week.

As I write this my good friend and best man Charlie Brown--retired chief Quartermaster, United States Navy, submariner extraordinaire, Pilot Major of the Western Seas, international nice guy and last of the big spenders--is lying in the intensive care unit of the Kansas Heart Hospital in Wichita recovering from the same triple by-pass operation I had in November. He texted me this morning. He had a hard first night, but he came though OK and there's no heart damage. He got lucky too.

He knew something was wrong because he was short of breath all the time, so he went in for a stress test which he failed, and they sent him straight to the big heart repair shop downtown. He was the last one off the table Friday night and doing well in ICU when his sister texted me. She had his phone and a list of four people to notify when he came out of surgery. I was honored to be first on the list and she caught me with a half-dozen of Charlie's U.P. friends at the Legion for fish fry. We drank his health. That's where John comes in. He was my nurse that first night I woke up in the ICU.

When I got out of the hospital I had the noble intention of writing nice notes to all my nurses and thanking them. But all I had were first names and, like I said, I had met more than twenty of them. I never found the time and the notes were never written. I consoled myself with the memory that I had thanked them all profusely at every turn of my care while in the hospital. They'd probably say that they were just doing their job. And they were, and they do their job very well.

The first six days in the hospital were a combination of boredom and terror sprinkled with pleasant conversation. The morning of my surgery, I remember showering with the smelly disinfectant soap they give you and then riding to pre-op in a gurney. There I met a nurse and a doctor, and several other people in scrubs and colorful hats, and then the anesthesiologist who only listened to one of my jokes before he shut me off and later that evening I woke up in the ICU. That's where I met John.

They give you lots of drugs before, during and after they saw your sternum in half, fold back your rib cage, stop your heart, deflate your lungs, and let a machine oxygenate your blood and pump it around your body for 4-6 hours while they replumb your heart. They warned me that the effects of those drugs would linger for 12-24 hours after surgery. When I woke up in the ICU I couldn't move and I couldn't hear. I could see OK and I knew where I was and why and I was immediately relieved. I didn't die, and I was not intubated.

John was standing next to my bed doing something with one of the monitors I was plugged into and he was talking but I couldn't hear him at first. Then it was like he had slowly turned up the volume and I heard, "how's your throat feel?" He was a young man, maybe 30, with short black hair and a closely trimmed beard. I tried to answer him, but I couldn't make any sound come out. He picked up a Styrofoam cup and spooned a couple of ice chips into my mouth. They melted and moistened my palate and throat.

"Thanks," I managed to whisper.

"Do you know where you're at?" he asked, and I nodded. "Doctor says you're going to be fine and there was no heart damage. Your wife and daughters were here until an hour or so ago. They'll be back in the morning. They've had a long day too." And then he walked away.

The room was beige and dimly lit. It did not look like an intensive care unit. Of course, I'd never seen one before except on TV. All the technology I expected to see was behind and above me. I wouldn't notice it until I saw the picture my wife took the next day. I had at least two IVs in each arm though, and in my peripheral vision I could see IV poles lined up on each side of the bed.

And then there was this big round clock on the wall in front of me with a second hand on it. I looked at it for the next six hours and could never once determine what time it was. My brain would not process the face of that clock into the time of day. But the second hand never stopped. John measured the hours for me. Every hour he took my vitals and pricked my finger and tested my blood sugar. Then he checked all the equipment I was plugged into while he talked to me.

"You want some more ice chips?" he asked.

"Please," I answered, startled, but also reassured by the sound of my own voice. He gave me a spoonful and I swished them around in my mouth until they melted.

"More?" he asked. I nodded and said, "Yes, please, maybe in a glass with a little scotch?" He laughed and adjusted something behind me.

"I can't move," I said, suddenly remembering.

"That's the anesthesia," he explained. "It'll wear off pretty soon," and he excused himself and walked out of sight again.

I lay there and took stock. I was lying uncovered in bed with my head up. I was warm, relatively comfortable and I felt no pain. I could move my head a little but other than that I felt nothing. I could see the chest bandage and, in addition to the IVs, there were tubes and wires coming out of every opening in my hospital gown. I was disoriented but euphoric. I was on the other side. The worst was over. I am not a religious man and I was not reborn that night in any Christian sense, yet I felt like a brand-new person when I woke up, experiencing the first minutes of my life. But I am a spiritual man and, somehow, everything was just different. The world was new and none of the old rules applied anymore.

John said later that I floated in and out of consciousness those first few hours, and in hindsight I recognize that I had been hallucinating, but I always woke up when he came to check my blood sugar.

"Ouch," I said as he pricked my finger.

"Drugs are wearing off," he said in a low monotone that was both calming and informative. "You're going to start tingling," he added and as if on cue, my hands and feet started to come back to life.

"Touch your nose," he directed a few minutes later and I did instinctively though it felt like someone else's hand. "If you start feeling any pain ring the bell," he said and put my hand on top of the call button.

"What time is it?" I asked, and he told me, but I don't remember what he said. It was like time was going forward but standing still at the same time, like a cartoon character who starts to run and his legs are churning but he's not getting anywhere. I think I asked him a dozen times. He always told me, but it just wouldn't stick in my head.

He had just started a 12-hour night shift when I came in and I was his patient that night. He told me the next morning that I finally drifted off about midnight and slept through the night. Those six hours seemed like a dream and they still do. I was there but I wasn't. I remember that I really wanted to see what was behind the wall the clock was on, but that was the outside world and I was safe where I was at. My bed felt womb-like and I knew there was no hurry. I would get there. I had time now. The pain crept in as the anesthesia wore off.

"On a scale from one to ten how's your pain level," he asked when I told him it hurt.

"Seven or eight," I said, and he gave me a pill that put me down for the night. I learned over the next five days to catch the pain at four or five so the pain killers would kick in before it got too bad. The pain woke me the next morning. I am a side sleeper and I had tried to roll over on my side. It hurt. I groaned and almost immediately John was there.

"Lie still while you can," he said. "They're going to make you get up today and walk around your room. You're doing really well so they'll probably move you to the step-down unit tonight." I got juice and a blob of oatmeal for breakfast and slept most of that morning.

The hardest part about getting out of bed the first time was not getting tangled up in all the tubes and wires stuck to me, into me and out of me. I felt like a Borg halfway through assimilation into the collective. But the two day-shift nurses who took over for John after breakfast had a schedule and having me get up and walk around was on it. I protested, but resistance was futile. I was getting up.

Getting out of the bed was the hardest part. Try rolling out of bed with your hands folded across your chest clutching a pillow. Once I was on my feet I was fine, but in order to walk around I had to drag an IV pole and push a wheelchair carrying a suitcase full of the bodily fluids draining from my chest tubes, along with a bag full of urine from the catheter, all the while trying to hold my gown shut in back. It was not a good look for me.

But I managed, and probably due to the high quality and frequency of jokes I began telling my nurses they kicked me out of the ICU that night. They needed the bed.

I had my own room in the step-down unit, right next to the door so I got to hear everybody coming and going and it was a busy place. But I had a TV in my room and I kept it on constantly if only for the distraction. I spent three days in there during which time they took out the catheter, which I could not feel until they removed it, gave me some stuff that got my bowels working embarrassingly well, pulled the electrodes that were attached to my heart out through the drain tube holes, a decidedly strange sensation, and then pulled the drain tubes out themselves.

The young resident who did that assured me that it wouldn't hurt and then she apologized when she was done for lying to me. I took a deep breath as directed and held it while she quickly and deftly pulled four inches of tubing out of my chest. It hurt like hell. I thought she'd yanked out a lung with it.

"It's always hardest on bigger guys," she said. "If I had told you that it was going to hurt you would have tensed up and it would have hurt even more," she explained in her defense. I thanked her with as much sincerity as I could muster as the pain subsided.

I was down to a heart monitor and one IV and, of course, the bandage. It was 12" square and looked like a piece of saran wrap with two rectangular vacuum pumps imbedded in it and I had to carry the battery-operated pump motor around with me. I got out of the step-down unit on the tenth day and moved back to a quiet room on the seventh floor.

Later that night a nurse came in and removed the bandage and the last IV and I finally got to take a shower. I felt almost normal as I put on skivvies and pajama bottoms and a t-shirt, the shirt being the hard part of the process. I could see and feel the staples in my chest moving as I put my hands over my head. It was painful and very disconcerting. They'd just put me back together and I was already wrinkling the paint job.

But as I crawled into bed with only the portable heart monitor left attached I felt so good I almost cried. I had the bed by the window and I saw the sun for the first time since I arrived. There was a brilliant sunset filtered through mountainous clouds that looked, well, almost heavenly, and I felt a measure of relief that I did not think was possible. I was going home in the morning. I had survived the ordeal and had a new lease on life.

I am 58 years old. My father died of a massive heart attack when he was 57. Physically at least, I have become my old man and I knew I had been living on borrowed time.

I am grateful to my cardiologist and my surgeon and to the rest of the surgical team. And I'm thankful for the physical and respiratory therapists, the lab techs and the transporters, the housekeepers and even the cooks, but it's the nurses that provided the hands-on care that got me through. That last night in the hospital I started writing this letter in my head to John, but it's for all the nurses who took such good care of me while I was there.

Dear John,

Thank you. I hope I was a good patient. I tried to be, but I never had heart surgery before. Sorry, I was scared.

Thanks for being good at what you do and thanks for caring so much about your patients. For most of our lives we don't notice the little things, but when you're measuring every breath and counting every second, the little things are all there is, so they're all that you notice.

Thanks for caring about the little things and doing them so well.

Thanks for understanding my pain and accepting my fear without judgement.

Thanks for laughing at my jokes. They were my defense mechanism.

Thanks for being perfectly calm and absolutely certain about everything you did. I was reassured and that means a lot when you're wounded and scared.

Thanks for your technical skill with the machines you use to save lives and help people get better so they can go home.

Thanks for the empathy you showed and the compassion that is a nurse's second nature.

Thanks for working a mandatory 12-hour midnight shift that

night for far less pay than you deserve.

Thanks for missing nothing even though you were all working short-handed.

Thanks for answering my questions honestly and in language I could understand.

Thanks for your steady hands and gentle touch.
Heart surgery hurts.

Doctors cure people. Nurses care for people. I talked to my surgeon twice in 11 days, once before surgery and once after. I remember his name, but I don't remember what he looked like. During the first of those 3-minute conversations he managed to convince me that I was a good patient, he was a good surgeon and I was going to be just fine. I was reassured.

During the second conversation he let me know that he had been right on all three counts. I was grateful, and I thanked him. But it was the nurses that I remember. They took care of me and got me through the hardest thing I've ever done, through the scariest days of my life and through the closest brush that I have ever had with death. You are angels, all of you.

Thanks John.

And Charlie, I've been down this road recently and your halfway there, shipmate. The storm is over, but you have a long voyage ahead. Don't cough any more than you have to for the next couple of months, and fergawdsake, try not to sneeze.

Life's Short! Drink the Good Scotch First!

Stop Helping. Please!

Disclaimer: No federal government employees were injured in the writing of this story. But I thought about it at the time.

In the end I just shook my head and walked away. I had tried to help, and I had failed. I couldn't get there from here. My efforts were worse than wasted, they had been counterproductive.

It started well enough. I had been swimming every day after work at Paradise, the rocky point northwest of Christmas where the locals have been swimming and bathing along the low sandstone shore for years. There's a small parking lot there with a couple of camping spots, a large community fire ring and a half mile of low cliffs over crystal clear water, perfect for diving and snorkeling. There are also several small inlets and coves with shallow wading pools that warm nicely in the sun. It truly is a Swimmer's Paradise and that had been its original name when the locals discovered it a century ago.

It was the summer of '96 and we were cutting down the Baker Grade. The weather was hot, and the bugs were miserable that year. Each day I came home from work, sweat-drenched and bug-bitten, wearing a sheen of bar oil coated with sawdust. Every afternoon I'd grab a towel and my shaving kit, two dogs and whichever kid was handy, and stop at the Hillside for a six pack on my way out for my daily dip.

There is no clean like Lake Superior clean and after scrubbing a day's worth of sweat and grime and sawdust away, I'd bask in the sun sipping a beer while I reduced the callouses on my feet by rubbing them on the coarse sandstone. Kids and dogs would swim and chase sticks and I'd completely unwind from the toils of the day. It had become a daily routine and I looked forward to it. One good thing about working in the woods in the summer is that you start at dawn and your done by two. That gave me the heat of the day to enjoy along the "long blue edge of summer" that the U.P. is still famous for.

We seldom had the place to ourselves, but it was never crowded. That summer was particularly hot, though, and we saw quite a bit of local traffic as well as a few tourists. I never litter, and I soon found myself picking up the trash left by other people; bottles and cans, wrappers and diapers, plastic and Styrofoam. It became part of my routine and daily I filled a small garbage bag which I carried around in the back of my truck until I thought to throw it away.

Paradise is within the Hiawatha National Forest and the popular swimming spot and campsites are designated primitive. There are no amenities; no outhouses or garbage cans. But the more I picked up trash the more I thought it would be a good spot for a large garbage can, something that would hold a week's worth of trash, so I wouldn't have to haul a bag out every day.

The next day it rained and I had a logger's holiday so I went to the Ranger Station and presented my idea to an acquaintance of mine who was of decision-making rank.

"Yeah," I said. "It's getting pretty popular with all this heat we've been having and I'm picking up a lot of trash. I'm out there every day after work and if there was a garbage can there I'd volunteer to empty it when it got full, if you'd give me a stash of bags and let me throw it in your dumpster that is." I didn't exactly expect affirmation of my noble intention or praise for my civic attitude, but I did expect serious consideration for the idea. The garbage would get picked up and it would only cost the government a few garbage bags. Instead, I got:

"Well, if we put a garbage can there, people would throw garbage in it," he said, and I nodded.

"Yup, that's the plan" I said, certain my idea had found fertile soil.

"No," he corrected. "If we put a garbage can there, people will start going there and dumping trash."

"Well, I hope so," I agreed, "but if they don't, I'll pick it up and if you give me some garbage bags I'll empty that trash can at least once a week."

"We can't do that," he said with finality. "Putting a trash can there without someone to monitor it could turn it into a wildlands dump site."

I understood him now. Before they built the new landfill, the National Forest was a free and all too convenient place for people to dispose of their trash. In my wanderings I would find these dumps and report them, and the Ranger District would map them and clean them up as they had extra manpower. It was a real problem for a while.

"Well, it's not the side of a side road well off the beaten track," I countered. "It's primitive but it's not remote and there's too much traffic there for anyone to try using it as a dump."

"Still, I can't do it," he said. "Regulations prohibit it." I walked away disappointed and a little irritated, but life goes on and I continued to swim out at Paradise and pick up the trash every day before I left. A week later I received a "Wild Lands Trash Reporting Packet" from the Ranger District in the mail.

I was familiar with the form, but I had refused to use it in the past. It was eight pages long which I thought was unnecessary, so I just used the 4-digit Forest Service Road number when reporting the dumps I found in person at the Visitor's Center. When necessary, I pointed to the site on the large map they had hanging on the wall and told them what they'd find there.

But I believe in working within the system when possible and necessary. Maybe filling out the form would change someone's mind, so I completed it in detail and mailed it back. A week went by. Nothing happened. Another week went by. Still nothing.

"Oh well," I thought. "I tried." Then one warm day I pulled into the parking lot for my usual swim and I noticed a new signpost had been set and there was an official looking notice posted on a small well-painted board. The sign said that I was the swell guy who graciously donated his time to keep this chunk of the national forest clean.

"Well, that doesn't help much," I told my dogs, but it was amusing so I gave it no more thought and I headed down to the lake. That was the day the trouble started.

I was in my second year on the city commission and had just been elected mayor for the first time. The commission was split and polarized along generational fault lines. The issues were divisive, meetings were contentious, and the debates were intensely personal. On any given day, half the people in town agreed with me and the other half hated my guts.

Before long, the sign in the parking lot became a magnet for extra garbage—bags of trash, junk and even old tires. People began cleaning out their cars and sweeping out the beds of their trucks in the parking lot. Dutifully, every day, I picked it all up and once a week I took a truckload to the landfill. One day the sign had been pushed over and there was a pile of garbage next to it. I picked up the trash and stood up the sign and on the next rainy day I went back to the Ranger Station and I told them they weren't helping, and would they please take the sign down.

The young lady I spoke with wasn't sure she could do that. What's more, she wasn't sure who would do that or even who should decide who would or could do that. It was a new problem for her. She was in charge of having the crews put up these signs and it had just never come up before. People were usually pleased to have the recognition. But she promised to check into it and get back to me.

A week went by and I continued to pick up the garbage. One day there was an unusually large amount of particularly nasty trash and the sign had been run over and was broken in two. So, the next day I brought the sign into the Ranger District office and I gave it to her and I said "stop helping. I can't afford the tippage at the landfill anymore."

And things quieted down a little. I continued to swim and pick up the trash and then one day I noticed a brand-new sign had been erected but this time they had sunk it in concrete. I checked and sure enough there was my name on the little notice. I shrugged and went swimming. The next day I pulled into the parking lot and noticed that, in addition to one other car, there was a beer box—Budweiser long necks--sitting next to the sign on which someone had written profanities that they had at least spelled correctly. The box was empty. I was relieved and tossed it into the back of the truck and headed to the beach. When I got to the point where the forest gives way to sandstone she met me coming off the rock. It was the nice lady from the Ranger District. She was carrying a bag of trash.

"Wow," I thought. "She's come out to help me," and I thanked her for taking the time to pick up the trash.

"Don't go down there barefoot," she said. "There are broken beer bottles all over the rocks. I picked up everything I could see, but there are shards and ground glass everywhere." Someone had launched the bottles randomly from the parking lot and deliberately spread broken glass over an acre of sandstone.

"Well, if you picked up everything you could see then no one will realize the danger," I pointed out.

"I hadn't thought of that," she said. It was Friday afternoon, so she promised to get a crew out there first thing Monday to try to sweep off the rocks. I was not reassured.

"What about this weekend?" I asked. "It's supposed to be in the 90s and this place willing be swarming with people."

"I don't know," was her reply as she put the bag of broken glass in the trunk of her car where I noticed she also had two full boxes of government-issue contractor bags.

"I'll take care of it," I said in frustration. "But stop helping. Please!"

With a screwdriver from my truck I pried out the staples that were holding the vandalized notice proclaiming me a swell guy to the signboard and I wrote "Danger! Broken Glass on Rocks" on the back and then I duck taped it to a piece of string and I strung it across the narrow trail that led to the rocks. I had an idea and I went looking for my friend Joe who was just getting off work.

Joe swam with his kids and dogs there too and he recognized the urgency of the situation. So, we made a few phone calls and before long we had a portable fire pump, 50 feet of inch and half hose and a fire nozzle in the back of my truck and we headed out to the scene of the crime.

With more than a little effort we drug the pump down onto the rocks, put the suction hose in the lake, hooked up the firehose and nozzle and fired up the old two-stroke motor. It ran fine but it rattled out a cloud of blue smoke through what was left of the muffler that gave an industrial quality to what was ordinarily a tranquil outdoor scene. However unpleasant, it was necessary.

For the next two hours we took turns, one of us on the nozzle while the other tended the firehose, and we systematically power washed an acre of sandstone. If you've ever used a firehose you know how exhausting it is, but we were fighting the dying light, so we kept at it without a break.

Just before sunset the parking lot began filling up with cars and before long twenty well-dressed amateur photographers were standing on top of the rocks staring at us with disdain. The Forest Service volunteer who was guiding them on what was supposed to be a serene and picturesque photography expedition glared at me through the blue smoke.

Seeing all those cameras I instinctively turned and saw the most beautiful sunset that we hadn't noticed at all as we did our best to finish our work. Right about then, the motor on the pump ran out of gas and it got eerily quiet. Joe and I were soaked from head to toe and we were exhausted.

"Good enough," Joe said and began to drain the pump and flake the hose. I expected her to at least ask us what we were doing, but as we lugged the pump back up to the truck all she said was "I hope you're happy. You've ruined our sunset and spoiled my class." I was just too tired to care, and I said nothing and walked away.

Two weeks later I received an official looking letter from the Ranger District Headquarters, signed by the person in charge of such things, in which I was advised that two-cycle engines were not permitted in primitive camping areas of the forest and then I was further chastised for interfering with the district's cultural affairs programs. I threw the letter away and the next year I bought a boat.

I have the greatest respect for federal employees no matter what they do. The Park Service and Forest Service staff work hard and try to be good stewards of the land. No one at the Ranger District did anything wrong and there was no malicious intent.

But sometimes the systems we build to make large bureaucracies work get too complicated and they get the best of us. At the federal level, one size is too often meant to fit all, but doesn't, and the systems and the rules become inflexible. Sometimes the people who work within those systems just don't know what to do. But everyone should at least learn to recognize when the best thing to do is to stop helping. Please!

Life's Short! Drink the Good Scotch First!

Life's Short! Drink the Good Scotch First!

Pigs in Space

The most traumatic thing I've ever done to my body on purpose was to launch it off the deck of an aircraft carrier. The scariest thing I've ever done was to land on one.

I've launched a half dozen times and it's not something you get used to. It's a great jolt to your body and you can hurt yourself if you're not ready for it. And I've landed, or "trapped," twice and that's an exercise in sheer terror. On all these occasions I was cargo in the back of a Navy C-2a, a Grumman Greyhound. Also known as a COD, for Carrier Onboard Delivery, the Greyhound is perhaps the ugliest and most beautiful airplane I've ever flown in.

It's ugly because it looks like a fat seagull with a box kite strapped to its ass, and it's beautiful because it was taking me off the ship and back to the land of room service and cocktail lounges, commercial airplanes and a long but much more comfortable flight home.

After nine years in the submarine navy, I was lucky to land a job when I got out with a marine engineering firm near Seattle with navy contracts, one of which was to perform vibration testing surveys on all the rotating machinery to be found on aircraft carriers. Now, aircraft carriers are wonderfully complex machines and there are hundreds of pumps, compressors, fans and motors ranging in size from three-story high forced draft blowers in the bowels of the ship to five horsepower aircraft defueling pumps scattered along the catwalk around the flight deck of a vessel 1,000 feet long with 5,000 sailors on it, supporting the busiest and most dangerous airfield in the world.

We did this work with a five-man crew over the course of a week of 16-hour days on a not-to-interfere basis with the ship's schedule. We went to wherever the ship happened to be and that often meant either the first leg or the last leg of a journey half-way around the world was in a C-2 COD.

The COD is the workhorse and whipping boy of the air wing and it can carry some combination of five tons of cargo or 24 passengers. The cargo goes in first. It has priority. Passengers are then squeezed into rows of very small seats four across in whatever room is left in the back. The seats face aft which is good when you're landing and go from 150 miles an hour to a dead stop in about 200 feet. It's not so good when you launch and your body is thrown into your five-point harness on the way from zero to 160 miles an hour in just short of two seconds.

The acceleration is so great off the catapult that your vision tunnels and it's like you're seeing the world through toilet paper tubes. It's an unpleasant experience. If you happen to have your head turned sideways when the catapult is fired, you can wrench your neck something awful. I did that once. Only once. And I learned to keep my eyes closed too.

The cargo bay of the Grumman Greyhound has one small round window, about five inches in diameter, on each side of the plane. In flight, the only other light came from the emergency control box for the rear ramp (which can be opened in flight so you can shove all the cargo out if you need to) and another for the escape hatch in the ceiling of the plane.

The trip to the ship was usually an hour or more of extreme turbulence followed by a terrifying descent in the dark to the controlled crash landing I mentioned. That ride down often got repeated by a waive off from the landing officer and then there was an ear numbing climb back up into the traffic pattern to fly in circles for a while before trying it again.

The bad thing about the COD was that it had the lowest priority for launching and recovery. I've spent an hour on the flight deck cinched into a five-point harness waiting for a catapult to clear and I've been "stacked up" and circling a carrier for just as long, endlessly waiting for the call to land.

The flight deck of an aircraft carrier is a pretty busy place and priorities for landing and launching aircraft are constantly changing so the poor COD sits in a lonely spot on the edge of the flight deck or flies in aimless circles in a high cap while the fighters and attack aircraft, submarine hunters and electronic warfare jets do their thing and hog all the glory.

Aircraft carriers were a culture shock to me. I had come from the diesel submarine navy, an enlisted man and part of a crew of 75. The old boats were small, and we literally had only one passageway fore and aft. From there I went to a civilian pay grade just high enough to berth and mess with the officers, and get priority for a seat on the COD, and they always put us up with the air wing where we were surrounded by officers, mostly pilots. On my first few surveys I needed a map to find my way around.

Navy pilots are an exciting and boisterous bunch and hands-turned-into-airplanes filled the air over linen-covered tables at every meal in the wardroom as they traded stories about that day's mission. They are also as macho as macho gets. Think Tom Cruise and Val Kilmer in Top Gun. That macho. They had to be. But they were a friendly and fun-loving bunch and they're still my heroes for doing what they did every day. And they liked catapults. They lived for them.

Of course, they catapulted while facing forward in a contoured bucket seat in a bubble canopy inside a $30 million strike fighter loaded with a couple of tons of death and destruction with thousands of pounds of thrust screaming behind them controlled with a joystick held tightly in their hands between their knees just waiting for the catapult officer to pull the trigger. It's just like in the movies.

They also prided themselves on their landing skills. Landing was, after all, an important part of the job. The goal was to catch the

Life's Short! Drink the Good Scotch First!

"three wire," the third of four steel cables an inch in diameter strung across the deck attached to arresting gear that caught the tail hook of a plane when it landed. If you caught the first wire you had come in too low and risked crashing into the stern of the ship. The second wire was more acceptable, but if you caught the third wire it was considered the perfect angle of descent. Sometimes you missed the third wire and caught the fourth, and that was OK. But miss the fourth and you "boltered" – you hit the deck and immediately took off again.

When a plane lands on the deck of a carrier the pilot goes to full throttle on impact in case they have to do just that. Any less speed and they couldn't take off again and would go over the side of the ship into the ocean and the pilot would have to eject. That was not good for anyone's career. Going to full throttle at the same instant you're stopping abruptly also makes the landing that much more intense.

I watched a lot of landings from "buzzard's row," a small observation deck on the back of the ship's island. And I got to meet the guy who pulled the trigger once. He's called the shooter and he had a really cool office.

The shooter and a couple of helpers work in the "bubble," an armored, Plexiglas hexagon that sticks up about 18 inches above the flight deck right between the bow "cats." He calculates the weight and configuration of each plane to be launched and then adjusts the steam pressure in the catapult cylinders to match. Not enough pressure, the plane gets shot into the ocean. Too much and the catapult rips the nose gear right off the plane.

The shooter lets the pilot know just before he pulls the trigger. A lot of other critical things happen on deck to get to this point, but hundreds of times a day the delicate ballet of an aircraft carrier flight deck gets to this point. The nose gear is locked into the catapult shuttle. The jet blast deflector is raised. Engines are run up to full thrust. Catapult steam pressure builds. The shooter gives the pilot a thumbs up. The pilot returns a salute, faces forward for launch and then there's a pause.

The shooter has a very important and serious job. He has the life of the pilot in his hands. Pilots also have a very important and dangerous job too. Launching and landing on the deck of an aircraft carrier isn't for the timid, and neither are the combat missions in between. But all these guys are naval aviators, a rare breed with a sharp and precise sense of humor that is also deadly serious.

I heard the shooter talking to himself that day as I slid into one of the two backseats in the bubble. "Don't turn your head . . . don't turn your head . . . " It was the late 80s and, appropriately, Kenny Loggins' "Danger Zone" was playing almost as loud on the speakers inside the bubble as the jet engines, muffled by an inch of armored Plexiglas, were roaring outside. Then bang! Roar! BANG! And the F-14 Tomcat was gone in a wisp of steam.

"He turned his head, didn't he? He turned his head! Didn't I specifically tell him not to turn his head?" the shooter chuckled at the first-class petty officer sitting next to me. Younger pilots were prone to turning and looking back over at the shooter to see if something was wrong if they sat longer on the catapult than they thought they should.

"You told him LT." he replied. "You told him twice. I heard you plain. He didn't listen though. Nuggets!" he shot back with a grin in what was obviously a practiced routine for the two. It was hard to talk with them as they were connected via headset and were pretty busy, but I was allowed to watch for a few minutes while they launched aircraft left and right into the night sky somewhere in the Arabian Sea.

Next up was an S-3 Viking submarine killer and the Beatles' "Yellow Submarine" came blaring over the speakers. The S-3 had an experienced pilot who received no invitation to turn his head. Thumbs up. Salute. Bang! Roar! BANG! And he was gone.

That pause and invitation was for the new pilots, or "nuggets," and though the crew in the bubble enjoyed the joke, it was actually very important training. Pilots had to be focused and patient under an incredible amount of stress. You cannot teach that in a classroom or in a simulator. The shooter told me later that most nuggets usually had to take the lesson several times.

For this shooter the strike aircraft, the Tomcats, Hornets and Intruders, got a variety of heavy metal "music to fly by" while the electronics aircraft, the Prowlers and Hawkeyes, always got something from Pink Floyd's "Dark Side of the Moon."

Just before I left the bubble, a COD waddled onto the catapult and its nose gear was coaxed into the shuttle.

"Oh no, they did not put that fat, ugly sonuvabitch on my catapult!" the shooter cried. "We cannot have this!" he added as he adjusted the pressure in the catapult. "Get him ready. He's leaving right quick!"

The turboprops on the COD screamed, the steam pressure built in the catapult and the shooter gave the thumbs up. The pilot saluted and turned his head forward. And then the theme song from the Muppets' "Pigs in Space" came over the loudspeakers, building slowly. The shooter smiled and warned "don't turn your head . . . don't turn your head . . . don't turn your head."

Bang! Roar. BANG! And the Greyhound was airborne.

"Good boy," the shooter said. "He didn't turn his head. He'll be back."

We had the good fortune of leaving the ship after that survey in a CH-47 Chinook helicopter and my body was spared from the catapult.

Life's Short! Drink the Good Scotch First!

Underwear and Satellite Radio

I bought a new truck this summer and it has me thinking a lot about my underwear when I'm driving. I generally don't think much about my underwear other than, you know, making sure I have on a clean pair every morning when I leave the house in case I'm in a car accident.

But my new truck came with three months free satellite radio, and I liked it so much that I paid $60 and got another year. The radio dial is pretty spartan here in the U.P. and I do a lot of driving. Now I get 150 stations. Pretty much anything I want to listen to. Depending on my mood I listen to bluegrass, old country music and old rock and roll, a little Sinatra, and on occasion, some big band and swing. And because I'm a news junkie I also tune in all the major news channels, left and right, real and fake.

And much to my surprise I'm now part of a radio advertising market group that I'm unfamiliar with. Nobody on satellite radio is trying to sell me cars and trucks, beer, car insurance, or new drugs that you should ask your doctor about. Instead, in satellite radio land I'm apparently in need of no-show socks, sheets that are endorsed by three presidents (whose names aren't apparently worth mentioning), runner's sunglasses "that don't look like a spaceship has landed on your face," office chair mats, job applicant recruiting services and really nice underwear.

Apparently, the maker of this underwear feels that playing the same advertisement every commercial break on ten different satellite radio channels for 45 days is a good way to get me to buy their underwear. It's not but it has me thinking about underwear every 15 minutes or so when I'm driving around the U.P. these days. It's not a productive use of my time, I know, but it's hard to avoid. And I drive a lot, so I have been giving my history with underwear considerable thought. I have evolved.

When I was a kid, I didn't think much about my underwear other than, you know, making sure I had on a clean pair every morning when I left the house in case I got in a car accident. Even into my teenage years style was never a concern let alone an issue. Underwear was tighty-whitey briefs. Hanes. BVD's and Fruit of the Loom. And underwear was white. We lived in a world of our father's and our grandfather's underwear.

I was, by any measure then, a simple country boy and it wasn't until I got to boot camp that I realized there was more than one style of underwear and that I had a choice. I was standing in line with a hundred other guys getting our first issue when I got to the underwear guy (I'm thinking not a very sought-after assignment) and he asked me "boxers or briefs?" So far, I hadn't been given much in the way of choices in the Navy and I had to think for a second.

"Briefs" I said instinctively, not entirely sure I had made the right decision. He didn't have to ask what size because we all had a tag hanging from our neck that told him what size everything we were. Over the course of the next ten weeks I spent a lot of time dressing and undressing in a big room with 80 other guys and I noticed that it was an urban-rural thing, a cultural difference. All the city boys, black, white, Asian or Hispanic, wore boxers. All the country boys wore briefs.

At the time I didn't understand why, and I didn't give it much thought. But recently I've been thinking a lot about my underwear and I have concluded that it might have been because city boys as civilians had worn slacks (and this was the age of polyester) and all the country boys wore jeans. That makes sense to me and I like it when things make sense.

I tried to wear boxers later on. I was, and still am, a man who'll try almost anything once. But they did not work well with navy dungarees, at least not for me, and I went back to briefs. And then there was a time when I was in the Navy when I wore no underwear at all. Blame it on the monsoons.

For almost five years I was deployed overseas where we spent a lot of time in tropical climates, mainly the Philippines, and when ashore we dressed as lightly as possible which meant a t-shirt, shorts (with lots of pockets for our stuff) and flip-flops. Underwear was optional and even counter-productive in a tropical climate where it was either a hundred degrees or raining buckets or both.

Being the submarine sailors that we were, we had a lot of adult fun and we were seldom properly supervised while on liberty. A regular toast at a Subic City bar full of boat sailors was a "skivvy check!" yelled by some drunk at which time everyone would take a drink and then unbuckle their shorts and let them drop to the floor. Any non-qual or Westpac newbie caught wearing underwear was shamed into doing the "dance of flaming asshole."

This involved going into the bathroom, stripping naked and tucking a six-to-eight-foot length of toilet paper between your ass cheeks, lighting the other end on fire and then running all the way around the pool table and back into the bathroom before you burnt your butt hair. It was a fun game. And I can say quite proudly, it was never me.

By the time I got out of the Navy men's underwear had evolved a little. We got bikini briefs. They weren't very manly, but neither were speedos and they were popular in those days. I wore these for a while when I was a lumberjack and still looked good naked, but they weren't durable enough for an outdoor lifestyle. They did come in colors besides white though and that was new.

So eventually, I went back to briefs until they made boxer-briefs. I think I bought my first pair from Michael Jordan and that's what I wear to this day. Now my underwear comes in every color except white. Which was probably more than you needed to know about my history with underwear. But as long as we're on the subject.

I like the TV commercials for Duluth Trading Company underwear. How could a guy not want a pair of "Buck Naked" underwear? "No pinch. No stink. No sweat," and that wonderful cartoon of "the boys" sitting comfortably side by side strapped securely in buckets seats. Like the Duluth Trading Company, satellite radio underwear is battling the demons of rolled waistbands, bunching in the legs and smelly sweat, and the advertisement gets into the specific features of the product for combating those underwear defects which includes having real silver thread stitched into them because it's a natural deodorant.

Pretty expensive deodorant, I'd say and thinking about it, the pitchman never tells you how much they cost. I guess if you have to ask you can't afford a pair. But if you don't love them, the first pair is on them. They'll refund your money and you can keep the underwear. Sounds fair. And there are some things you just don't return. But I hear this ad a lot and the thing that strikes about it the most is the opening pitch.

"Guys, you spend 90% of your day in your underwear. It's literally the foundation of your wardrobe."

Yes, your underwear is the foundation of your wardrobe. You put it on first every morning, or at least most of us do, but 90% of your time leaves you 2.4 hours each day when you have no underwear on at all. That's an intriguing amount of time. I like sauna, but two and half hours is a very long sauna. And it's quite a few, or even several, long, hot showers or an awful lot of sex each day, or both.

Either that or the guys who buy this underwear spend a couple hours a day just hanging out naked, maybe so they can better appreciate their underwear when they put them back on. I wonder now that I'm in the satellite radio listening audience if I'm being profiled. If so, I've joined a pretty strange bunch of potential underwear purchasers.

As I was writing this story, that particular ad buy ran its course and the same guy is now trying to sell me sweatpants that are so stylish and comfortable you'll want to wear them to work. When I'm not on the road I work out of my home and admit to sometimes working in my pajamas, so they have my attention this time. And who doesn't want to be more stylish?

But at least I'm back to only thinking about my underwear once a day, you know, by making sure I have on a clean pair every morning when I leave the house in case I'm in a car accident.

Life's Short! Drink the Good Scotch First!

Life's Short! Drink the Good Scotch First!

U.P. Road Warriors

Welcome to the U.P., land of ice and snow and armored mailboxes.

I was reminded that winter is on the way the other day when I saw a pick-up truck with an old Western snowplow on the front heading up Scaffold Hill on Highway 13. Early October is a tad early for mounting plows, but I guess this guy just wants to be ready. We sometimes get snow this early. In fact, it's not uncommon, but you really don't need a plow until Veteran's Day.

But it got me to thinking about driving this winter. After more than 500 days locked down working out of my house my job has me once again driving the U.P. from end to end and top to bottom. And one of the constantly changing parts of the very rural scenery I enjoy so much is the armored mailbox in all its thousand iterations.

Your average U.S. Postal Service-rated, sheet steel mailbox doesn't stand a chance along the highways and byways the U.P., not without some stout defense from the county plows. Mount a new one on a 4x4 post and you may get one winter out of it, or at least part of one winter, but you'll be replacing it in the spring and adding at least some measure of protection.

If the county plow hits your mailbox the county will replace it if there's direct contact. They're obliged to. It's also the least they can do, since you now get to spend an afternoon trying to dig a hole in the frozen shoulder of the road to install the new one. But it happens sometimes.

If they damage or destroy it with the snow and slush they throw at it, well, then you're on your own. Municipal immunity they call it. That's insurance talk for giving units of government protection from liability while they do dangerous things that only they can and will do. If you ever get hit by a police car or a fire truck you're out of luck too.

And it's why almost all mailboxes you see when driving across the U.P. are armored with something. That something ranges from a pallet nailed to 4x4 posts stuck in the ground up to and including elaborate and artistic pieces of personalized roadside engineering. The variety makes for a constantly changing side show of postal fortresses to keep you amused when you're on the road four days/week.

I once postulated that your average Yooper tries to avoid fame and notoriety and doesn't feel the need to stand out from a crowd. For most of us it's enough to just stand out a little from the landscape so that our friends can find us. Mailbox armor is perfect for that. People build little shrines to their postal selves along the highway and paint and decorate them to suit their own personal tastes.

Life's Short! Drink the Good Scotch First!

Many proudly display the name and fire number of the architect. You can tell the Lions fans from the Packer fans (often right next door to each other) and the Wolverines from the Spartans. People are proud of their heritage up here too and both the Finns and the Italians are well represented. There's plenty of both and we love them all.

Some people use brick and mortar. Some mailbox forts even have built in flowerpots because, after all, you leave them up year-round. Actually, you appreciate them more in the summer. So, I always keep my eye peeled for any new and innovative way that people come up with to keep their mail and the box it came in from becoming wind-blown paper trash and twisted wreckage in the ditch.

There are other things to keep an eye out for as you travel Michigan's Upper Peninsula. Like deer. The two-lane black top in the U.P. is not fenced like the freeways below the bridge but the rights of way along the highway are cut back as much as fifty yards on each side which lets you to enjoy three or four majestic leaps before the deer lands in the lane in front of you. Dodging deer is a skill you learn in driver's training up north. Brake but don't turn.

You need to keep your head on a swivel, tree line to tree line when driving, especially during the prime deer dodging hours, dawn and dusk. And you don't ride a motorcycle after dark in the U.P. unless you want to be an organ donor.

My friend Dave Aho once described riding a motorcycle in the U.P. at night as "deer Nintendo." Deer vs. motorcycle is an even match. Many of the nurses I know refer to motorbikes as "donorcycles."

I have hit three deer and I've had two deer hit me since I moved back to the U.P. 30 years ago. When you hit a deer, it dies a traumatic death and leaves a big mess on the side of the road. Fear not though because the eagles, ravens, buzzards, and coyotes will make quick work of the carcass and after a few days there will only be a large blood stain left on the highway. But it can also mean thousands of dollars' worth of damage to your truck. Both realities will ruin your day.

When a deer hits you they most often survive, but if they break a leg they will not survive long. The wolves and the coyotes in the U.P. are hungry and efficient. And you might have to live with a little dent in your buggy.

I hit a deer on H-58 just past Melstrand one summer morning when we were logging out on the Baker Grade. It was just before dawn and the instant I saw the deer the whole world turned gray as the hood of the Dodge Colt I was driving folded up over the windshield. I instinctively locked the brakes and skidded off the shoulder and into a field. The front clip was crumpled but the radiator was intact so the engine was fine, but I needed some help to pound the hood down so I could see to drive.

Life's Short! Drink the Good Scotch First!

I knew my friend Rob would be along shortly with the work truck, so I grabbed my flashlight and knife, found the yearling doe on the shoulder and I salvaged the backstraps. Venison tenderloins were small consolation for the damage to my car but in the U.P. you take whatever you can get from whatever life throws in your path.

The absolute worst day to hit a deer is when you're driving your new car home from the dealership. I got lucky that day because the young buck running at me full speed across US-41 just grazed my rear bumper, tumbled a few times and then ran off into the woods.

The rest of the roadkill in the U.P. is comprised primarily of skunks, racoons, porcupines, and the occasional squirrel. They usually don't do any damage. Snapping turtles are a regular road hazard along the Seney stretch in June, though, but people are pretty good about avoiding them. I've even been known to stop and help them across the road because, after all, a man needs all the good Karma he can get. If my wife is with me, it's a given that we stop and help.

The road-kill ratio is the highest in the Spring, for deer and all the other critters, most of whom have spent the winter underground. The highway corridors are wide and the first green shoots of spring are found along the side of the road. Baby racoons seem to be the most common casualty. By the end of summer you'll see about one per mile. I think the term "a coon's age," as in "I haven't seen him in a coon's age," is indigenous to the U.P. and comes from the fact that the average racoon lives about six months before it becomes roadkill.

It's rare to hear of anyone hitting a moose. Good thing too as those collisions are often fatal for the driver and the moose. My wife's uncle did hit a 700-pound calf one spring day several years ago at the bottom of the Shelter Bay Hill. Fortunately, it hit the passenger side of his brand-new truck. It totaled the truck, but he walked away, quite shaken. Surprisingly, I see very few road-kill turkeys or sand hill cranes in the U.P. even though there are lots of both and they frequent the highway rights of way to forage. They must have good traffic sense.

Dodging critters will keep you alert when you're driving up north, but there are other road hazards to be watchful for too.

Log trucks would be right near the top of my list. I think I've heard of only one recorded case of a log truck spilling its load and crushing someone in a car. I'm sure there have been more so I don't like to follow them too close. I make sure I have rolling-log-dodging-distance between me and all the log trucks I encounter when I'm driving. Even when they're coming at me, I hug the fog line and tense up until they go buy. It it's raining heavy or snowing it sucks to get behind a log truck because they throw up so much water or snow that you can't see to get around them.

There are lots of other big trucks on the road to watch out for too. State highway M-28 across the U.P. from Sault Ste. Marie to Wakefield is the primary connecting route for Canadian truck traffic coming across the International Bridge headed for US-35 in Minnesota. Truckers hang a left there and then it's a straight shot to the Mexico border. These "Canadian Cowboys" like to run at night and they're always in a hurry.

Because of the heavy truck traffic, the older two-lane blacktop that links the U.P.'s towns and villages is rutted just enough for water to pool in a heavy rain. To keep from hydroplaning you have to straddle the ruts which has you either crowding the center line or else hugging the shoulder of the road. If you can see good and there's no one coming at you, hugging the center line is probably safer, but keep in mind that any oncoming cars are likely gonna' claim their half of the middle too.

Visibility is always an issue when driving in the U.P. Even a short trip on a summer night can coat your windshield with bug guts so thick that it takes an ice scraper to get them off if you can smear them sufficiently with your washers and wipers to find your way to the next pit stop.

In the Winter it's the snowplows. There's is a serious business and these guys are professionals. They're also fearless. The law of the land and the law of gross tonnage are both on their side. It's illegal to park on the street, the highway, or the shoulder of the road overnight because plow truck drivers work on the assumption that they're not going to have to watch out for anybody that stupid. They can't slow down and they don't like to go around.

And they are their very own mobile whiteout—a portable snowstorm two or three hundred yards long. If you meet a plow, get as far to the right as you can and guide yourself off the snowbank until you get by. You can't stop and you won't see anything in front of you for the several seconds (that seem like an eternity) it takes to come out the other side. We learn not to stop in a whiteout in driver's training too. If you stop, you'll never come out the other side.

If you get behind a plow, you'll most likely never see it for the whiteout it causes. One minute it's clear and then you're driving in a snowstorm. If you do see it, you're way to close. It's suicide to try passing—think several seconds of whiteout (that seems like an eternity) while you're accelerating in the wrong lane. The only thing to do is to slow down, fall back, and give yourself the extra time.

"I got stuck behind the plow" is a common excuse for being late in the U.P. in the Winter.

"I didn't have cell service" is why you didn't call to let people know. Neither excuse will be questioned, and people will nod knowingly. Going slower, you'd think you'd have time to enjoy all the many and variously constructed armored mailboxes I was talking about except you can't see them in the winter because they're coated with all the ice and snow that the county plow threw at them.

And that's how they came to be.

I know a couple of people who also travel all over the U.P. for their job and I'm thinking of starting a club; the U.P. Road Warriors Association. To be a member, you have to average a thousand miles driving across this splendid peninsula each week and have hit at least three deer.

Life's Short! Drink the Good Scotch First!

Life's Short! Drink the Good Scotch First!

The Old Soul

I see him walking along the highway every afternoon when I take my dogs up the hill to Hanley Field for their daily run. I don't know who he is, but I call him the Old Soul because he's like an apparition, a mere ghost of a man. He seems just barely there.

He walks every day with measured steps, head down. He's never in a hurry and he never looks up to make eye contact with any of the passing drivers. I see him either on M-28 or walking to the top of Scaffold Hill on Highway 13 where he turns around and walks back down. I haven't figured out where he lives. I've never seen him on any of the sideroads along either highway. He's just there on the shoulder of the road when I drive by. Every day. I would guess his age at 70.

I used to call him the Lost Soul but after many months of watching him I decided I was being unfair. After all, I didn't know him. I saw him every day, but I didn't even know his name. I knew nothing of his life story or his circumstance. He might be the most contented man in town, the epitome of self-actualization. How was I to know? I just saw him, every day, walking.

I suppose it was his appearance. At first glance, he looks every bit the bum. He is slightly built with a scarecrow frame, and he wears the same thing every day. Old blue jeans that are faded and baggy and pleated at the waistline where a brown leather belt is cinched tight to hold them up. His blue work shirt is always partially untucked and nearly as faded as his jeans. He wears an old pair of brown shoes, and in the summer, a straw hat that looks like it had a bite taken out of it. When it's cold, he dons a faded gray overcoat that looks like it has seen 20 winters, the hood pulled up over his head.

His appearance, his gate and his manner seem forlorn to me, like his daily walk is a meaningless habit. He keeps a slow pace and is always facing traffic, but he never looks up. He can hear me and other cars coming, and he moves from the fog line over to the grassy edge of the shoulder in plenty of time, but he never hurries. There is no sense of urgency. His pace never changes. And he never looks up.

At first, he reminded me of the old winos I knew when I was a practicing juvenile delinquent, lost men who had sleeping rooms at the Bellevue Hotel and who spent what little extra money they had on white port wine. Each day they'd get drunk and ruminate about their life and the path it had taken. They were sad and broken old men.

And he reminded me of the younger old men I worked with at community mental health, men who aged quickly and died early, their lives lost in a foggy alphabet soup of mental disorders and mind-altering medications. I've known many lost souls in this life.

He just looked the part I guess, but there had to be more than that. There had to be a story in this Old Soul.

So, I looked hard at him again. His clothes were worn and threadbare, but they were always clean. His walk, though it seemed to lack purpose, was steady and deliberate. He did not weave and he did not stagger. I decided to break the stereotype I had built. I decided he walked for his health and had a home where he was safe and warm and loved and cared for. I decided that he was retired from a long and meaningful career, a merchant mariner perhaps, who missed the exotic lands that had been his life and his purpose.

The sadness I noticed, or else invented, was just a longing for the sea and foam and the distant and enchanted places he had seen. I could relate to that.

And I added a broken heart to his burden, the recent loss of a wife and lifetime companion, or the bittersweet memory of a tropical maiden he had loved and then left behind. Such heartache and pain can leave a man lonely and longing and thirsty for whiskey. It can strip the very purpose from his step. Yet this was not such a man.

I made him a veteran, scarred by war who walked to forget the things that kept him awake at night. I gave him signs of a chronic illness and made walking his therapy. Each day I gave him a new back story to explain the sadness I saw on his face, a sadness that I wasn't sure was real because I never got to look into his eyes.

Maybe the reason that he didn't look up was because he'd seen it all before and he'd rather keep his eye on the planet instead. Sometimes you have to watch it to keep from falling off and it certainly could use some more looking after.

I asked a few friends about him, but no one recognized my description of him or his daily route. No one else had seen him which I found hard to believe because he walked every day and there's a lot of traffic along that stretch.

He might have been a husband. He may be someone's father or brother. He was certainly someone's son. After a while I quit asking and decided that he wasn't real after all, that he was just an apparition that I'd created to remind me of the approaching winter of my own life.

I missed him on days where our schedules didn't quite overlap—never more than two days in a row. We were both that regular. He became a marker along my trail. There he is. The Old Soul. Walking through another day without comment or complaint. Adding a couple more miles to a lifetime spent out wandering.

I've come to see him now as just another pilgrim on his daily journey, a humble man with a good heart and noble intentions on his way somewhere. It doesn't really matter where. And that's his business anyway. His modest attire is the modern-day equivalent of a robe and sandals. His quest is simple and something common to us all—just another mile, Lord, and give me just one more day. And so he walks. I hope that it helps him find peace.

Winter is here and I don't run the dogs at the airport anymore, so I don't go up the hill very often. I don't see him every day. I haven't seen him in weeks. I hope that he's alright. I hope that he keeps going and makes it through another winter. I hope we all do. I hope that I see him in the spring.

If the blessings I've been given in this life are free to give away, and if the honest prayers of a common man are any good anymore, the Old Soul can have some of mine.

Life's Short! Drink the Good Scotch First!

Life's Short! Drink the Good Scotch First!

A Random Chorus of Trumpets

It's mid-March and I'm sitting at the kitchen table at camp on a cold and sunny, Sunday afternoon. I came out for the day to get camp ready for the girls who will be out later for sauna. I hauled water from the spring, tended fires, took care of a few small chores, and went hunting for walking sticks in the swamp.

I find myself making excuses to go to camp these days to pick up this or drop off that or else tend to some small job that warrants the 20 mile drive out from town and back. I'm here at least twice a week for this reason or that excuse and every Sunday for the whole day.

I sit here thankful for a Winter that was both mild and short. I needed spring and it's coming early. It's been a long year. Coronavirus and cancer treatments. Travel restrictions, Closures. Shortages, Lockdowns and a million COVID refugees trying to escape the big city and find a few weeks of safety and sanity "Up North."

It's been a year of going nowhere, working out of my home, and living a truncated social existence that would have been intolerable were it not for the safety bubble and sanctuary of this camp.

Camp rescued me this winter and I feel better for even a brief visit this spring. We're planning a couple of weekends here in April including the last Saturday for the opening day of trout season. The snow will be gone by then and there will be a new list of chores to tackle. But camp chores are not work. They are exercise and they are therapy. Just being at camp improves my outlook on life.

Hell's Kitchen sits on the south side of the road at the bottom of the hill on the Munising side of Trout Lake. The road was named for the lake, but the camp was not. Hell's Kitchen got its name from a couple of tent camps we hunted out of down the Stillman grade before we found this piece of land and the building five years ago.

Those camps were named after a section of pothole country just south of Christmas by my brother Darrell who hunted that area for most of his life. It's god-awful terrain that was known locally as the Devil's Kitchen, but my brother corrupted the name and passed it on to the big MASH tent that served as our deer camp for two years.

So, when we built the camp on Trout Lake Road, the old name came with it because A: we're not very creative and B: Trout Lake Camp on Trout Lake Road just east of Trout Lake would probably qualify for a department of redundancy department award. We just call it camp.

Camp is a sacred word in the U.P. and it's so much more than just a place in the woods or on a lake. It's a way of life. A state of mind. Another point of view. Although our camp is new it has already acquired a spiritual presence with the power to relieve stress and reduce tension, to lighten burdens and gladden hearts, to conjure smiles and make the walls ring with laughter. Friends and family and people passing by are welcome here. No one goes away hungry or thirsty and those who stay find a warm dry spot to fall down.

Despite it's dark and somber moniker, Hell's Kitchen is a comforting and restful place that became my refuge during the Great Pandemic of 2020 (as I'm sure it will be called a hundred years from now). This past year has been spent working and playing here with a small group of family and friends, all members of our "pod." During that time, we doubled our living space, added the sauna, and turned a seldom used deer camp into a comfortable winter retreat.

We'd planned to add on the year before. We even poured the slab that November. Our intention was to dry it in and then work on it over that Winter, but it took us six months to get a variance from the township. That's another story that involves some discrepancies with our current variance, a property line shared with the federal government and a township zoning board that existed only on paper, a puzzle that required equal amounts of administrative patience and social grease.

So, the serious work didn't start until about this time last spring—the Ides of March to be exact--when the coronavirus had already spread to all 50 states. Michigan was hit hard early, and the most egregious restriction was a ban on travel between two residences in the state. This was meant to stop the trolls from escaping the mitten and coming to their camps in the U.P. bringing the COVID up here with them. That made sense and it mostly worked, but the governor had no authority to ban interstate travel, so it did not stop people from out of state from coming to their camps in the U.P. This they did, in droves, beginning last March.

And for a while it kept us from going to camp which was and still is the preferred venue for Yoopers who want to socially distance. It took a fair and loud amount of yelling and screaming before the governor saw the wisdom of changing that policy. She finally did so in April and last spring we began spending most of our weekends and some of our workdays at camp. By mid-March we were already bending the rules somewhere between a misdemeanor and a mortal sin when I spent a couple of afternoons shoveling the slab we had poured in November. It was a big job because we had shoveled all the snow off the roof onto it in late February. But gravity was on my side and I had it cleared off in a weekend. Two weeks later we got a snowstorm that covered it up again and I left the second chorus of that chore to the younger members of camp.

Like most spring storms it was wet, heavy "heart attack" snow that broke off limbs and bent over saplings blocking the old logging road that follows the railroad grade down the valley. Where the valley narrows the road carves its way up the side of the ridge and through the mature hardwood on top of the hill and then runs the rest of a mile north and the back down to camp on the old wagon road.

Life's Short! Drink the Good Scotch First!

It's our firewood loop and much to our surprise cleaning it up had us making wood in the spring, which is something that no one does in the U.P. unless of course, they run out, which is something that no one in the U.P. does. We spent a day clearing the road, me out front cutting and dicing brush with the chainsaw and Pat working behind me throwing everything out of the way. It took the whole afternoon and three tanks of gas, but we got some easy firewood as a bonus, filling the bed of the side-by-side a couple of times with dead poles that had fallen across the road.

By walking the whole route, we also found our winter firewood seasoning happily on the stump, ironwood and hard maple mostly, none of which needed to be split and most of which had lost its bark--dry poles that would fall right in the road. There are skills needed for making firewood but there is an art to making firewood easy and it doesn't get any easier than that.

In May, my brother and his crew laid the block, framed the walls, set the trusses, and sheeted and roofed the addition which took a couple of days. Then it got piecemealed here and there all summer. As fall approached the project gained momentum and we had it buttoned up before November leaving bare studs inside.

So instead of hunting last fall, we spent the first week of deer season finishing up the inside and, most importantly, making the sauna work. Preoccupied as we were with our labors, the deer were safe from our trusty bunch of nimrods. We added a propane heater and had the gas company set a 500-pound pig in the yard in January. A third large marine battery boosted our power supply and with our solar panels we hardly ever need to run the generator anymore. We deliberately did not plumb the sauna, content to use five-gallon buckets of water drawn from the spring rather than deal with plumbing on both ends of the building.

But at least we had sauna for deer season! It was heaven, made more so because the project had hung out on the back burner for four years. It also made weekends in winter that much more enjoyable.

We made a half dozen cords of firewood before the snow hit and we thought that would be enough, but we were feeding two stoves now and using camp almost every weekend. By New Year, our woodpile was shrinking at an alarming rate, but we got lucky with some nice weather in January. Pat had put tracks on this side-by-side, so we could go anywhere we wanted in the snow-covered world and we added three more cord of wood which will take us into summer.

Now that the world is opening back up, we're all pretty busy and it's been a month since anyone spent the weekend at camp. But someone is out most every Saturday or Sunday night for sauna and like I said, I've been making excuses to get out here at least twice each week just to fill the bird feeders and feed the swans, our rowdy winter neighbors.

Trout Lake is long, narrow, and very shallow. It's divided near its northern end by a causeway with two large culverts under the Trout Lake Road that drain the flow from the springs that feed it. The water flows the length of the lake and into the East Branch of the Whitefish River three miles to the south. There's a good current on either side of the culverts and a large portion of the lake stays open all winter. Because of that a bevy of trumpeter swans call the lake home from November through March. Their numbers have grown from a dozen five years ago to 56 this year with 14 cygnets. They are noisy neighbors for creatures so graceful and elegant. They're always out of tune, a delightful chorus of one note wonders, and they are always loud. They've also gotten used to being fed.

Cars stop on the causeway several times a day and the birds honk for a handout. We can hear them from camp, so we always know when someone has stopped to feed them. They've become a local attraction and the excuse for a drive through the woods on winter day. We give them frozen peas and carrots or cracked corn which they like, and which is good for them. I bring them an ice cream bucket full each time I'm at camp. They recognize me and they tolerate my dogs, but sometimes they won't feed until we leave and head back up the road. While walking back to camp we're always serenaded by a random chorus of trumpets, singing out a thanks for their supper. It's a joyous noise that's become our COVID anthem and winter theme song.

Nights at camp are quiet and still save for the distant yelping of coyotes and, occasionally, the long mournful howls of a pack of wolves that call the river valley home. Their song is as old as the rocks and the trees and it echoes up the valley and across the lake. In the morning, we're greeted by the whistle of blue jays and the staccato hammer of pileated woodpeckers.

I asked my friend Edgar who is 95 what kind of fish were in Trout Lake. He looked at me with a grin and said "trout." There may have been trout at one time but not anymore. The only fish I see these days are white horse suckers that come all the way up from Lake Michigan each April to spawn. We see them schooled up near the culvert and I suggest to my nephews that we should catch a mess of them for the smoker like their Grandpa Louie and I used to do when I was a boy. So far, I have had no takers.

I canoed into the north end of the lake from the small pond that feeds it one spring and found a pile of fish cheek plates and back bones. Otters like suckers and we have a few of those sleek black visitors each spring when the fishing is good. We also have a growing colony of beaver in the lake. I guess no one is trapping anymore.

The original half of Hell's Kitchen was the Grand Island Ferry Office and Gift Shop in its first life. It's a 16'x44' structure that we moved 20 miles south from Lake Superior very early one Sunday morning in late October five years ago. We kept the sign because, well, it's a really nice sign and it makes a good conversation piece.

We framed in a bathroom and an 8-man bunkroom, put the kitchen on the opposite end and the rest of the space is dominated by a table with a lot of family history in it.

It came out of the schoolhouse on Powell's Point during the years when that venerable old structure, itself built from shipwreck parts and salvaged lumber, also got a second life as a deer camp for my uncles from downstate when they hunted on Grand Island in the 50's and 60's. It seats eight and I relish the snowy nights when me and my nephews gather around it drinking cold beer and warm whiskey knowing that my grandfather and my uncles rested their elbows and raised their glasses on this same table some 70 years ago.

The addition is paneled in cedar and pine and perfectly fits a mismatched set of overstuffed leather furniture that's cracked and weathered over the years to a perfect stage of supple. The whole camp is dog friendly.

There's an old amp and turntable in the new living room and we have accumulated what is arguably the finest collection of vinyl on the planet. Heat comes from an air-tight stove in the old section and then the sauna stove on the other end. Now that we have a gas heater to keep the place above freezing, it warms up in about an hour when you fire both stoves on a cold winter day.

The addition is separated from the original camp by a half wall with two doorways and an opening behind and above the stove. It's surrounded by an odd collection of chairs where we gather on cold winter evenings. An old padded armchair faces the stove and is the preferred spot at camp. You usually have to kick a dog out of it if you want to sit there.

The final piece of furniture to find a home there was a 100-year-old chaise lounge that came from the lobby of the Hotel Williams on Grand Island and spent 20 years in my sister's basement and then ten years in mine. It has an old whorehouse look about it and fits perfectly beneath the coat rack by the front door where it's real handy for catching backpacks and putting on your boots. You might say that it ties the whole room together.

The addition has a 14'x14' overhang that overlooks the yard and it will make a good spot to watch thunderstorms. There's covered firewood storage and a tool shed, a five-foot fire ring and a gently used buck pole. The grass we planted last spring came in thick and green and the back yard will hold a half dozen pickup trucks. Camp is complete.

It's more than complete. It completes me. It is my happy place. No harm can befall me at camp. I am at peace and at ease whenever I am here.

It's April now and I stopped out again today just to take a ride. I needed to drop off an old lazy Susan from the Munising Woodenware given to me by my realtor when I bought my house ten years ago. We never used it and I thought camp was a good place for it and that I should take it here today. I also needed to take stock of our provisions for this weekend.

It's cold and rainy and going to camp and building a fire to warm the place up seemed like the right thing to do, even though I couldn't stay. As the fire got going, I walked down to the lake. From high overhead came the lonesome and faraway sound of Canadian geese and I looked up and saw hundreds of birds in wide V's heading north toward the refuge at the south end of the Forest Lake Basin.

The lake itself was empty and the surface was choppy beneath the stiff north wind. The trumpeters had dispersed to other lakes and ponds nearby for spring courting, mating and nesting. Just when I felt alone, an eagle dropped from a branch below the tree line on the other side of the lake, circled aimlessly a few times and then landed in the top of the same tree.

I've seen him on my last three visits, and I assumed he was fishing, but I hadn't seen any fish in the lake yet. I was confused until I looked hard at the big spruce tree he flew back to and saw what looked like the beginnings of a nest. She would be doing more than fishing. Oh well, there goes the neighborhood.

By the time I got back to camp the fire was crackling and beginning to roar so I sat at the table and wrote a note in the log. Then I chucked the stove full, dampened it down and left with the satisfaction of knowing that if someone else felt the need to drive out from town on some important errand, to drop off supplies or pick up a tool, or do some little chore, they would come into a warm camp. And there is no better feeling than that on a cold and rainy day in April.

... and I Learned it All in the Navy

I have a running joke with everyone I know and everyone I meet long enough to have a conversation with that I "ain't right in the head" and I got that way in the Navy.

I joined the Navy when I was 17 and spent most of the next nine years poking holes in the western pacific on old diesel submarines. I learned a lot on those old boats. It's where I spent my formative years and it marked me forever. You cannot squeeze yourself through the unique environment that is a submarine and not come out a changed man, physically, mentally, emotionally and even spiritually.

But I also learned a lot while I was in the Navy. Some of it was in classrooms, but most of it was on the boat and the best of it was "on the beach," which we defined as any place that was not the boat. Much of what I learned was useful, at least it was then, but much of it had no practical application later in the civilian world. On the other hand, some of the skills I learned and some of the lessons I took have guided me my whole life. And for most of it, you just had to be there to understand.

In a Navy classroom in Orlando, Florida in 1977, I learned the "Law of Gross Tonnage."

I was in Quartermaster 'A' school and we were learning the Rules of the Nautical Road. The chief teaching the class asked me who had the right of way between a sailboat and a cargo ship in a crossing situation.

"The sailboat would have the right of way," I answered correctly. "The cargo ship would have to 'give way' and change course for the sailboat who would 'stand on' and maintain course and speed unless of course the cargo ship was not under command, was constrained by her draft or otherwise restricted in her ability to maneuver and flying the correct signal to indicate her privileged status" I explained.

I was such a smartass at 18.

"So, if you were in a 20-foot sailboat in a crossing situation with a 100,000-ton cargo ship you would stand on and assume the right of way?" he asked.

"Yes, I would," I replied. "Relative size doesn't matter."

"And if the cargo ship could not stop or change course in time and you collided who would be at fault?" he asked.

"The Captain of the cargo ship would be at fault," I insisted.

"And where would you be?" he finished and it took a minute, but then came my awareness of the law of gross tonnage. I understood and I've tried to heed this law ever since.

I always stand up for what I believe in, for my own rights and for the rights of others, but I do not stand in the crosswalk and demand the right of way from oncoming traffic, especially if that oncoming traffic is a semi-truck. That discretion has helped me get old. Pedestrians and those who ride bicycles in traffic would do well to learn the law of gross tonnage too.

In the Navy I learned how to "grease the skids."

My very first day on my first boat, the Sailfish, we were loading torpedoes and the Chief of the Boat was in charge topside. The Mark 14 torpedoes we still carried in 1978 were 21 feet long and weighed a couple of tons. They were lowered by a crane from the tender and then slid down a track of mahogany skids and steel rollers through the side hatch of the forward escape trunk into the torpedo room.

"New guy," the COB yelled at me. "Get over here. Your job is to grease the skids."

"What do I grease them with," I asked.

"Grease, you dumb shit," he replied.

"Where do I get the grease?" I asked innocently and he pointed to a five-gallon bucket full of thick grease.

"What do I put it on with?" I asked again.

"Your hands dammit!" he said. "Go get one great big handful of grease and don't touch nothin' with that hand except the skids. Don't touch nothin' greasy with your other hand either and don't step in any grease or you'll end up on the torpedo room deck. And, dammit, don't you touch any of them lines with your greasy fingers!"

So, I jumped and went at it. I had to grease the skids a couple of times those first few months. It wasn't hard and I even got good at it. Then we got a new guy and he had to grease the skids. Because I wasn't yet competent to run the capstan or be a phone talker or handle one of the lines, I was promoted to standing around pretending to be busy until somebody in the torpedo loading party needed something or the COB needed a cup of coffee. I haven't had to do it literally since then, but I'm still pretty good at greasing the skids and it's still not hard. Doing the small things in advance that make everybody else's job a little easier makes your job easier too, this time and next time.

In the Navy I learned to mind my bubble and to never chase it or lose it.

Minding your bubble was good. Chasing the bubble was bad. Losing the bubble could get you a figurative slap upside the head.

You wouldn't think it, but the newest, least experienced guys on a submarine get to drive. And yes, we were closely supervised by the diving officer who was either;

A: a junior officer who was hypervigilant and provided a never-ending stream of unnecessary and often contradictory directions and instructions, corrections and dire admonitions or else it was,

B: a crusty old chief petty officer who wasn't above slapping you upside the head, figuratively of course, if you didn't mind your bubble. This combination of style and technique was not conducive to efficient learning, but it was how we did it in the old Navy and I somehow learned to drive submarines just the same.

There are three control surfaces on a boat. The rudder, which controls your direction, the bow planes, or fairwater planes on nuke boats, which control your depth, and the stern planes which control your angle. The stern planesman stared at an inclinometer and endeavored to maintain a "zero bubble" when at prescribed depth. When increasing or decreasing depth he had to "mind his bubble" as he pointed the nose of the boat up or down at somewhere between a one- and 25-degree angle. That angle varied by how fast the skipper wanted to go up or down and it was easy to "lose the bubble" and let it get away from you. Then you'd end up chasing it and short-cycling the hydraulic plant while you flapped a couple thousand pounds of stern planes around like flippers.

Losing the bubble coming up you could "broach," and the bow or the sail would come out of the water instead of just the periscope which is the instrument you came to periscope depth to use. This got the officer of the deck and the diving officer hollered at and got you a slap upside the head, figuratively at least.

Losing the bubble going down could mean losing control of your descent sending you deeper than you wanted to go, which, on a good day would get you another slap upside the head and on a bad day could sink the boat. We tried to avoid that. I was a good planesman, but I preferred the helm. I liked to steer. Still, to this day I always try to keep a zero bubble despite the distractions and commotion of daily life in our increasingly uncertain world, and on those occasions when I do have to change depth, I work hard to mind my bubble and never lose it.

I learned to shoot stars in the Navy. And the sun and the moon and the planets too.

I did not learn this in school. I learned it on my first trip across the Pacific Ocean. Whiskey Charlie taught me celestial navigation on the Darter when I was still a seaman. He had learned it from Ricky Tic years before on the Grayback where my friend Denise also learned it. Charlie Brown learned it on Darter, but I don't recall if he learned it all from me and how much I had to beat into his head. I do recall he was very good at it. A few years later on the Barbel I taught Swanny and Carl T. how to shoot stars.

At first, I was disappointed that I would not be learning the constellations when I learned celestial navigation. You shoot stars at twilight, before the constellations appear and all those extra stars confuse identification.

Instead, I learned the names of the 57 brightest stars in the heavens. Some you know, like Polaris and Regulus, Vega and Antares. But I also learned where to find Pollux and Betelgeuse, Arcturus and Denebola, and my personal favorite, good old Formalhaut. Each time I pulled them down to the horizon, flipped my sextant over and then rocked them in the cradle was a cheap thrill.

A sextant is an elegant and precise instrument and the Weems and Plath Mark III's we used were World War II Vintage. They had charted some sea miles. Being able to measure the angle of a few stars, mark an exact moment in time, reduce the sight though 20 steps of arithmetic and create a line of position to plot on a chart and know exactly where we were on the planet was tremendously gratifying. And I got to spend a lot of sunrises and sunsets on the bridge of a submarine, steaming on the surface in the middle of the ocean, just staring at the sky waiting for the first or last twinkle in the heavens. That will change a man's perspective significantly and forever. It did mine.

I have lost that skill and celestial navigation is officially a dying art, replaced by the modern GPS system installed on every cell phone in use today. We don't need to know how to shoot stars anymore unless, of course, all those satellites fall from the sky some day. Then it will be a good thing to know if you want to go anywhere across the ocean in a boat.

I also got some very specialized technical training in the Navy.

I spent a whole week in "high speed, low-light, black and white underwater periscope photography school" just before we left San Diego for Sasebo, Japan, in 1979.

The intent was to sneak up behind enemy ships while submerged and take pictures of their propellers, the configuration and design of which is secret technology on all warships. I never actually got to do that. We tried once in an exercise, but we just couldn't go fast enough on the battery to sneak up behind anyone.

As ship's photographer I did get to use a really nice German Hasselblad camera and I also learned how to use a darkroom, develop my own film and make prints. I was able to re-use that skill when I was a young reporter in the late 80's and again after I moved back to the U.P. and became the Yooper at Large for the Porcupine Press.

I retrieved the pieces of that camera from the periscope well one day when a curious junior officer, who will remain nameless, decided to see if he could lower the periscope with the camera attached. He should have talked to me first and I could have saved him that explanation to the captain. I still remember the look on his face standing in the wardroom passageway outside the captain's stateroom with an armload of very expensive camera parts.

I learned to drink professionally while I was in the Navy.

Now you gotta' remember this was the "old Navy" and drinking too much was not only acceptable behavior, it was a required part of a sailor's basic skill set which also included swagger, irreverence, cussing colorfully, talking like a pirate and charming young women who didn't speak very good English. I got good at all those things and though I don't drink like I used to I can still stand at the bar with the best of them. Just ask my son and my nephews and the boys at camp.

I learned to play pool in the Navy.

I don't like pool and I'm not very good at it, but I learned quickly that a pool stick was a handy thing to have in your hand if a bunch of marines or fleet sailors walked into the bar. Every bar in the Philippines had a pool table where we would congregate and let the girls run the table while we stood around drinking cold San Miguel beer and leaning on pool cues.

I'm proud to say that I never had to bust a pool cue over anyone's head. It was usually enough to admit to the loudest guy with the biggest mouth that you didn't know if you could whip his ass or not so you weren't sure how the fight was going to end, but you were damn sure how it was going to start. As a survival measure, we also made sure we knew where the back door was as soon as we walked into a new bar and to this day, I still do that. I cannot sit in a bar with my back to the door either. You need certain skills if you're going to get old.

In the Navy I learned that frogs have water-tight assholes.

I'm not really sure that this is true, but we used the democratic process to reach that conclusion during one of our trips across the Pacific. I forget which boat and I don't remember how the subject even came up, but the question of whether a frog's asshole was water-tight, or they equalized with sea pressure when they dove felt like an appropriate subject for submarine sailors and the debate ran non-stop for 20 days.

This was before the Internet, of course, and we had no encyclopedia or other reference books onboard, so we merely argued the point, honing our logic and debate skills in the process. The two sides quickly formed, and the crew was equally divided. In the end we put it to a vote, and it was a tie, 43 to 43, and we were obliged to ask the Captain to act as tie breaker.

He listened politely to representatives from both sides and eventually decided in favor of water-tight assholes. He said it just seemed right to him. That issue being fairly resolved, the crew moved on to other weighty subjects like whether you could ever get a chicken's foot clean enough to cook and eat and why you would ever want to.

In the Navy I learned about "good order and discipline."

The navy has lots of extra rules that civilians don't have to worry about, and we were reminded of that every day. Published in the boat's Plan of the Day, which told everybody what we were doing that day and also what we were going to eat, there was always a paragraph about 'good order and discipline' just to remind us that breaking those rules had consequences.

After specifying the rank of the individual and the infraction he was guilty of, it would note that this sailor "was awarded punishment" of reduction in rank, forfeiture of pay, 90 days in the brig, etc. It always struck me as funny that the navy considered punishment an award because the sailors who received it sure didn't see it that way.

Fraternization was a big deal when I was in the Navy as more and more women were being integrated into service. Fraternization between officers and enlisted was strictly taboo. Even socialization of officers and enlisted of the same sex was discouraged, but on the boats, we pretty much ignored that. I recall more than one occasion being half of the team that carried one of our officers back to the boat after a large time ashore. He may have been an officer, but dammit, he was our officer and we were shipmates.

But fraternization between the sexes was especially prohibited. Enlisted men did not have social contact with female officers and male officers did not have social contact with enlisted women. Hormones be damned. When I was on shore duty, I had a very cordial and professional relationship with a female lieutenant who worked down the hall from me. I worked in Port Services and she ran the separations unit, processing sailors out of the navy at the end of their enlistment. She supplied me with a never-ending cast of temporary help for my office and we also stood duty together. She was a reservist who went on active duty while her husband, also a navy officer, was deployed overseas.

The building where we worked was half military and half civilian and one day I asked her why all the civilian women in the building spent their lunch hour in the restroom. We didn't call it the "head" on shore duty. It was like a daily pilgrimage and there wasn't a female to be found during lunch time.

She told me they were in there watching soap operas and while I was still trying to figure out what particular piece of porcelain would be best to hold up a TV set, she explained that there was a lounge in there with couches and easy chairs and a fridge.

I found that hard to believe so she offered to show me. Being the adventurous young submarine sailor that I was, off we went to the ladies' room. After checking to see if the coast was clear we went in and, sure enough it was as she described, quite comfortable and well-appointed right down to magazine racks and lace doilies on the arms of the couch and chairs.

We made jokes and were having a good laugh as we walked out into the hall just as the captain and executive officer were walking by. They were both grizzled old four stripers at the end of their careers and they were less than impressed by what they must have seen as pretty questionable fraternization.

I was not awarded any punishment for my tour of the ladies' room, but I did receive a stern talking to with a wink from the Port Services officer who had been instructed to provide me with some general military training. I'm sure that she had a blemish on her fitness report, too, but she didn't really care because she was a reservist.

In the Navy I learned that you never piss to windward.

On an unnamed submarine in an unknown straight near an unidentified foreign country, an unnamed officer was conducting a burial at sea and made the mistake of dumping the box of ashes to windward, thoroughly dusting the forward deck and the honor guard with the remains of the dearly departed. As the story goes, the guys were brushing themselves off before they came back down the hatch and they had to dive the boat to rinse it off and complete the burial at sea.

From that story, which may or may not have happened, I learned that no matter what the endeavor or the circumstance, no matter what the tactic or intent, it is never a good idea to piss into the wind. You will just get it all over yourself and maybe even some on your friends. Jerry Jeff learned that in the Navy too.

In the Navy I learned just how much a shitload is.

But before I give you the now standard measure, I need to explain a little about the nature of sea stories.

In the Navy I learned the difference between a fairy tale and a sea story.

One starts out 'Once upon a time' and the other starts out "this is no shit.'"

The gold standard of sea stories, at least for China Fleet sailors, was the "Hong Kong no shitter."

If it was a Hong Kong no shitter it was true. It really happened. Or, at least some of it happened and the teller of the tale was actually there, or else he heard about it from someone who was actually there. The person or persons in the story really did do what they did, or said what they said, or something close to that depending on who is telling the story and how many times you've heard it before. Of course, all sea stories are open to a certain amount of embellishment, a detail added or altered here or there to make the story more interesting, especially if the tale is dog eared and well worn.

All good sailors will take a few liberties with the details of sea story. It's expected, but the core of the story cannot change because if it does it's no longer a "Hong Kong no shitter." Then it becomes "bullshit" and the quality control guys of sea stories—those who were actually there or who at least know that the teller of the story was not—will make the necessary social correction.

I am some forty years removed from those days so some of these stories have faded into echoes of themselves. Was I really there or did I just hear that story from someone else who wasn't there either? I was recently reminded of that uncertainty by my good friend Charlie Brown who remembers stuff better than I do. Really. He does. Go ahead. Ask him. And that gets us back to the definition of a shitload.

Trash on submarines if stored in steel cans or mesh bags which are weighted and then shot out of the bottom of the boat in the Garbage Disposal Unit which is, essentially, a vertical torpedo tube. The cook shoots the trash, but he needs the Captain's permission to do it, so he calls the chief of the watch on the sound powered phone and he, in turn, asks the officer of the deck who calls the Captain to ask for permission because the Captain likes to know when you open up an eight inch hole in his submarine.

Our friend John was chief of the watch one night and got the call from the cook requesting permission to shoot trash. John asked the officer of the deck who called the Captain for permission and the Captain asked the officer of the deck how much trash there was to shoot because the Captain was interested in details like that.

Well, the officer of the deck asked the chief of the watch who called the cook back and asked him and then he told the officer of the deck that there was a "shitload" which the officer of the deck, in turn, reported to the Captain who, of course, asked just how much that was.

Whether our friend John made the number up or the cook told him how much trash he had to get rid of is a flexible part of the story. But John said, "eight cans and five bags" and that's what the officer of the deck reported to the Captain and from then on it became the standard measure for a "shitload" amongst all my old shipmates in Squadron 7, if not the entire submarine Navy.

Now, a month ago I swore that I witnessed this first-hand on the Darter when John and Charlie Brown and I served on her, but Charlie Brown swears it happened on the Queenfish and Rojo, who served on that boat with John, told us both that story one night at his house in Pearl Harbor when we were all drunk.

I'm not sure anymore and when I asked him, John, always the diplomat, was open to the possibility that he had said the same thing on both boats and in both cases the Captain was not amused. In the Navy I learned the difference between a fairy tale and a sea story. One ends with "they all lived happily ever after" and the other ends with "and that's a Hong Kong no-shitter."

Sometimes I miss those days so very long ago when we were young and foolish, and submarines were still named after fish.

Life's Short! Drink the Good Scotch First!

Buckets of This and That

All hail the five-gallon bucket, that humble vessel of practical utility and the world's most reusable container. May it take its rightful place of honor alongside the duct tape and WD-40 on the shelf where we put those things that no person should be without.

Everyone has a five-gallon bucket laying around somewhere and everyone needs one from time to time. We don't know where the one we're using came from, what its original contents were or what company made the bucket or the stuff that was in it. And this one might not even be your bucket. It might have been mine. It's hard telling where it came from. They're all so different that they all look alike. I might have borrowed it, or it got left at my house or in the back of my truck. All buckets have an uncertain lineage.

They sure come in handy though, every time you need to move something, liquid or solid, from here to there in five-gallon increments. Five gallons of anything is about the most weight you want to carry with one hand. And they are one-handed tools. In fact, it's easier to carry twice as much of whatever you're moving if you're using five-gallon buckets to move it. They're meant to be carried in pairs. There are short ones and there are tall ones but, miraculously, they all hold five gallons.

Everybody has at least one five-gallon bucket, maybe not handy when they need it (oh man, we should have brought a bucket) and they may even have quite a few (grab some of them buckets out of the garage). In fact, I'd bet the average American household has somewhere between a couple and several buckets in their possession at any given time. Notice I didn't say "owned" because buckets are communal property in our rural society, kind of like beer koozies are or butane lighters used to be back in the day. No one puts their name on a five-gallon bucket.

You might use one every day for several months, or it just might ride around in your truck all summer long doing nothing, but that doesn't mean it's yours or that you will keep it for very long. Eventually it will be passed on, full of something, to the next user in the circle, a floating link in the chain or the matrix or the orbit that makes up the bucket-sphere. We're talking about buckets here. Pick your own metaphor.

Or they will be gathered from several sources to be filled with something in common, moved and then dumped, and from there they go back onto the bucket grid. Buckets exist in a just-on-time universe. You don't usually get them or have them until you need them. They wait patiently in a shed or a garage, a basement or the back of a truck, until the day in the not-too-distant future when they're needed again.

But we treat them as valuable possessions. They are useful. Guys will pull over if they see one lying on the side of the highway. But we will not develop a personal affinity for them. We like buckets and will save and even hoard them according to our own needs or habits, but we will not become attached to any particular one. There are no family heirloom five-gallon buckets.

They're handy and at times indispensable (think sinking boat), but this one is just as good as that one as long as they still have a handle, and they don't leak. Even if they do leak, they can still be used to bail and to haul dry stuff, rocks or apples for instance, but if they've lost their handle they are soon discarded. Buckets do not merit loyalty from their human users.

Unlike many other common objects, they're easy to store because they're all the same size, at least in diameter, making them easy to stack. Beware, however, if two of them decide to stick together. There is no force on earth or tool in your garage that can separate them. I think they're mating when they do that, or bonding, or melding in some fashion that's essential to their collective survival, because one day the two that were stuck together will simply slide apart.

Flip it over and a five-gallon bucket can also be used as a seat. Add a wide board and you have a comfortable seat (add a wide board and you don't even have to flip it over). With buckets and boards you can make temporary furniture, from benches to shelves, and you can cut the bottom out with a sawz-all and stick it over a freshly dug hole for a primitive latrine in the woods. Bring along a toilet seat and you're sittin' in high cotton.

All buckets were at one time filled with some industrial volume product, usually a liquid; paint, glycol, hydraulic oil, floor wax, detergent, cooking oil, cake frosting, bearing grease; you name it. If you need a lot of something, we can get it for you in five-gallon buckets. Once empty, the lids need to be cut off and they're usually thrown away. The bucket needs to be cleaned and rinsed thoroughly and even then your average five-gallon bucket is never used for drinking water.

But they're good for just about everything else that will fit in them. I once hauled a basketball-size rock that my wife took a fancy to for a quarter mile, barefoot, along a rocky beach, in a five-gallon bucket. Who loves you baby? It still guards our front door and was much prettier when it was underwater.

Mostly we put smaller things in them from gravel and sand and wet cement to tools and nails and deer bait. Aside from wet cement, they seldom get rinsed after each use and they often pick up a second skin on the inside, a layer of residue from everything they have ever carried. Sometimes it's colorful. Sometimes it smells bad. I give those buckets away as soon as I get the opportunity.

"Here, you could use this bucket of dirt."

But we use them again and again and they reproduce endlessly and circulate through our society until they wear out or get lost, or else we throw them away because the last thing we put in them won't come out.

We had a good stash of twenty at camp this summer—we were bucket rich--and I used them to haul clean sand for fill. I shoveled the sand into the buckets instead of filling up the bed of the truck because that way I only had to shovel the sand once. I made two trips and covered all the rubble we used to fill in the hole in the yard. I salvaged another ten buckets of topsoil to cover that, threw down some grass seed and spread some hay and now we gotta' mow that spot. I kept the buckets in my truck and used them this fall to gather windfall apples at the family homestead on Powell's Point. It was a bumper crop. A tree that usually produces small, wormy apples gave me 35 buckets of the cleanest, sweetest apples I had ever picked and fed to deer. We didn't have to buy much else for bait.

That started a bucket depletion that lasted all deer season. I left the apple buckets in the shed at camp alongside the bags of corn, carrots and sugar beets. We mixed a bucket each time anyone baited their blind and more often than not, the bucket didn't make it back to the shed. It's either in a deer blind or the back of someone's truck, buried in snow for the winter. It's that way with five-gallon buckets. They're nomadic in their natural environment.

We did pick up a few new ones, but right now I couldn't scare up a half dozen on a bet. I'm not worried though. When you need to bring something to camp often times you use a bucket, so I'm confident that all our buckets, or at least a similar amount, will make their way back to camp before spring.

I found a steel five-gallon bucket this summer. It just appeared magically in my back yard one day and I'm not sure where it came from. I brought it out to camp for hauling the ashes in the stoves. We had been using a plastic bucket but it had holes burned in it.

That steel bucket, a rare find in the age of plastic, reminded me of when I was a young boy growing up on Powell's Point in a shack that had no plumbing. The walk to the outhouse was an unpleasant one in the middle of the night in the Winter so there was a "honey pot" on the front porch. First boy out in the morning carried it to the outhouse. It was an old steel paint bucket with a lid with tabs you bent over with a screwdriver. We moved into a house with plumbing before I got old enough to grow into that chore.

I do remember hauling water from the lake with my older brothers, or at least tagging along when they went for water. This was before my dad put in the well (and I learned about dynamite!) We had a pair of galvanized buckets for that chore and some days in the Winter the hardest part was chopping a hole in the ice. Times were hard in the U.P. back then, and we were poor, but we were not so poor that we only had one bucket.

I bought my very first ever "new" buckets at Madigan's Hardware when we put in the sauna at camp last year. We have eight now and they're only used to haul water from the spring to use in the sauna. They'd never had anything in them. Nothing. Ever. They're red and white. Pristine. Virgin buckets. It was a novel concept for me, but I gladly paid $2.99 each in trade for the comfort of knowing that I wasn't leaching some chemical into my body at 180 degrees. They're tall ones and they're just as sturdy as any bucket that has ever carried toxic waste. And we got a sponsor too. No extra charge.

Ace Hardware is now the official water bucket of the sauna at camp.

Makin' Wood

I stood back, brushed the sawdust off my pants and admired the piles of firewood we had made. There was a half a cord tightly stacked near the main stove, a full cord in the rack by the sauna and half a dozen more beneath the overhang out back. We had enough for Winter. And it was good wood too; the best you can get.

Putting the addition on camp had doubled our square footage which had also doubled our need for firewood. The sauna doubled that again and using camp more often multiplied that amount by even more. But getting more wasn't very hard. We know where it grows. Hell, at camp we're surrounded by it so every weekend we spent there last fall we laid in another load.

In years past we only needed enough wood for deer season and maybe one Winter outing. But now we expected to use camp most every weekend and last Winter we did. The sauna was the game changer. Someone was there every weekend through March, if not for a Friday night bonfire in the yard and a Saturday night session around the kitchen table, then at least for a Sunday night sauna.

Making firewood for camp is my job and I am rather particular. You might even say I'm a firewood snob. And given the leisure I had to gather it last year, and the need for a whole lot more, I took my time finding it, cutting it, and hauling it back to camp.

Pat and I got most of it driving the firewood loop in his side-by-side drinking beer and stopping when we found dry poles in the understory--ironwood or hard maple with no bark left on them. They were clean and dry as a bone and when you knocked two pieces together, they sounded like bowling pins. It's a good sound and it makes a hot fire and a warm camp on a cold and snowy winter night.

I've been making firewood for more than 50 years and it's something that I really like to do. It's a humble enough skill, and a lifetime of experience has made me pretty good at it. I grew up swinging an axe and a splitting maul and I'm a fair hand with a chainsaw. And I have my eye out year-round for easy fire wood.

There are skills to "makin' wood," but there is an art to it too. I learned the skills the hard way and I've grown to appreciate the art. Making firewood is not work to me. It's more like therapy and the reward for a day of uncomplicated and very social manual labor can be measured in cubic feet that later gets turned into BTUs. And you get to do it beneath the gold and scarlet cathedral of the hardwood canopy in the fall.

Makin' wood is old pick-up trucks and chain saws and a couple guys down an old back road for an afternoon's useful and productive diversion. No TV, Internet or cell phone service. Add a dog or two and a shotgun ready for the chance encounter with a stray grouse and top it off with a couple cold beers over the rail of the truck when it's full and you've got a simple man's slice of heaven. It's not work. It's play. If you're gonna' go make wood, color me in.

I didn't always feel this way. Makin' wood used to be work for me and it was work that I hated. I grew up making firewood with my dad and my brothers on Grand Island. Each summer we made a couple hundred face cord for the Island residents and then we made a Winter's worth of wood in the fall for my older cousins John and Ted who both had farms up the road from where we lived.

My dad cut and split the wood we made on the island and us boys were the "woodchucks" throwing it into and out of the truck and stacking it where we were told. As we grew older, we all graduated from chucking and stacking wood to splitting cook stove wood with an axe, slabbing shorter rounds of clean grain maple that split easily. These short slabs were later split into smaller pieces with a hatchet on a chopping block and fed into the nickel-plated cookstoves that dominated the summer kitchens in every cottage on the island.

As each of his boys reached that age when we got "too big for our britches" the old man would hand us the maul and say "have at it" while he filed his saw, drank coffee and smoked a cigarette. An 8-pound splitting maul is a serious tool and as I grew older, I took my turn at slabbing the big beech rounds lined up in a row. I'd think highly of myself if after 20 minutes I had managed to whittle ten pieces out of one round only to have the maul bounce harmlessly off the heartwood several times before I gave up. Then I'd look at the line of "hockey pucks" I'd stood up, put the maul down and go back to loading the truck.

An 8-pound splitting maul is also an excellent tool for taking the piss and vinegar out of a 13-year-old boy. My dad would take over then and he'd walk around each piece swinging the maul effortlessly, like an extension of his arms, carving chunks off each round down until only the heartwood was left. Then he'd split the center in half with a grunt and move on to the next round. It would take me a lifetime of splitting wood before I realized how he did it and made it look so easy.

I still count my fingers and wonder every time I think about making wood on the farm. As my cousins got older my dad did what heavy lifting there was left on both farms, making a barn full of hay and a few bushels of potatoes each season. Come fall, we'd pick apples and make firewood. We used a 1946 Ford tractor with a 36" buzz saw on the PTO to make wood. It had a rocker table that would take 8' logs which we bucked onto 16" pieces. My dad and my cousins would man-handle the logs onto the table and rock them into the blade slow enough that we didn't lose our RPM. Every so often a bigger log would make the tractor cough and spit if they fed it too fast and my dad would bump the throttle up a little. I stood on the other side of the blade and threw the pieces into a trailer as they were cut. There was no guard of any kind on the saw and my eyes never left that spinning wheel of death. Like anything though, I got used to it and it didn't scare me, but I never took my eyes off that sawblade.

Remember when you were a kid and your dad tried to teach you something and he would tell you to pay attention? That's where I learned how to pay attention.

I hated makin' wood as a kid. In the spring and summer, it was the black flies and mosquitos when I should have been playing baseball, and in the fall, it was wishing I were wandering the woods with my shotgun and my dog. But firewood was necessary for survival and there was no discussion. It was going to be a long Winter. I received annual assurance of that. And I never earned a cent.

"You eat, don't ya'?," my dad would say every time I suggested that my labors were worthy of a day's wage.

"Ya' slept in a warm bed last night, didn't ya?" he'd add and then he'd go on a not-so-serious rant about the trials and tribulations of raising eleven kids on a workman's wages. We would tune him out at this point and wander off, but it didn't matter because he was talking to himself anyway. When he needed us he'd holler and we'd come running.

When I moved back to the U.P. 30 years ago I went to work in the woods on those frequent occasions when I found myself between professional positions. I started piling pulp for a friend who was a small jobber, and I took turns piling for the two sawyers he had cutting for him. I was their "pilot," (as in "I cut it and you pile it") for about six months and I learned a lot about felling trees just by watching them do it.

Anything smaller than 8" had to be piled and that could mean five or six sticks in each tree that the sawyer didn't have to put down his saw and pile. He could keep cutting and I'd pile everything behind him. Flipping and sometimes carrying 8" maple logs will build muscle, sinew and character in a hurry. We eventually got into some bigger timber and one day Tom, my boss, said "I need you to pick up a saw."

The old man had never let us touch his chain saw when we were kids other than to fetch it. So, one day I started on a deck of dry firewood logs we'd culled from the section we were cutting, and it took a couple of tanks of gas before I loosened my white-knuckle grip on the handles of the old Jonsered they gave me. But I got the hang of cutting with the tip that first day and the next day Rob showed me how to fell a tree. We started with a big hemlock.

"Which way does it want to go?" he asked me as we walked around it.

"Right there," I said, and he nodded.

"Which way do you want it to go?" he said as we walked around it again and considered the other trees we would have to cut in the vicinity, where they were likely to go and where the Tom would need to put the forwarder to pick up the pieces.

"Right over there" I said pointing 45 degrees to the left of my initial line.

"Go ahead and notch it," he said, and I did. "Now make your back cut level and split the face of your notch. Leave a good hinge." I did as I was instructed, and the tree fell with a mighty crash right where I wanted it to go. It was the first big tree I had ever felled and having it land where I intended was tremendously rewarding.

"Now go cut it up," he said and walked off toward his own strip. During the six months I had spent piling pulp I'd also learned the basic safety precautions about checking escape paths and watching for widow makers and spring poles and my last instruction that first day was "now think three or four trees ahead." That was my training.

In a week I had gained a certain level of confidence and the saw didn't scare me anymore. Inside of three months my output was comparable to the other two sawyers on the job. I worked for Tom on and off for four or five years and we usually cut pulp and logs for the company three days a week and then made firewood on state land the other two days. Logs and pulp paid the bills, but firewood paid the crew.

We bought stumpage from the state on tracts they wanted thinned, and we took woods-run timber. The oldest complaint in the firewood business is "there sure is a lot of cherry in that load." When there was too much cherry marked, we'd complain, and the cruiser would blend more maple and beech into the mix. Tom had an old Iron Mule and he decked the wood near the road where we could get at it. On firewood days, we'd have some mix of the four of us cutting wood on the deck, running the wood splitter, swinging a splitting maul and loading a six-cord dump truck. We tried to deliver three loads each day.

Now a chain saw is a murderous tool, and it is to be treated with respect. It's also a noisy machine and when a saw was running there was no conversation. When I was felling trees, I used to sing just as loud as I wanted to because I had perfect pitch when accompanied by a chainsaw. But when we were splitting the wood and loading it, we were at ease and light chatter and hearty laughter marked the hours. Once the saw stops, makin' wood is a right social undertaking, whether you're getting paid to do it or not. We made firewood on Thursdays and Fridays and sometimes on Saturday if we got rained out during the week.

Friday is a special day for a lumberjack. It's payday and there's the weekend to look forward to and plan. The Fridays we made firewood were even better. Rather than being alone in the woods with a screaming chainsaw for company, those days makin' wood were spent as a crew, competent and productive at our task, content with each other's company sharing old stories and future plans. The days that I spent working on that crew with Tom and Rob and Steve were some of the best days of my life.

I deliberately don't own a chainsaw anymore. I don't need one. I don't burn wood myself, at least not at home. I have access to a half dozen saws if I do need one and I only need one if I'm felling a tree for a friend or making someone else's firewood. I used to help my friend Joe make thirty cord each Winter for his house. I traded him the chain saw work for the repairs he was always doing on the junk I drove back then.

Joe could fell trees and was a good man in the woods, but his real skill was with a splitting maul. He was a machine and reminded me of my dad the way he just walked around in a circle slabbing off pieces before whacking the heart wood in half. I'd fell a tree and he'd let me cut ten rounds before he started splitting behind me and then the two of us would keep our three boys busy loading until the truck was full. It usually took us two weekends to get the wood he needed for Winter.

I still make most of the wood for camp though, and that chore gives me a month of good weekends each October. Fall is the usual season for firewood. Unless they do it for a living, no one makes wood in the spring or summer, and if you're makin' wood in the Winter, you're not doing something right and your life is way out of balance. I like the work and the company and I relish those weekends at camp.

Along with a few basic tools and some essential skills there's some art to making wood, too, an intuitive method that utilizes gravity to the maximum extent possible while minimizing the number of times you touch each piece. And the type of wood you burn is important too. In this neck or the woods (pun intended) the preferred firewood in order of desirability is ironwood and then hard maple.

Ironwood (eastern hop hornbeam) is an understory tree that never breaks the canopy. It rarely gets larger than a foot in diameter and if it gets that big it tends to be hollow. Lacking adequate sunlight, it grows exceedingly slow and then dies. Then it stands there forever, slowly shedding its bark and waiting for the discriminating woodpecker to cut it down, cut it up and take it home.

"Woodpeckers" are guys like us who road-hunt their firewood and take a casual approach to the task. You can tell when we've been by when you see sawdust in the road.

But ironwood is as hard as a rock—one of the hardest woods on the planet and we are blessed with a lot of it near camp. Hard maple is a distant second and it's considered excellent firewood itself. We have lots of that too.

After that, oak, beech, ash, and soft maple are all about the same quality and all will do if seasoned properly. Everything after that—cherry, aspen, willow, fir and pine—we refer to as gopher wood as in "put a piece on the fire and go fer another." We burn gopher wood in the fire pit to get rid of it, but no self-respecting Yooper would ever burn it in the woodstove or, God forbid, in the sauna.

When you're making firewood, there are a couple of rules to follow.

Rule #1; downhill wood is the better than uphill wood. Gravity is our friend and if we can roll it, throw it, or carry it downhill to the truck, that's preferable to rolling it, throwing it, or carrying it uphill to the truck. Uphill wood is acceptable only if it's very high quality and not very far away. We try hard to cut those dead trees that will drop in or very near the road and when we can't get them in the road or very close, then a tree length away is as far as we'll go.

Rule #2; Touch each piece of wood as few times as possible. The least labor involved in burning wood is to cut the tree down and have it land in the fire, but that way won't keep your shack warm in the Winter. The most labor involved in burning wood is to cut the tree down, cut it into pieces, stand each piece up, split it (sometimes standing halves or quarters back up to be split into smaller pieces), throw it out to the road, toss it in the truck, stack it in rows in the back of the truck, throw it out on the ground when you get it home, stack in it piles outside and then eventually carry it into a rack or a wood box in the house and then throw it in the stove.

Eliminating as many of those steps as possible is the art of makin' wood. For instance, throwing it loose in the back of the truck and not stacking it eliminates one step, but you can't carry as much wood. Picking it up off the ground and stacking it directly in the truck eliminates two steps, but the pieces need to be close by. And that man is an artist who can split a block of wood without having the pieces fall over (so he can split them again if he has to without having to stand them back up). The more you make wood, the better you get doing that.

We found this year's wood in our travels this spring. It's ironwood and hard maple again and there's not much to split. The nice thing about cutting poles out of the understory is that you can push them in almost any direction you want so most of these will drop right in the road. And that's right where we want them.

The season is changing up here on the north coast. The burnished hues of late summer have given way to autumn's painted splendor. Shadows have begun to lengthen and storm clouds are gathering. Days are getting short. Mornings are brisk now and the grass is heavy with dew. The first frost is not many days away and I've been harvesting the last of my tomatoes to wrap in newspaper and ripen in boxes. The boat and the camper are ready for storage and we're starting to put the yard away for the winter.

Fall is upon us with all its sweet and ripening melancholy. It's time to enjoy the forest one last time before the cold, north wind blows the last rays of gold away for another winter. It's time for hiking boots and flannel shirts, well-oiled shotguns and good-natured dogs. The woods smell of mushrooms and dry leaves and the fading glory of the hardwood canopy beckons us to the annual ritual. I'm looking forward to the smell of sawdust and wood smoke again. I

Life's Short! Drink the Good Scotch First!

long for the sound of bare branches rattling overhead and the rustle of dry leaves beneath my feet.

So sharpen your chain saws, boys, grab the gas and oil and the splitting maul and let's wander down the river valley and up into the hardwood. The hell with football, it's time to make firewood.

"Wanna' go camp, make wood this weekend?"

Life's Short! Drink the Good Scotch First!

Life's Short! Drink the Good Scotch First!

Guardrails
(With thanks and apologies to Bob Seger)

We all have waypoints along the roads that become our lives, milestones reached, and markers passed; achievements and failures, forks in the road, bridges burned or crossed.

Some of them are planned. Some aren't. A man dies. A child is born. You get married, divorced, and retired. Some are fleeting and your life changes in an instant, but others last whole seasons, and often we don't recognize them until many years have passed and we've earned the clarity of hindsight.

For me, 1976 marked the first real turning point in my life, the first fork in the road. Looking back, I've steered a seemingly random course since then, across distant seas and down paths less travelled, around the world and back home again, and it all started in the summer of my 17th year. It was the hottest summer anyone could remember, and Bob Seger sang the theme songs or our generation from 8-track tapes in car radios as we lived out the blossoming drama of our teenage years.

I took some hard lessons that summer and by year's end I had made some hard choices. By fall I had left the boy I was behind and began the journey forward to the man I am today. And it all started with a new job.

Kids in the 70's with the wrong last name from the other side of the tracks were also the kids who had long hair and got in trouble. Most of my friends were also practicing juvenile delinquents by the 9th grade so we were "guided" down a vocational track in our high school education. I had four years of welding, two years of wood shop, a year of drafting and a year each of small engine and automotive repair at dear old Mather High.

By 1976 I also had a probation officer who was certain that hard work would make me a better citizen and she reinforced the vocational choices that were being made for me in school. I was 16 at the end of my junior year so I was provided gainful employment that summer by the state of Michigan through a government funded Youth Corps program working on a labor crew. I considered myself lucky because it was full time job and it paid a little better than the minimum wage I'd made in my other summer jobs, threading well pipe and glazing windows up at Jack Denman's Hardware, and unloading trucks and hawking produce down at Big Pete's Bushel Basket.

We were a motley crew, Harold, Greg, and I, clueless and cocky, classmates who between us already knew pretty much everything and we had most of it figured out too. The state put us to work for the Alger County Road Commission and the shop engineer/manager at the time was Mort Hendrickson who gave us our marching orders every Monday and our paychecks every Friday. Old Mort just shook his head that first day at the trio of long-haired wannabe hippies in tank tops and bell bottom jeans that he found standing out behind the county garage smoking cigarettes. At least we were there on time.

"You the new crew?" he ordered rather than asked and jerked a thumb toward his office inside the garage where he introduced us to Dennis, our crew leader. Dennis was clean cut and wore straight leg jeans as most farm boys did back then, and we didn't trust him at first. We were hoping he wasn't as big a redneck as he looked. He was older and had gone to school in Eben, so we didn't know anything about him. We weren't sure if he was a former juvenile delinquent in training or a college kid with a summer job. Over the course of that summer, we got to know him pretty well, but we never did find out. In the end he would prove to be good leader and even a kindred spirit.

The county gave us a surplus Rambler Ambassador station wagon with a State of Michigan logo on the passenger side door. It was shit-brown and perpetually dirty, but it carried the four of us, a wheelbarrow, and all the assorted shovels and rakes and hoes that Mort figured we'd need to begin our new career as "erosion control technicians."

That first week we started on M-28 at Deer Lake spreading gravel and topsoil on the shoulder of the highway where the spring rains had washed it away. Mort went with us that first day to explain the job to Dennis and make sure we all knew what was expected from us.

Mort was a competent and likeable enough guy and a loquacious fellow too. He possessed a large vocabulary of which he was rather proud because he always seemed to use as much of it as possible. He strung extra words on a sentence like he was hanging wet laundry on a line. As the three of us stood on the side of the highway leaning on shovels that first morning, Mort explained the job to Dennis who listened patiently.

"Now you can observe here that the copious precipitation we had this spring drained off the bituminous surface with such volume and force as to erode the dirt and gravel and create these gulches, defiles and crevasses which have denuded the gravel shoulder along with all the organic cover further on down the slope," he explained as he pointed at the side of the road.

We all listened intently. This was starting to sound complicated.

"So, the heavy rains ran off the road and washed out the shoulder," said Dennis and we all breathed a sigh of understanding.

"That's right" said Mort, "now every 30 minutes or so a county dump truck is going to transport a load of 22A road gravel with a clay mixture out to your location and deposit it on the shoulder. When the truck is here your crew is going to have to provide traffic control while the trucks maneuver perpendicular to the edge of the road and discharge their load into small mounds along the shoulder. Every third truck will have topsoil."

At that he pointed at a couple of Stop signs on a stick and a wad of orange vests he'd thrown in the back of the Rambler.

"They'll disburden their loads into a half dozen piles maybe 30 yards apart or wherever you observe that the erosion is most pronounced and direct them," he added. "And your guys will have to redistribute it to match the grade, so the asphalt doesn't begin to crumble and wash away the slope any further."

"So, I'll show the truck drivers where to dump the dirt. We'll stop traffic for them and then we'll spread the gravel and dirt around," Dennis echoed back.

"Precisely," said Mort with finality and he jumped in his truck and drove away. It was on that very first morning we considered the possibility that Dennis had been to college.

As Mort was leaving the first dump truck of gravel arrived. So far, the job didn't look too tough. I grabbed a vest and a stop sign at a signal from Dennis and he stood in spots on the shoulder where he wanted a pile of gravel. As soon as we had stopped what little traffic there was the truck driver dumped a yard or two in front of wherever Dennis was standing. And then they'd move down the road and dump another. This was kind of fun, I thought to myself. I was already feeling important standing in the middle of the highway with my sign making people stop and wait.

Once the truck left, we attacked the closest pile, first with shovels and then with rakes and hoes. We weren't half done with it when the second truck showed up. Well, we dropped our dirt wrenches and two of us grabbed vests and signs while the third man moved the Rambler up the road and into the shade. It was going to be a hot day.

"Were going to have to pick it up a little" said Dennis with encouragement when the second truck left. Then he dug in like he meant it. We took it as the challenge that it was and we responded with enthusiasm, tearing into the pile with gusto and purpose. Gravel flew. When the third truck came with a load of topsoil we were drenched in sweat and sucking wind, and we were still working on the second pile from the first truck.

"Alright, let's get him dumped" Dennis said with resignation, "then we'll take a break and make a new plan. We're gonna' kill ourselves trying to keep up with these trucks." So that's what we did for 20 minutes until the next truck arrived. We got two more after that, set a steady pace in between, and heard "that's all you get for today," from the driver of the last truck as he pulled away with a wave.

It was late morning by now and the four of us gathered around the station wagon in the shade, smoked cigarettes and drank water from a big plastic cooler. My feet hurt and my hands were beginning to blister. This was getting to be less and less fun and I no longer felt particularly important. None of us had brought any lunch and we were ten miles from anywhere. Not that it mattered because between the four of us we didn't have so much as a dollar in our pockets. We kept a slow but steady pace for the rest of that first day and when Dennis dropped us off back at the garage, I didn't have enough juvenile delinquent left in me to head downtown and raise any hell, so I just walked home.

My dad dropped me off the next morning wearing the closest thing to work boots that I owned and with a grocery bag full of bologna sandwiches and cold drinks to last me the day. He had watched me tending the blisters on my hands the night before and had said nothing, but as I got out of the truck, he handed me a new pair of heavy cotton work gloves.

"You're gonna' want these," he said.

Our on-the-job training as erosion control technicians went on for a couple more weeks and I soon grew accustomed to the work. I'd grown up with six brothers, some combination of which were my dad's crew, so I was no stranger to working hard. We spent two weeks spreading gravel and topsoil along M-28 between Deer Lake and the Laughing Whitefish River and we took our lunch each day at the river. It was cool sitting on the big rocks under the highway bridge and somedays we soaked our feet in the gurgling stream.

One day during the second week Dennis suggested we take a drive for lunch. He'd forgotten his so we drove back to Christmas and stopped at the Brown Derby where he knew they had nickel sandwiches. He went inside and tried to get a handful of the pickled bologna or egg salad on cocktail rye snacks to go. The bar was just opening, and the bartender explained to Dennis that the nickel sandwiches were only a nickel for the customers drinking in the bar, so he came out and got us.

As we slid into a booth, he ordered a beer for himself and cokes for the three of us and asked for nickel sandwiches all around. Without enthusiasm, she brought us a dozen sandwiches wrapped in waxed paper on a plate and went back to her bar opening routine. We savored our lunch that day and talked about girls and cars and rock and roll music. We drank RC Colas, smoked cigarettes, and played all the Bob Seger songs they had on the juke box.

I stood there boldly
Sweatin' in the sun
Felt like a million
Felt like number one
The height of summer
I'd never felt that strong
Like a rock

I was 16
Didn't have a care
Working for peanuts
Not a dime to spare
But I was lean and
Solid everywhere
Like a rock

Our boss had already earned our respect on the job, working just as hard as we did, and lunch that day had us all thinking that he was also a pretty good guy.

Most of that first Friday paycheck went for new boots at the People's Store, along with a couple pair of gloves, and a thermos that would fit in the top half of my dad's old lunch pail. Instead of sleeping in, I was up early in the morning with him now. We got ready for work together. He gave me a ride. I started drinking coffee and I began to see both him and each day in a different light.

We were rebuilding the motor on what was to be my very first car. It was a '62 Plymouth Valiant station wagon that we had salvaged from the boat house on Grand Island when it blew down in a rare tornado that spring. We were working on the island that day and I remember huddling beside the truck where we were parked making firewood up the center road. When it had blown itself out, we drove back to the landing and saw a pile of lumber where people had parked their island cars and stored their boats in the winter.

My dad got the salvage work on the boat house, so we got the old Plymouth for nothing. We dug it out and brought it home. I got to steer as he towed it with his truck through town. The motor needed rebuilding and we worked on it as he found the time. I spent a lot of nights handing him tools and holding the light or the dumb end of the other wrench while he pulled pistons and changed the rings. We never had much to say to each other and I tended to wander off at those moments when he didn't need me.

The following Monday, Mort had us follow him out M-94 about a mile south of Wagner Falls to where a grassy slope drained down to the ditch alongside the road. A cement trough split the slope in two. It was about 100 feet long, six feet wide and rose at a steep angle draining the hillside above the slope that had been cut into the ridge to put the highway through. And it had washed out.

Mort explained. "That drainage trough catches and channels the hydraulic discharge from the watershed above that drains this whole hillside, and it prevents this slope nearest the road from washing out. When it rains hard, the water cascades under the top of the trough undermining the construction leading to weakness which is collapsing the structure rendering it counterproductive."

"I need your guys to pulverize the remaining conglomerate so we can pour a new aqueduct on top of the rubble," he added.

Dennis gave us a sideways glance and half a smile and told Mort, "So, the water washed out the trough and you want us to bust it up."

"Exactly," said Mort and he jumped in his truck and drove away. He left us standing there leaning against the side of the Ambassador looking up at what I now saw as Alger County's equivalent of Roman ruins. My training in erosion control was about to take on a whole new dimension.

"Well, now we know what those sledgehammers are for," I said walking to the back of the wagon to grab one and get started. It was going to be another hot day and I wanted to get on with it.

"Now, let's just hold on for a minute," Dennis offered, still leaning on the hood of the old Rambler with his arms folded. He was quiet for a moment, like he was trying to make up his mind about something, and we stood there waiting for instructions. We were well trained by now.

"This might take us all day" he said, "so whaddaya say we smoke a joint and think about it for a minute," and then he pulled a joint out of his t-shirt pocket, held it up and asked if anyone had a light. He was immediately offered three lighters.

Being just paranoid enough to be discrete, we climbed to the top of the hill before we sparked it up. On top we had a nice view of the Anna River valley and Perch Lake swamp and when we came down ten minutes later, we had gained a better understanding of how our little crew fit in to the larger rural road maintenance picture while also devising a plan for tackling the day's work.

We had to go at it from the bottom where we could swing into the hillside, but it was only wide enough for two men to swing a sledge, so two of us went at it from the sides which meant standing on uneven ground swinging an eight-pound sledge at an odd angle. We took a smoke break every half hour and switched off. It was back breaking work, but with patience and lots of breaks we got it done before the day was out. Just as we were finishing Mort pulled up and took a minute to admire our work without comment, positive or negative.

"Good," he said to Dennis. After our first meeting, he never spoke to us directly.

"Now we can pour the new cement tomorrow. The first load will be here at eight."

Then he jumped in his truck and drove away.

He left us all staring at the hill and the long row of rubble we had just made and each of us, in our own way and at our own pace, came to the realization that we would play a significant role in getting that cement up that hill.

As it happened, the next day it rained and we busied ourselves tidying up tools, equipment, and materials in the garage. We even washed the Rambler. It was the only rain day I remember from that summer, though I'm sure that there were more. We relished the light work and got to take our lunch with the guys in the shop where we were teased like news guys everywhere get teased. But they saw the hard work that we were doing--work that they didn't have to do—so they overlooked our hairstyles and accepted us as part of the crew that day. That meant a lot to all four of us.

The next day we met the first cement truck at eight armed with a dozen 5-gallon buckets. Dennis stuck a trowel in his hip pocket and carried the first two buckets up the hill and started spreading the cement over the rubble as we brought him more. We dug steps into the turf with the toes of our boots over the course of the morning hauling cement up that hill. The first truck got us a third of the way down, and by the time we got to the last truck we could daisy chain the buckets up to Dennis as he worked his way down the hill. We had just enough cement to finish and we were done before lunch. And we were exhausted.

Mort showed up just as we were rinsing buckets and admired our work. It was not a thing of beauty, but it was functional. But we had also screwed up his plan for us that day. This was supposed to be an all-day job.

"Well, I'll have paint for you in the morning," he said, "and you can get started reconditioning the guardrails. Take the afternoon and go inventory the material condition of the camp sites at the Forest Lake campground. Compile a summary of what you'll need for maintenance."

And then Mort jumped in his truck and drove away.

In those days, the Michigan Department of State Highways and Transportation was also in charge of the state forest campgrounds. I remember that MDSH&T was painted on, carved into, or burned onto every piece of equipment they had. We joked about being paid by an organization we referred to as "Madshit."

The campground on the Forest Lake Basin was just past the dam and a couple of miles south of the highway. We decided to take our lunch there as part of our afternoon assignment. There were few campers that early in the summer, so we made a loop of the twenty or so sites and picked the best empty one for our lunch break—just down from a family with a pair of teenage daughters who seemed to enjoy attracting our attention.

We did not work hard that afternoon. We did do a thorough inventory and assessment of all the picnic tables and fire rings, outhouses and garbage barrels and we managed to look as official and important as possible in our orange vests while doing it. Once finished we made a list of the tools and materials that we'd need to fix or replace everything that was broken or missing. It was a group effort, and it took us the rest of that day. We knew this project would have to wait, but we agreed that there were many days of important work to do at this campground and that it should be made a priority. Dennis would talk to Mort about it.

It would take a while, but we made it back and as the summer went on it became our afternoon work site after mornings on the highway. First it was weekly, on a Friday, but then it became daily as painting guardrails became our morning routine. And there were lots of guardrails to paint.

Driving south from the intersection with M-28 just east of Munising, highway M-94 runs through hills and crosses ravines from several watersheds for its first half dozen miles until it climbs the grade at 7-Mile Hill. At least half of that stretch is lined with guard rails on both sides of the road.

Guard rails in 1976 were still post and cable with ten-inch diameter posts buried into the ground as far as they stuck out of it. Two rows of one-inch galvanized wire rope were strung through eyebolts on each post about eight inches apart and at bumper height. The bottom of each post was dipped in creosote and the top was painted white. Some were rotted almost in half at the demarcation line where the creosote stopped and the paint started. It was 1930s technology and the guardrails on M-94 were probably installed right after the war when they built the highway so most of the paint had peeled away. With a post every six feet there were, well, you do the math; 880 posts per mile times about six miles equals somewhere between a shitload and a gazillion.

The next day we found four 5-gallon buckets of white latex paint and a new box of four-inch horsehair brushes in the back of the station wagon when we got to work. Mort didn't need to tell us what we were doing that day. He just said, "start at M-28 and work your way out to 8-mile Corner. Don't stop until you run out of paint."

"Well, we won't get too far down the road with this much paint," I said just as I noticed the pallet right behind Mort stacked with five-gallon cans that looked just like the four we had in the Rambler. We all looked and did the math; 3 by 3 by 3 cans high, there were 23 more five-gallon cans of paint left on the pallet. And there was another pallet right behind the first one. And it didn't rain for a month.

We reconnoitered the whole stretch that first morning and I boldly predicted, staring at all those guardrails, that we would never make it all the way to 7-mile Hill. There were dozens of sections from one hundred yards to almost a mile long, more often than not on both sides of the road. We started at M-28 and worked around the corner to Wagner Falls, our first waypoint.

As we opened those first cans, we noticed that the heavy latex paint had separated and required a half hour of vigorous stirring for which the yard sticks they had given us for the job proved entirely inadequate. So, we cut some stout saplings and watched the people driving by watch us as we sat on the guardrail and stirred our respective pots.

The painting itself was neither easy nor hard. There was no prep. We painted over the original paint which was often peeling in spots, non-existent in others, and we didn't have to clean up our drops in the gravel. In those days, the state used liberal amounts of herbicide on the shoulders of the highway, so we had no weeds to contend with either. I tried to make a clean line around each cable at first and not paint the eyebolts, but that attention to detail fell by the wayside the first day. Painting a post efficiently means circling it as you go, finishing where you started. Not so with guardrail posts as you had to step over the wire ropes twice and spend half your time on the narrow shoulder inside the rail with your ass in traffic.

So, we had to stay on the outside of the wire rope rails and reach over and around. This also meant standing all day on a slope just steep enough to require a guardrail between it and the moving traffic above. It was an ankle bending and back breaking job made worse by the menial nature and repetitive monotony of the work, the indignity of which was magnified by the public spectacle we quickly became doing it.

People would toot their horn when they went by, and we knew not why. Was it to say hello? Was it in jest? Were they encouraging us or recognizing a job well done? Were they admiring our bronze torsos? Were they jeering at us?

I swore that everybody I knew with a car drove by once a day just to make fun of us. It felt like we were on a chain gang. Every day we were hot and stiff and sore, covered in heavy white paint and bristling at all the attention we got.

Dennis was not immune to this, but he just told us to ignore the traffic and paint one post at a time. So, I applied myself and before long I could paint a post in under ten minutes. I started counting. A half-dozen an hour, maybe fifty posts each day with breaks. I made that my goal. Sometimes I'd lose track of how many posts I'd painted and would get mad and go back to where I started and recount the ones I had painted that day.

On the third day I found an old floppy felt hat with a red polka dot bandana tied around it. It was cool. It looked relatively clean, so I put it on. It fit like it was mine and in addition to being cool, it kept the sun off my head and neck which was also cool. It became a part of my wardrobe on and off the job and I was careful not to get any paint on it.

It took two days to get to Wagner Falls, three sections and about a quarter of a mile. Then came the long straight stretch along the Annie River and the railroad tracks. It was endless, almost a full mile on each side that seemed to stretch all the way to the horizon. The only break was at the quarter mile mark, the finish line for testosterone fueled muscle car races on hot summer nights. It took us two full weeks.

I was painting 50 posts a day the first week, and the second, but at some point, I stopped counting posts and started counting paint cans. We were down to the bottom row on the first pallet. After a couple of weeks our days got broken into two unequal sections. Because of the heat, Dennis had gotten permission for us to paint in the mornings only. Each day we painted for five hours and then took our lunch at the campground where we worked a short afternoon.

We replaced rotten boards on the picnic tables and straightened the cooking grates on the fire rings. We swapped out rusty 55-gallon drums that served as trash barrels and painted the outhouses. We made that work last as long as we could and then we put our newly acquired erosion control skills to good use filling potholes in the road. We brought sickles and shears and trimmed the empty campsites and the shoulder of the access road—anything we could think of to keep us in the shade and off that highway.

July gave way to August as we started the guardrails on 7-Mile hill. We were down to ten buckets of paint, and I started wondering if old Mort was a genius and had given us exactly enough paint to finish the job. We almost made it. We ran out of paint with a couple dozen posts left on each side of the road. I felt cheated. After not caring for a month, now I wanted to finish the job just to see it done. I wanted to paint that last damn post.

But it was not to be, and in the end, it didn't matter because they began replacing those guardrails the very next spring. And I lost my hat somewhere that day.

Our last two weeks were spent playing at road maintenance on the campground road, digging drainage ditches and trying our best to fill in the never-ending series of dried-up potholes that were the roadbed. The county had no gravel for that thoroughfare. We finished that summer by taking our last afternoon off and having a little party at the campground. We had earned it. We lounged in the sun and swam in the basin. Dennis brought and shared a 12-pack of Stroh's and said he'd have brought more but it wouldn't do for us to go back to the garage drunk.

I never saw Dennis again. I saw Harold and Greg the very next week at school. It was our senior year. I had just turned 17 and I'd grown used to getting a paycheck, so I took a job pumping gas at the Holiday Station. It was a good job for a guy who had his own car. And then life got complicated.

That first week of school I blew the engine on my new ride. The old man had warned me several times to take it easy until it was broken in, but there was a carload of girls I had to catch one day, and the engine seized up in a cloud of blue smoke on the Forest Lake Road. I steered as my dad towed it with his truck through town to the junk yard. He didn't say a word. He didn't have to.

Then, to stem truancy and juvenile delinquency in general, the school began factoring unexcused absences into our grades. I was one of those lucky kids who got it the first time and I only went to class on days when we had tests or quizzes. I went from straight A's to failing most of my classes in one marking period. It was not fair.

I had just been elected president of the senior class, but I quit school anyway and wrote a scathing letter to the editor that was never published. I began working full time and put off the decisions I knew I had to make. I proposed to my girlfriend. She wisely turned me down. I got my GED and joined the Navy that December and delayed entry until the following spring.

An old Navy man himself, my dad happily signed my enlistment papers. He died a month later. That was hard for me. I owed him. I still do.

I had a job I considered easy, and I played hard and led a carefree life. No school. No study. No choices to agonize over. I had cast my lot, quite literally, upon the water. I watched my classmates sweat the decisions they had yet to make, and I fancied they envied me my freedom. Spring came and I went away. My journey had begun.

Now, almost fifty years later, I remember that summer, the work that we did and the things that I learned, especially when I hear an old Bob Seger tune on the radio.

My hands were steady
My eyes were clear and bright
My walk had purpose
My steps were quick and light
And I held firmly
To what I felt was right
Like a rock

And I stood arrow straight
Unencumbered by the weight
Of all these hustlers and their schemes
I stood proud, I stood tall
High above it all
I still believed in my dreams

That summer I learned to work hard.

I learned that there is satisfaction in hard work, well done.

I learned that hard work earns respect.

I learned that there is nothing more important than a good pair of work boots.

I learned to work as a team and to feel the warmth of being accepted as part of a crew; to be treated as an equal by men I looked up to.

I learned that I didn't want to do manual labor for the rest of my life, and I realized that I was just smart enough to not have to.

I learned that sometimes you don't get to finish the job. You can work really hard for a very long time and never see the final product. Life is like that. Get used to it.

I learned that sometimes it's best to take a minute and make a plan.

I learned that everyone needs some form of guidance.

I learned how to eat an elephant. One bite at a time.

I learned that there is Zen in everything, be it a shovel and a pile of dirt, a sledgehammer and a cement trough, or a paint brush and a line of guardrail posts stretching to the horizon. You just have to find it.

I learned that life is not fair and most times there isn't a damn thing you can do about it.

I learned that there is more than one way to measure anything. Everyone measures progress differently.

I learned that appearances are almost always deceiving and that kindred spirits seldom look like you.

I learned that my dad was a good man and I still owe him my best. I try hard to be the kind of man who would have made him proud.

I drive down M-94 a lot these days. It's the road to camp and to the Buckhorn Lodge and it takes me to many other places I like to go. I looked at just the right time the other day and I caught a glimpse of the cement trough we had built on the side of that hill. The grassy slope has long since grown up into a thick stand of mature red pine and spruce.

I pulled over and parked at the end to a new sheet-steel guard rail, galvanized and corrugated, and went back to take a look. The cement was completely covered in thick moss beneath the trees locked tightly together overhead. You had to know what it was and that it was there before you saw it.

You could walk by and not notice it. It had aged well and was intact, right up to the top. There was no erosion evident. None of it had washed away.

It was standing the test of time. My own personal Parthenon.

"I built that," I said out loud to nobody and pointed absent-mindedly up the slope as cars whizzed past me on the highway. I smiled at what those drivers might be thinking but I didn't care.

"I built that," I said out loud again and my mind wandered back to that summer so very long ago. I thought about my dad and the things he tried to teach me. I'm older now than he got to be. And I miss that old hat too.

And then I jumped in my truck and I drove away. The radio was on, and I caught the end of an old Bob Seger song that had been stuck in my head all day.

40 years now
Where'd they go?
40 years
I don't know
I sit and I wonder sometimes
Where they've gone

And sometimes late at night
Oh, when I'm bathed in the firelight
The moon comes callin' a ghostly white
And I recall
I recall.

Life's Short! Drink the Good Scotch First!

Life's Short! Drink the Good Scotch First!

No Snot, No Lace Panties

I made my way slowly in the dark to the stove, guided by the faint light from the last dying embers of the fire. Contrary to their own good sense and more than casual past instruction, the boys had all left camp without putting any wood in the stove. There was already a chill in the air as I raked the few coals that were left, opened the damper, and added an armload of dry maple and ironwood to the firebox. I watched for a minute until the first small flames began to flicker.

I circled the kitchen table and turned on the single bare bulb above the sink which gave me just enough light to find my coffee cup in the cabinet and draw a hot cup of Harbor Girl from the carafe the boys had filled before they left. At least they had made coffee. There was hope. I added a generous amount of Irish cream and then slid into the green armchair opposite the fire. It was going to be a good day.

The flames caught quickly and then gathered on the dry wood I had added. In a minute the fire was crackling so I dampened down the flame. The camp had cooled off a little, but it was warm before the fire. Charlie Bear groaned and stretched on his pad next to my chair, so I helped the 15-year-old dog get up—his back legs get numb when he's been sleeping--and I let him outside for his morning walkabout. He never goes far but he takes his time doing it and I took comfort from the fact that he would thoroughly examine every new scent in the yard.

I sat back down and planned my morning. It was odd being at camp alone. We had put five hunters in the woods before dawn and that's not like us. Ours is traditionally an afternoon and evening crew, but they'd been excited all week by photos of a 9-point buck that kept haunting their game cameras. For the last few days he'd been showing up just before dawn and that had convinced them to get out early.

I savored the coffee as it cut through the fog of the night before. The Handsome Johnnies had been flowing freely and we had stayed up late. I had short circuited any hangover I may have earned with three shifts in the sauna before going to bed. I felt good. I was at camp where I'd spend the weekend with my nephews and great nephews. I had come out, not to hunt but to process the 4-point buck I had shot opening morning. Other than that, my only job was cooking breakfast and maybe some odd chores if I felt they were important enough to get me up out of my chair by the fire. It was roaring now.

As I lingered over my coffee, the darkness outside slowly gave way to the cold gray light of a November dawn. The air was still, and it was snowing lightly. But camp was warm and snug now and I was at peace with the world. I was exactly where I wanted to be, immune from and impervious to all the world's endless troubles and unnecessary concerns. They were still outside my door, but they could not get in.

My internal clock told me that an old black dog was staring at the other side of the door handle, so I finished the last sip of coffee and let the old boy in. He immediately found his bed in the corner, strategically located where he could see the counter, the stove and most of the kitchen table. He did not get to be old and fat by missing much kibble. I'd left the wolf hounds at home. They're too high maintenance for deer season and the "old Bear Dog" was enjoying the peace and quiet along with exclusive access to the bounty of table scraps of which there is never any shortage at camp.

In the growing light I charged the third and fourth pots of coffee and put them on the gas stove to perk. Then I dug through the stack of vinyl we had played the night before and put an old Gordon Lightfoot record on the turntable. Rich Man's Spiritual was a good start to my day. The boys said they would be back by ten which gave me a couple hours. I was used to an inpatient audience sitting around the table on their second cup of coffee watching me make breakfast and I was looking forward to flying solo this morning and taking my time.

There are few things in life that I enjoy more than cooking a hearty breakfast for a bunch of guys. Today would be the standard feast for a crew of hungry hunters; fried potatoes and corn beef hash, bacon, sausage, biscuits and gravy, pan fried toast served with fried eggs that were always over medium, "no snot and no lace panties."

It's a running joke at camp that you can have your eggs any way you want them as long as you like 'em "over medium, no snot and no lace panties." Though I also make soup, breakfast is my specialty. My bacon is always perfect and I fry eggs so that the white is completely cooked, no snot, and they're not crunchy around the edges, no lace panties. The yolks are just right for dunking your toast. It's no great feat. Many a line cook has mastered it, but it takes some practice and just the right temperature. I learned the term for it from Captain Dave who was a breakfast cook at Mrs. Claus' Kitchen in Christmas after he got out of reform school back in the 70's. I poured another cup of coffee and colored it with another generous dose of Carolyn's.

Some things you don't scrimp on when you go to camp. Coffee is one of those things. There's always an assortment of fresh ground blends in the cabinet. Bacon is another and I went outside to the meat cooler and grabbed a pound of locally raised and smoked bacon, a pound of fresh ground pork sausage from IGA Bob's, along with a dozen farm fresh eggs and I set them on the counter.

I turned my attention to the stove before I started my prep. It's an old four burner propane stove with a full oven which I turned on and lit with a kitchen match. The temperature control is a mystery of calibration, and it takes a good half hour to get it somewhere near the temperature you need. I needed 350 so I started at 250.

What makes it unique are the two side burners with their own firebox and chimney. It has an adjustable grate that can burn either wood or coal and it makes a great spot to keep food warm or let dough rise. A small fire keeps the cast iron top warm for an hour after the fire goes out. I'm also the camp baker and I love this stove.

I threw in a fire starter and covered it with kindling. It was roaring in a minute. I checked the oven and it was warming nicely. First the biscuits, then the potatoes.

I pulled down a stainless-steel bowl from the rack above the sink, measured the biscuit mix and added water. Once I got the desired consistency I blended in some shredded cheese and spooned the mixture out in lumps on a greased cookie sheet. While the oven searched for the right temperature, I grabbed a pile of Yukon Gold potatoes and a big yellow onion from the basket on the counter and started dicing up a panful. I oiled and buttered the cast iron skillet, added the potatoes and onions, sprinkled on the salt and pepper, and then turned the gas down to medium so it didn't burn. I had lots of time.

The oven was close to temperature, so I slid the biscuits in and set a timer on my phone. Both coffee pots had perked a while by now and I used one to refill the carafe while the other one found a trivet on the wood stove. Now for the gravy.

I opened a packet of white gravy mix, added water to it in a saucepan and whisked it smooth. Then I covered it and set it on a low burner. I put half the pork sausage in another skillet, added a few diced onions and minced it all up with a spatula and then kicked the potatoes. They had browned well on one side. I now had Charlie Bear's full attention and he tracked my every move.

Gordon Lightfoot had given way to John Prine on the stereo, and it was now, officially, a Big Old Goofy World.

I finished the sausage, drained the excess grease, and then mixed the sausage in with the gravy which has already started to thicken. I added a good dose of pepper and set the pan on the front of the wood burner. On the back I put what used to be an electric fry pan that we've had for more than 30 years at two different camps.

It's rectangular, about 10 inches by 16 inches with a tall aluminum cover. We busted all the electrical parts off it, and we use it as a warming pan. It fits on the back half of the side burner perfectly and that's where I put it just as my alarm went off. I pulled the biscuits out and shut off the oven. Then I brushed them with garlic butter while they were still warm and stacked them on one end of the big pan.

I kicked the potatoes again, made patties out of the rest of the pork sausage and arranged them in the frying pan, pushing them around and turning them with a wooden spoon as they sizzled.

When they were done, I added them to the warmer and I wiped out the pan with a paper towel.

I unwrapped the home-cured bacon and cut it in half. Herein lies the secret of well-cooked bacon. You have to cut it in half. Long pieces of bacon in a round frying pan just don't work. They buckle and curl and you can't cook them evenly. Cutting the bacon in half lets you fit more in the pan where it cooks more evenly and produces the holy grail of breakfast; bacon that is both chewy and crunchy.

I added half the bacon to the pan, kicked the potatoes again and decided they were done. I scraped half into the warmer and added canned corned beef to the rest. I stirred that while I tended my bacon, transferring each piece as it reached that perfect texture to a pad of paper towel. Then I drained the bacon grease from the pan and added the other half a pound. The hash was done now and I added it to the warmer. It was almost full.

Guy Clark had relieved John Prine on the juke box and we were waiting on a train somewhere in Texas, 1947.

The rest of the bacon cooked quickly and when it was done, I wiped out the frypan and melted a couple of pats of fresh churned butter (always invite farmers to deer camp). Then I added thick slices of Trenary wheat bread which browned quickly. I toasted half a loaf and the warmer could hold no more.

The boys would be back soon, so I poured another cup of coffee and made some notes in the log while I waited. I was satisfied that they would come into a warm camp filled with the heavenly smells of fresh coffee, bacon, and hot biscuits.

Guy Clark had turned the table over to Blaze Foley (if that's a pun it was intended) and we were now Living in the Woods in a Tree.

Charlie Bear, rightly, got the first piece of bacon. He was thankful and remained ready for another. It is likely his last deer season, and I will miss him, but for now he was as happy as a well-fed dog in a warm kitchen at camp. My coffee cup was full, breakfast was ready and I was as happy as a well-fed dog in a warm kitchen at camp too. We both sat quietly by the fire and sighed contentedly.

I finished my third cup of coffee just as the boys started coming in, not one of them dragging a deer. Within a few minutes the table was filled with three generations of red cheeked deer hunters, talking and laughing, cold hands wrapped around steaming mugs of hot coffee. The joyous noise almost drowned out the music.

Of course, I felt obliged to remind them frequently that until somebody else shot a deer bigger than mine, I was still the senior hunter in the forest and winner of the buck pool too. Then I got up, lit a burner on the stove and asked the standard question.

"So, how do you boys want your eggs this morning?"

Life's Short! Drink the Good Scotch First!

I Knew Your Dad

I was at the credit union today and I went into the lobby for the first time in several months because I had more business than I wanted to do at the window. I was waited on by a polite and pretty young lady whom I did not know. I had to tell her my name and then I had to spell it for her. To make it easy I just handed her my driver's license, and she got the information she needed to complete the transaction.

She smiled and gave me my receipt and we thanked each other but it was very formal and a little awkward because the pleasantries we exchanged were those of strangers and it bothered me that I did not know her. After all, Munising is a small town. And then I looked around the room and realized that I didn't know anyone there. The credit union merged with the credit union in Marquette a while back and most of the staff I was used to doing business with pre-COVID, had retired or moved on to other jobs.

It was somewhat disconcerting because I do all my banking there and I used to know everyone who worked there. Going to the credit union used to be a social event. I knew all the tellers and the loan officers. The manager, Rick, was a classmate and we were both post officers down at the legion. His sister is married to my brother and his wife Terry's twin sister Mary is married to by cousin, Bill. I knew everyone there on a first name basis. I spotted one familiar face on the way out the door and she confirmed that, yes, there had been a big change over since the merger.

I remember calling the credit union in Munising from my office in Marquette one day to transfer some money to my son's account. Kitty answered the phone and we chatted for a few minutes. I asked her how her husband Dan was doing and did he and Gene get a bear yet? They didn't but they were out hunting again today. I asked her to take $100 out of my checking account and put it in my son's account and she said OK, sent her best to my wife and we said goodbye.

One of my colleagues was in my office at the time, she overheard the call and she asked me how I did that.

"Did what?" I asked.

"How did you transfer that money without telling her what your account number was, what your son's name was and his account number? How did she know it was you?"

"It was Kitty," I explained. "She knows me, and my kids and I only have one son. I've known her and her husband Dan for, I don't know, most of my life I guess."

"Doesn't the bank have any policies about phone transactions," she asked somewhat confused.

"Oh sure," I said, "She knew who I was and what I wanted to do and she did it. My son will have that money this afternoon."

Now Marquette is not a small town. It's a small city. And it's intimate for its size and you will likely run into someone you know while you're out doing your business, but you're not going to know everyone you do business with like you do in a small town like Munising. And many times, you're going to know their parents and their kids too. That's the best part of living in a small town.

"I knew your dad," I would hear repeatedly from his peers when I met them. He died when I was 17 and in the years that followed I met a lot of people who knew him. He was a somewhat colorful man and people knew both his good and his bad side. They were mostly World War II veterans and it was important for them to tell me they knew him. It was statement of recognition, a building block of trust between two generations and, in many cases, two families. Knowing my dad was an invitation to a circle of friendship that was multi-generational.

"I knew your dad," was all it took to establish a bond and make a new connection in the complicated and intimate network of relationships that are the hallmark of small towns.

Kayleigh, who I've known since she was a baby, is one of my favorite bartenders at my nephew's pub. She's working on her master's degree at NMU and she's a very smart young lady. Her dad, Chad, and I are friends because his dad, Dave, and I were friends. I also knew her great grandparents, Bill and Dolly, and I have fond memories of hanging out on the hill that still bears the family's name. Bill and Dolly also knew my dad. That's why I came back to the U.P. That's why I came home.

All friendships are special, and I made many good friends in the 15 years that I was away. But there are friends whose bond of friendship is inherited and passed down to sons and daughters, to grandsons and granddaughters, almost like a birthright. The old Finns up North have a saying, "omena ei putoa kauas puusta," when talking about the children of people they know well.

"The apple does not fall far from the tree." It's a double-edged observation, not always a compliment, and it generally brings out nods of agreement. We are very much like our parents without trying to be.

"You're one of Louie's kids," was how the conversation started before moving on to "I knew your dad." Well, Louie had eleven kids and none of us fell far from the tree, at least not as far as our appearance is concerned. People see both my mom and my dad in all of us and I see my old man in the mirror every day.

I left my hometown when I was 17 and I came back 15 years later so I missed the acquaintance of a whole generation of people whose parents I knew and whose older siblings I had gone to school with. Though I would not know them when we'd meet, I could usually identify them by their physical appearance and in some cases even distinct family traits. This multi-generational recognition and affinity is downright genetic for me because my family has lived in this sheltered little harbor on Lake Superior since 1840. I like to say that I'm related to the patron on every third barstool in town and it's not far from the truth.

There's a running joke down at the pub that every night is family night. Bring a cousin and get a free beer. That reward is always redeemable tomorrow, but on any given Thursday night more than half the 20-odd patrons at the pub are related to me, though most are from the younger generation, nieces and nephews, younger cousins and great nieces and nephews. I'm always eager to explain to my many cousins how we're related.

"Your great grandmother, Annie, was my grandmother Mary's oldest sister," I reminded Rob, our prosecuting attorney, the other night. Rob went to school with my daughter Vicki. They're third cousins.

Or, "your great great grandpa, Aaron Sr., was my great grandpa Curran's youngest brother" I explained to young Dimitri one night. I went to school with Dimitri's dad Scott. We're fourth cousins. Ours was a prolific family.

"I knew your grandpa," is what my nephews hear when someone mentions my dad and another strand is woven into the tapestry of small-town living. Several years ago I was paying birthday greetings to Beo Mitchell on her 104th birthday. She lived to be 109. She didn't recognize me though she had seen me around the Health Haven where she was living and so she asked who my dad was.

"Louis," I said.

"I don't remember him," she said. "What was your grandpa's name?"

"Clarence," I replied.

"Oh yes, I knew him" she said, "and your grandma too. We used to buy fish from him. Such a tragedy," she added. "I don't know how she did it," and she patted my arm with great care and affection.

She was referring to that May afternoon in 1959 when my grandpa, my great Uncle Louie and my uncle Harvey drowned when their fishing boat sank in the west channel during a sudden spring squall. My grandmother lost her husband, a brother and a son that day. I was born four months later so I never knew any of them. That pat on the arm from someone who did know them was heartfelt and sincere and it perpetuated that intergenerational bond. By the way, my nephew Jim's wife Tristan is Beo's great great niece.

I met my wife 12 years ago when I officiated a friend's wedding. Andrea, the bride, introduced us, and as I always enjoy doing, I explained to this delightful woman who would later become my wife how Andrea and I were not related.

"Andrea's mom's sister is married to my brother and her dad's brother was married to my sister." It makes perfectly good sense to me.

I needed to refill my prescriptions the other day, so I called the pharmacy (there's only one in town), and my next-door neighbor answered the phone.

"Carla, I need my drugs," I said jokingly. "I'm almost out."

"Let's see," she said while she looked up my prescription. "OK," she said after a minute. "But you're out of refills. I'll call Dr. Kurt's office and see if he will phone in the new script."

"Thanks neighbor," I replied. "We can't have my cholesterol and blood pressure getting out of control. Dr. Kurt frowns on that." So, I went to see Dr. Kurt last week for my annual physical so he would renew my prescriptions. He's been my primary care physician for the 30 years since I moved back to the U.P. We call him Dr. Kurt instead of Dr. Olson because he shares a practice with his brother, Dr. Mark. They're about my age and while we chatted Dr. Kurt mentioned that his son had recently joined the practice as a nurse practitioner. I saw a young man who resembled both Dr. Olsons on my way out, but I didn't get a chance to meet him as he was talking with a patient.

I look forward to asking him one day soon if he will be my primary care provider when his dad retires. And I'll also let him know that his grandfather, Dr. Walter, was my doctor before his dad took over that responsibility.

I have good health care.

Life's Short! Drink the Good Scotch First!

The Last Ride

I had hoped that I wouldn't have to write this story. I prayed that he would die peacefully in his sleep with the wolf hounds next to him to see him down the final hill and across the last bridge. But in the end we had to take that last ride together.

The ride itself was easier than the decision to make it. I had contemplated it for months and procrastinated on it for weeks. Once I made it I couldn't think about it for the 48 hours we had to wait for an appointment. When I did I choked up and couldn't talk and I just went and sat with him, petted him, and spoke all the magic words that he knew.

Id' been helping him into the truck for the past three years. His back legs wouldn't get him up on the seat anymore, so he'd put his front legs on the running board and I'd lift him into the passenger seat. He always rode shotgun. Each day these past few months it got progressively harder for him to even get his front legs up and in the end he couldn't, so for the last month I had to pick him up rather unceremoniously and put him on the seat. He didn't care. At least he got to go. I took to lifting him down that last month too. He could still jump down but he could no longer land gracefully. He collided with the ground and did a face plant. He never hurt himself, but it embarrassed him. He would look at me and I could see it in his eyes. So, he waited for me to help him down with as much dignity as the could muster.

His last "good" run with us was about six weeks ago. The wolf hounds and I turned around just short of a half a mile, as we usually did, and we met Charlie Bear lying in the snow-covered road at the top of the last hill. He liked nothing better than just lying in the snow. He looked like a lump of coal in all that white. He always watched us do the last couple hundred yards from there. He knew we we'd turn around and he waited for us and caught his breath.

That last day he jumped up to meet us and trotted out in front of me. Murphy gave up the lead and let the old dog set the pace. His trot lasted about three steps and we all slowed down and gave him the moment. It was a cold sunny day. After twenty yards or so he gave up and slid to the back of the pack where he tagged along behind as he normally did at the best pace he could manage. He'd been bringing up the rear on our hikes for a couple of years and he knew where we were going and he kept his own pace. We waited for him at each bend in the road and at each hill to make sure he was still following.

His decline got more noticeable each day and I finally had to leave him at home. For his last two weeks I had to sneak the wolf hounds out of the house without him. It killed him to be left behind. It killed me to leave him behind. But it had gotten to the point that he only made the first hundred yards from the truck before he was hurting himself trying to keep up.

When he walked with us Shadow would always stop and wait for him. She'd look back to make sure he was coming before I could coax her into the truck.

"I won't leave old Charlie Bear," I'd have to reassure her. And we all waited until he came plodding along steadily. He had no hurry left in him.

The wolf hounds had no closure and they're still confused. They didn't understand that final morning that Charlie Bear was not coming back from that ride. They couldn't know. They had been staying close to him those last few days, especially Murphy. They sensed the end was near and if he would have died at home they would have accepted that he was gone. Dogs know death. To them he didn't die. He just went away and they're still looking for him.

It has been my great good fortune to have spent my life in the company of several good dogs, all loyal and true as well as first rate companions. Because of that lifelong love of canine company, I have been present at the death of many good friends. It is never easy, and it gets harder as a man gets older. It started when I was five and the only boy small enough to crawl under our house on Powell's Point yet strong enough to drag out the body of our old dog who had found a quiet spot under there to die.

I don't remember the dog or even its name, but I do remember dragging him out by his tail. I guess if I had been a little older it might have traumatized me, and it did leave a marker back there on the edge of my memory.

Then when I was ten, our mix-breed collie, Sparky, got hit by a car and we tended him on the kitchen floor for the hour or so it took before he died. I didn't see him get hit, but I heard it. I still remember that sound; the screech of tires and that final yelp. The nearest vet was fifty miles away and all we could do was make him comfortable and be with him. I watched him take his last breath.

The constant companion of my adolescence and teen-age years, a small sheltie mix named Smoky, died after I had left home and joined the navy. I was not there when she died. I got the news in a letter from my mom. The ten years I spent in the navy is the only time I didn't have at least one dog living with me.

When I got out and settled in western Washington we adopted a Benjie-looking dog from somewhere and Ginger lived with us through the move back to the U.P. Our last year there we adopted an old ridgeback mix, who just happened to be named Spice, from our neighbor who had recently got divorced and had a new lifestyle with no place in it for an old dog.

Spice hung out at our house and her and Ginger were buds. We fed her and let her stay the night on those occasions when my neighbor didn't come home. We had told him we would do that, so he wasn't being completely irresponsible. Eventually she just moved in. She spent her last year with us, and I took her on that last ride on my way to the airport for a two-week work trip. I finally came home, but Spice didn't, and Ginger looked for her for weeks after that.

We had Ginger for ten years. We never knew how old she was. We knew that she had been clipped by a UPS truck when she was young because for the rest of her life that big brown truck threw her into a rage. She was a very good dog, otherwise, and bringing her to the U.P. was like taking her to dog heaven. She had been a suburban dog on a leash, and she relished the freedom of her new home. Together we rediscovered all the old haunts of my childhood.

I took her on that her last ride in our old white van and the vet came outside to the parking lot to send her on her way. When I slid open the side door she lifted her head up, crossed her paws in front of her, laid her head on them and died. The vet was relieved to refund our money. We buried her in a little clearing near camp.

During her last few years she had the company of a mixed-breed German shepherd who we named Fred for obvious reasons. He protected our family for ten years before his back legs quit working. Virgil went with me the day the vet set him free in the back of my truck parked in the alley. We buried him next to Ginger which was a chore because he weighed 130 pounds and we had to carry him a hundred yards through the woods. Everyone needs a friend that good by the way, someone who will give you their day to help you say goodbye to and then bury a member of your family. Virgil is that kind of friend.

For his last few years Fred had the company of a pure-bred yellow lab named Jake who was small for a Labrador retriever. He was actually a cross between a chocolate and a yellow lab and his nose was liver instead of black. He was a very good dog and he loved to hike with us. He lived to be afield all day, every day and he was joined two years later by Charlie Bear. They were a good pair. Jake died early of liver failure. It was Winter when I took him on his last ride and he died with his head in my lap. We couldn't afford an exclusive cremation after the thousand dollars we spent trying to save him, so I took a snip of his fur to place next to Ginger and Fred in the spring. Charlie Bear lived alone with us after that until we got the wolf hounds, and he has lived the best life that a dog can have.

I have written about him several times and I will write about him again. In telling his story, I tell a few chapters of my own. He and I walked a thousand trails together and swam at a hundred beaches. He was my boon companion and I miss him dearly.

I stopped and bought a bunch of beef sticks to share with him on the hour-long ride to the vet. Without the wolf hounds in the back, I lay the passenger seat as flat as I could to give him room to lie down. He did not know that it was the end. He munched contentedly on the beef sticks and tolerated me lifting him out of the truck when we arrived. I had put his collar on before we left, something he's rarely worn for the past five years. He let me snap on the leash, something he had never known, and then he followed me dutifully to the door.

All the girls in the reception area greeted him without sorrow and we were led to an examination room with a small blanket on the floor. He immediately laid down which he always did if he wasn't actually in motion.

The vet gave us a few minutes, but not too many for which I was grateful, and then came back and gave him a strong sedative. I cradled his head in my lap and said all the words that I know he loved while he drifted off to sleep.

"That's a good boy Charlie Bear. You rest now. When we leave here we'll get in the truck and take a ride out to camp. When we get there we'll take a hike through the woods down to the lake and go for a swim. Then we'll fry up some bacon for dinner and have an ice cream treat for dessert."

He sighed deeply, closed his eyes and he was gone. He was 15.

Death is so permanent. I'm still coming to terms with his absence. Instead of ashes I had four paw prints taken, one for us and one for each of my kids. He was a big part of their lives too. My wife is going to make them into memorial plaques.

Murphy and Shadow are slow in adjusting. For weeks Murphy would not eat out of Charlie's spot on the two-dog food and water station in the back room. He had spent his whole life eating at a separate bowl off to the side. As a pup he had been corrected too many times by the old dog for even sniffing at that dish. But he's finally made the adjustment.

Shadow just keeps looking for him and waiting for him. At camp last week, she stayed fixed on the couch as we packed up to leave. She wouldn't move and I thought she was hurt. I looked her over and then finally had to coax her off the couch and out the door. Later I figured out that she was just waiting for Charlie Bear. She wasn't leaving without him. It was our first trip to camp since he'd been gone and she figured if he wasn't at home then he must be around camp somewhere.

Our daily walks are longer now that we're not limited by Charlie Bear's lack of endurance. But when we get back to the truck she still lingers and breaks my heart when she looks back over her shoulder, longing for a glimpse of her old friend trotting down the last hill, ready to ride shotgun on the way home. Then she looks at me with eyes that ask, "where is he?"

And I keep looking for him too.